A Silent Killer Among Us

KSPUBLISHING, LLC. ATLANTA

TAMYRA
WALKER

A SILENT KILLER AMONG US

KSPUBLISHING, LLC.

Publishing Since 2001

www.kingdom-scribes.com

Library of Congress
2016917875

Walker, Tamyra

A Silent Killer Among Us / Tamyra Walker,

ISBN 978-0-692-79856-0

Editor

Barbara Joe Williams

Photographer

Michael Moorer

Graphic Designer

Justin Q. Young

This book is dedicated to all foster children nationwide.

Right now three things remain: faith, hope, and love. But the greatest of these is LOVE 1 Corinthians 13:13 (International Standard Version)

 SILENT KILLER AMONG US:

DEPRESSION SINGS THE BLUES

Acknowledgement

First, I give honor to God who is the head of my life. In His image he created me and blew into my nostrils the breath of life. Everything that I am and have or will be is all because of Him. I thank Him for his grace and mercy. I thank Him for life. I thank Him for this gift of writing that He has bestowed upon my life and that it was tailor made just for me. I thank Him for allowing me to go through the things that I went through so that I may be able to reach out to other people who are going through similar things. I take no credit for any of this. It is all because of God who loved me so much and thought enough of me to deliver me from all of those things that were hurting me so badly.

I have always been a very private person. It was hard to conceive the idea of sharing so many intimate details about my life with people who I assumed would not understand

and who would only judge me. When I wrote this story I was thinking, *My God, I'm baring my soul. People are going to see my scars, my feelings of insecurity. I'll be naked like Adam and Eve in the Garden of Eden with nothing to cover my nakedness.* God said, "In all things I must get the glory. Your healing is not for you to be selfish with." I didn't think any more about it. I wrote, and I wrote, and I wrote some more. I knew I could relax when God said, "Stop here, Tamyra. This is the end."

I want to thank my mother, Lydia Fair, my twin sister, Tamara Walker, my classmate, Clifford Jackson, and another friend who I practically grew up with, Twanda White for encouraging me to write this book. All of you could see the vision and you assured me that I was doing the right thing by writing this book. I want you to know that you were the wind beneath my wings when it came to bringing this project to life. I will always cherish and appreciate you as long as I shall live. I pray that God will bless each of you richly.

Thank you to my editor, Barbara Joe Williams, who toiled relentlessly with this book. You went over every word with such grace, treating my book as if it was your very own book. I am so blessed to have had someone with your expertise who was willing to take on the awesome responsibility of making sure my book was as good as it could possibly be. I thank God for you and pray that he blesses everything that your hand touch.

Thank you to my photographer, Michael Moorer who did an awesome job on capturing the perfect picture of me for the front cover. You are truly one of a kind. I thank God for you and your beautiful gift.

Thank you to my graphic designer, Justin Q. Young. You are truly gifted...not talented, but GIFTED. I love how you brought life to my book cover. I was wowed at the first sight of it and I know that so many others will be too.

Thank you for doing this for me. You have no idea how much I appreciate you. May God bless you now and forevermore.

Thank you to Racquel Williams for just being the epitome of encouragement. I have never seen you in person. But I have never witnessed a person who goes harder than you do. You have overcome so much and I see a bright light of hope shining in you. There was not a single day that went by that you did not seek to encourage everyone else when sometimes you probably needed to be encouraged yourself. I just want you to know that I listened to your words. They saturated my soul and I took heed to your advice. I thank you so much for overcoming. Because you overcame, you are assuring that so many others overcome as well. I thank God for you and I wish you nothing but success in all your future endeavors. Because you shared your testimony I believe that I can conquer the world.

To my publisher, Jenine May, none of this would be possible if you hadn't taken a chance on me. There are no words to describe how much I appreciate you. I thank you for believing in me and allowing me the opportunity to see my dream of being an author come to pass. Thank you so much. God has his hands upon you. He hasn't failed you and I know he never will.

To my readers, and to all who support me, I just want to say thank you so much. I truly hope that this book touches your heart. Whatever you are going through, you can overcome. All you have to do is believe in yourself and take the necessary steps to make it happen. May God bless you and keep you in all of your ways.

Right now three things remain: faith, hope, and love. But the greatest of these is LOVE 1 Corinthians 13:13 (International Standard Version)

No, No, No! It Can't Be True.

I changed the name of the suicide victim in this prologue to keep his identity private.

August 2014

I awakened that morning, on a crisp day, with the annoying buzz of my cellular phone ringing in my ears. It penetrated my eardrums fiercely, almost as if to say, "Who do you think you are to be lying here so peacefully as if the world revolves around you? Well, I'm about to show you, it doesn't." At that moment, I considered my phone, normally attached to my palm, to be an evil culprit. I would give anything to silence its rage. Just allow me a few more moments of solitude.

Was it so bad that I wanted to make up for the sleep I had been deprived? Sleep had only found me no more than three hours before. Despite the fact I had to sleep with one of my nostrils plugged with Kleenex to keep it from running and the insanely embarrassing snoring, resulting from my less than perfect breathing, I was somewhat in a peaceful mode.

The two extra pillows I propped under my head the night before were doing their job. Long had my pulmonologist, Dr. David Franco, assured me after ordering me to undergo a sleep study in which I had to sleep with electrodes and glue in my hair that I had a mild case of sleep apnea. This meant at certain periods throughout the night, I stopped breathing. Sadly, I would have rather not be able to breathe at all than to wear the contraption he prescribed for me to put over my face during the night. There, on the couch, I lay with my almost six-year-old son lying on top of me. We had decided to camp out in the living room since it was where the flat screen television was housed. I found, if I entertained myself with a couple of comedy movies, it would distract me from how badly my sinusitis was kicking my butt. I had been dealing with this particular flare-up for about three weeks. Sinusitis, coupled with asthma, and a mild case of sleep apnea was not a good combination.

I allowed my voicemail to take that call, quickly readjusting the pillows under my head so I could once again fall into a deep slumber. I knew I would not have much longer to enjoy it. My daily duties would subpoena me. Without reservations, I would have to answer the call. So, without further ado, I closed my eyes and inhaled deeply. Just as I was drifting off, there it was again, my phone blaring loudly.

"What's the use?" I finally muttered, feeling drained as if energy would not grace me with its companionship. I hit the "Answer" button on the phone.

"Hello, hello." I frantically answered, my voice filled with the slightest tinge of aggravation.

"Tamyra," the voice came alive on the other end. I knew right away it was my twin sister, Tamara.

"What do you want, Tamara?" I answered with my eyes still closed. *I know she doesn't want anything, probably just bored.*

"Tamyra, I've got some bad news."

Instantly, my eyes sprung open. Obviously, those words were the only words I needed to hear for sleep to pack up and leave me lonely. But I was too afraid to sit up, thinking the strength of the bad news I was about to hear would knock me back down.

"Tamyra," she said again. Suddenly, I knew she was crying. *Oh, my God*, I pondered, bracing myself.

"What's wrong?" I mustered the strength to ask. I was nervous as ever, swallowing hard to ward off the feeling of nausea creeping into my space. By now, Tamara was sobbing uncontrollably. I was left feeling uncomfortable. It was cutting off my ability to relax just the same as a swollen airway would cut off one's ability to breathe. After a couple of minutes of listening to her relentless crying, she said, "Tamyra, Jae is dead."

"Jae who?" I shrieked, now sitting up. I flung my son off of me like a blanket which had gotten too hot during the night. I could feel my hands shaking, influenced by the rhythm of anxiety.

"Jae who?" I repeated, thinking to myself, *Girl, if you don't hurry up and tell me, I know something.*

"Jae Wright," she responded.

"Whaaaaaaat?" I screamed, now jumping up off the couch. Like clockwork, I began pacing the living room floor.

"What happened?" I wanted to know.

"He committed suicide."

Her words were barely audible. But I heard what she said. I just had to ask her again to make sure. Maybe my ears had deceived me. "What did you say?" I repeated, my voice trembling. "He did what?"

She paused for a second before continuing. "Tamyra, he committed suicide."

"Oh, my God," I managed to say before dropping the cellular phone on the couch. By now, I was hyperventilating. It seemed as if my heart stopped. I kept saying, "No, no, no! It can't be true! It's not true! I know it's not true! Please, Please, God, don't let it be true."

But it was true, so painfully true. As I sat in the middle of the living room floor, trying hard to compose myself, I wondered how could something like this come along and tear apart our little community. I grew up with Jae. He was only a couple of years younger than I was. It just didn't seem real that he was dead. Why would Jae Wright, of all people, commit suicide?

Truthfully speaking, he was one of the sweetest persons I had the divine pleasure of ever knowing. He always seemed to flaunt a carefree demeanor, an attribute of his I admired and was envious of because I could never be carefree for an extended period of time. There would always be something, regardless of how big or small, to rip off my peace of mind. This wasn't the case with Jae. Every day, he went with the flow. Nothing appeared to get him down.

As I pondered on those things, the tears continued to fall down my face. I sighed heavily as I remembered how I always counted on Jae to say something nice about a picture I posted on Facebook. He wasn't ashamed to compliment anybody. That alone, let me know how special he was.

The muscles in my face forced a half smile as I reflected on how Jae had dubbed me, and Tamara, as his favorite twins. Back in the day, when we attended church together, many Sundays I walked up to him as he sat in his wheelchair. Just before the deacons proceeded to sing, "A Charge to Keep I Have," during devotion, I leaned over him and pinched his cheeks. Knowing that I was being mischievous, I broke into a devilish grin, turned around, and walked over to where the youth choir was seated. Jae never said anything. He watched in awe. I saw the hint of his own smile making its debut on his face.

We lost touch for a while, reconnecting years later when he randomly commented under a picture I posted on Facebook.

"Aren't you the twin who used to always pinch my cheeks? I've been waiting all this time to get my payback," he concluded.

I snickered as I thought about the memory. The fact he remembered assured me of how it obviously meant something to him. That alone, meant something to me as well. I couldn't remember anyone being so moved about anything I'd done.

He later moved into an apartment next door to Tamara. The excitement he felt having the opportunity to finally have a place of his own, with a couple of his buddies, was very noticeable. I smiled to myself every time he made a post about it on his Facebook page. That little small milestone was equivalent, in his world, as an unlikely kid having the chance to go to Disney World for the first time.

By that time, I had a son. Jae had no problem at all entertaining my little guy, telling me that my son's smile was just as bright as mine and that he looked just like me.

Wait a minute, I thought with a heart pounding like a bass drum. My retrospective walk down memory lane was interrupted by a new set of thoughts. *I know this has to be all over Facebook.* I ran over to the couch and retrieved my cellular phone. With one click of a button, I was logged on. Sure enough, social media (Facebook) was lit up with distraught individuals expressing their condolences and telling Jae to rest in peace on his page. Even one of his sisters had changed her profile picture to a picture of him. The sight of the picture startled me. As I looked into Jae's eyes, I could have sworn they were looking through my soul. It was an eerie feeling, causing the very core of my soul to quiver. I hurried up and clicked the "Like" button and scrolled further down my newsfeed.

I read each post carefully, allowing the tears to continue spilling down my face. My eyes came upon his very last post. I felt as if I would die a thousand deaths. The silent tears were now heart wrenching sobs. He had left his suicide note on Facebook. I couldn't get the last sentence, "Tonight all of that ends," out of my head.

I was totally speechless, tangled in the arms of grief. I knelt on my knees with my face buried in the carpet, wishing I could unread the words I had just read. This had to be a nightmare. I was so ready to wake up. Besides, the abundance of tears were making my breathing even more difficult. Not knowing what else to do, I picked up the

Kleenex box off the coffee table and threw it across the room. Rage then took over my mind. I started damning Tamara for waking me up to tell me this horrible news. I mean, didn't she have the slightest inkling of how it would affect me?

This was the kind of thing I read about on the Internet or heard about on the news. I had just gotten a dose of it when the comedian, Robin Williams, who had made me laugh so many times, especially with his roles in *Mrs. Doubtfire,* committed suicide. Also, Lee Thompson Young, an actor who played the lead role in *The famous Jett Jackson,* and later had a role as a detective on *Rizzoli and Isles*, had committed suicide a year earlier. I felt bad for them, even shed tears on their behalves. As sad as it was, it wasn't supposed to hit this close to home. We were country people! We were close knit. How could something like this creep up on us?

Thankfully, my son was still sleeping soundly. God knows I didn't want him to see me so torn apart. "Man, this shit ain't fucking fair," I screamed as loudly as I could, not caring at all if my neighbors heard me through the walls of my apartment. More than ever, I wanted to question God. I wanted so badly to ask him, "Lord, why would You allow Jae to take his own life when You had the power to stop him?" As much as I wanted to do it, I knew it wasn't my place to do such a daring, yet blatantly, disrespectful thing.

The hours ticked by slowly. They eventually turned into a couple of days later. I'd had a hard time falling asleep ever since learning of Jae's death. Every time I closed my eyes, I could see him. I imagined how he must have been crying so hard in those last few moments before his life ended. I imagined how lonely he must have felt. I imagined how he probably didn't really want to do it but felt as if he couldn't deal with the pain.

My tears were few at that point. Still, I harbored a broken heart, seeming to weigh a ton. Again, I allowed myself to visit his Facebook page. The posts were still pouring in. I'd been collecting my own thoughts to pay my respects on his wall. I had to ask myself, why was I so angry? Yes, it was normal to be upset when finding out something as tragic as someone taking their own life had occurred. The truth of the matter was, I had gone slightly overboard.

Was it because I didn't notice Jae's pain before it was too late? It wasn't my fault I didn't see the suicide note he posted the night he died. But there was no denying I had seen the posts leading up to that point. I clearly saw he was hurting by the words he posted. Yet, I chose not to say anything. I, like so many other people, thought he was only venting. What if I had said something? I almost said something. It's too bad almost saying something didn't save his life. Almost saying something is the same as not saying something.

After reading his posts, I read again the posts of his friends and family who were grieving over his untimely death. "This is really true," I sadly mumbled to myself, sniffed, and wiped the new set of tears descending down my face.

Soon enough, night fell over the city. Still, I suffered with an immeasurable amount of insomnia. The moment my eyes became heavy, I immediately saw Jae in my thoughts. He came to me with his arms outstretched the way a baby stretches out his arms when he wants his mom to pick him up.

"I needed you to rescue me," it seemed as if he was saying. "You know firsthand how it feels to think no one loves you, but you didn't say anything," he continued talking to my mind. Jae was gone from earth. Yet, I felt his presence. His words were so true. I did know how it felt to think you were all alone in the world, feeling as if it was beneath you to truly be loved. I, too, had considered suicide, feeling like my pain would be over if I was no longer in existence. I'd been barricaded for so long in the prison of depression. At times, I felt I couldn't escape, even if I tried. It had snarled at my pain. It had made me it's captive. The last thing it wanted was for me to be free. So, yes, I knew how he felt. I knew so well.

The days approaching his funeral drew closer. I realized I could've been the one lying in that casket with people praying and singing over my soul. I could've been the one lowered into the ground, while the preacher murmured, "Ashes to ashes, dust to dust." I could've been the one gone from life too soon. I could've been the one.

It was only by the grace of God I didn't commit suicide. Even so, I believe my story should be told. Perhaps, it will help someone else thinking of committing suicide. It will help Jae's death to not be in vain.

Once Upon a Time, When I was Carefree

Beautiful Beginnings

The journey began on February 26, 1980. It was a beautiful Tuesday morning nestled within the bitter cold season of winter. The wee hours of the morning approached with my mother awakening with labor pains at their peak. Though it was a new day, never before seen upon the eyes of any, darkness was still projected across the sky. The moon lingered in its place. So did the stars. They shined brightly, their light beaming down through my mother's windowpane. Beads of sweat poured out of her skin as if she had been drenched with a water hose. She sat on the side of the bed, breathing heavily, trying hard to wrap her head around the fact she would soon give birth.

Slowly, the contractions increased to five minutes apart. Though she was toiling with everything within her, wincing as the pains hit her hard, time wasn't waiting for her with a smile. If she didn't get to the hospital soon, an epidural would not be administered.

Before the moon had time to bid farewell to the darkness of the night, my mother journeyed to Jackson Hospital, located off of Mulberry Street in Montgomery, Alabama. She wrestled uncomfortably through the pain. But in the midst of the toiling and all of the pain, soon enough the blessing would come forth. I was born.

It was a special day carved in the hearts of mankind; for it was not only the day I was born; it was also the birth date of my twin sister. She was the oldest, making her grand appearance in the world thirteen minutes before I stubbornly came out of the womb. But first, the doctor had to attach forceps to me so I could be turned into a head down position. I was a breeched baby, wanting to come into the world feet first.

Our mother decided to name us Tamara and Tamyra. Tamara weighed five pounds and six ounces, while I weighed four pounds and thirteen ounces. I'm sure I considered myself to be a blessed newborn. Not everyone was so lucky to enter the world with someone who was their first friend, an identical clone, baring the same DNA, except with a unique personality which classified her as different from me.

When we became older, it always brought a smile to my face when Tamara and I played tricks on unsuspecting individuals who didn't have a clue we were twins. Or when people who only knew one of us, found out for the first time we had a twin. The look of sheer shock on their faces was downright hilarious. All of their responses were pretty much the same. “Why the heck didn’t you tell me you had a twin?”

“You never asked me if I was a twin,” I responded, sarcasm dripping off of my lips like glaze dripping off of a doughnut.

For nine months, I shared the womb with Tamara. When sustenance was passed to me while in the womb, it was passed to her as well. We grew together from a zygote, to an embryo, to a fetus, and then at last together, we left the incubator when we were deemed ready to live outside of the womb. We slid into the world, crying as we were smacked on the bottom by the doctor.

The time had come for the debut of the beautiful beginnings. Life for us had just begun. There were so many things we would have to learn in order to stay afloat. Thankfully, we had each other to be an anchor of encouragement when the other was feeling weary as if life was too hard to continue holding on.

The month I was born turned out to be quite the month in history as well. Michael Jackson's hit single, "Off the Wall," was released twenty-four days preceding my birth. I imagined there had to be a countless number of people who were bumping that song on their radios as our mother rode home from the hospital with two bundles of joy to care for.

In the weeks to come, there was no time for peace and quiet. Sleep deprivation was our mother's new best friend. All of the attention we didn't require was selflessly given to our other siblings, which included two sisters. Their names were Pamela and Sharmeen. We also had a brother. His name was Jarrett.

We adored our sisters, desired to be in their presence at all times. Oftentimes, we considered our brother to be our nemesis. Tamara and I craved his attention like it was the air we breathed. Many days, we looked longingly at him sitting in the living room watching *GI Joe* and *He-man* on television, until finally, he broke down and played with us.

The drawback was, it was usually games you would play with another boy. We didn't complain. We realized beggars couldn't be choosers.

We knew Jarrett would never, in life, come near one of our dolls unless he could do serious damage to her. Many times, he did just that. I can never forget the look of terror I wore on my face when one afternoon, he threw my cabbage patch doll I'd just gotten for Christmas on top of the house. When I begged and pleaded for him to get her down, he pointed his finger at me in a taunting manner and laughed in my face.

"Na na na na na, why don't you make me, if you can?" he asked. I sat down and began to cry. Mom wanted to know what was wrong. The next second, after I laid all of my troubles in her bosom, she was breathing down Jarrett's neck, ordering him to rescue my baby doll. The idea of me not being able to hold my precious doll again created serious stress in my life. I clutched her like she was a real child when I finally did have her once more in my little arms. Jarrett looked at me with disgust. I knew he would soon devise another plan to destroy my doll. He would do so when he was certain mom wasn't around to correct him.

As the months were constructed in our lives, like a honeycomb hidden within a tree, we thrived in many ways. Before turning the tender age of one, Tamara and I were placed into our first foster home. In later years, Carolyn, our biological mother, relayed to me that she was the one who called The Department of Human Resources (DHR) to turn us in. She said we were too much for her to handle. Apparently, all of her children were too much for her to handle. She didn't keep any of us. Instead, she passed the buck of responsibility on to somebody else and went back to leading the carefree life where she was only concerned about what she wanted.

I don't remember much of what transpired in my life from the point of birth up until I turned four-years-old. Tamara and I were briefly in a foster home somewhere in Millbrook, Alabama. That placement lasted until November of 1984, when we were placed in a permanent foster home in a small town, called Whitehall.

In our little neighborhood, the trees were never-ending along with some long winding narrow roads with no street light in sight. Plum trees bloomed alongside the streets. I had my days when I stuffed my jaws with the sweet plums I pulled off the trees. All that I couldn't fit into my mouth, I put into my shirt as if it was a bag to shield them. Besides, I knew if Nana saw me walk into the house with a big bag of plums, she would make me hand it over so she could be the one to distribute them amongst me and my peers.

I had a field day with the blackberries as well. It absolutely felt like I was in heaven when my aunt made blackberry pies for me and my siblings. We hardly ate our dinner as the anticipation of getting a hefty slice of the pie was beyond overwhelming. We behaved pretty much the same way when it came to the abundance of sugarcane mom constantly had. I always stayed hidden in my room while everyone else shucked the sugarcane. It should come as no surprise how I made my presence known when it was time to eat up.

We got used to eating watermelon, too. During the summer months, we counted on mom stopping by the fruit stand every other day on her way out of Hayneville. She purchased the biggest watermelon she could find. We rolled that sucker in the house as soon as she drove up in the yard, fetched her a knife, and watched with excitement dancing in our eyes as she cut us a piece of the juicy sweetness. Afterwards, we stood under the carport having ourselves the time of our lives as the juice from the watermelon got all over the front of our shirts. We even had seed spitting contests to see who spitted their seeds out the farthest. The only thing we hated to do, was take the bucket of watermelon rinds out to the pigs when we were done. *They are so uncouth,* I thought, *and beyond nasty.* I could never understand why they always wanted to roll around in mud. Their snorting just about drove me insane.

Life in the country was considerably different from life in the city. We didn't have sirens to wake us early in the morning the way it often panned out in the city. If ever there was a time you heard a siren in the country, everyone within earshot gazed nosily out of their windows, wondering what was going on. It had to be something serious. For all who didn't know what was unfolding in our little world, they picked up their phones and dialed the number of someone else who was sure to know. There were at least two people in the neighborhood that had scanners. Everyone else considered them to be the neighborhood news reporters.

Also in the country, everyone knew each other. Many, in one form or fashion, were related to you. I can't remember how many times I heard someone referring to me as cuz, and I didn't know we were related or how we were related. Instead of being rude, I said, "Hi cuz." I feigned a smile and hugged him/her back, if they hugged me.

It was very easy for one prominent individual within the area to be the jack-of-all-trades, meaning a police officer, bus driver, mechanic, and so forth. The local store was the place to hang out. Everybody who was anybody had their birthday parties at the store. When it mysteriously burned down, it broke the hearts of many. We felt as if we had lost a part of our livelihood.

After conversing with Mrs. Lydia Fair, my new foster mother, I learned she was my second cousin. Her mother, Mary Walker, was my great aunt. We called her Nana. Nana was the sibling to my biological mother's father, Eddie Lee Walker, my grandfather, who I sadly have no recollection of. She was one of my primary caregivers throughout my days of youth.

The only thing I knew about my grandfather, was that he had two brothers. Their names were Willie Walker, better known as Man and Aaron Walker, better known as Lil Buddy. My Uncle Willie had a great sense of humor. He loved to crack jokes and make everybody laugh. As a child, he picked on his brother, Aaron, doing such things as striking matches under the bottom of his feet because they were very dry and scaly. He fell out laughing after doing so, becoming more tickled when he saw how angry it made Uncle Aaron. On the other hand, my Uncle Aaron had a tendency of being very loud and sometimes obnoxious. He wasn't into hearing anybody out about anything, had to have things done his way or there was hell to pay. A lot of that could probably be attributed to the fact that he drank like a fish and most of the time, he was intoxicated.

My grandfather also had another sister. Her name was Flora Walker. She was known as Ms. Mobile to a lot of people. She was Nanny to us. How ironic was that? We had a Nanny and a Nana.

One thing I can say, and if I could, I would give him a pat on his back, my grandfather definitely took God seriously when he said to be fruitful and multiply. He fathered a total of eleven children. His oldest daughter, my Aunt Minnie, died when she was only four-days-old. In later years, my grandmother miscarried another girl. Afterwards, there was a son who was stillborn.

His other six sons grew to be adults. Two of my uncles were in the Army. My Uncle Eugene was honorably discharged while my Uncle Willie Cee, was killed in the Vietnam War in December of 1968. He enlisted in the Army in 1966 and was trained to be a paratrooper. The day he died, he jumped out of a plane and stepped on a landmine. He was twenty-years-old at the time of his death.

Upon learning of his death, Carolyn was listening to the radio. At the top of the hour, there was breaking news. The news reporter said, "This just in, Private First-Class Willie Cee Walker has been killed in Vietnam." Carolyn froze as those dreadful words resonated in the air, piercing her heart. She decided to wait until the next hour before panicking, knowing that if it was true, it would be announced again.

Her eyes then averted to the front door as she heard someone busting through the door. It was my grandfather. He, too, had been listening to the radio and heard the news. "Did you hear that?" he asked Carolyn. The color had completely drained from his face.

"I heard something," she admitted, nervously. A few days later, there were some military officials who came to their home and confirmed what they both had heard on the radio was indeed the truth.

My mother (Carolyn) wasn't my grandfather's only living daughter. He had another daughter who was three years older than she. Her name was Dorothy. She succumbed to death also at the young age of twenty from cancer in November of 1970. Her death came a few months after my oldest sister, Pamela, was born in August of the same year.

By the time she was diagnosed with cancer, she was already near death, even though she appeared to be as healthy as a horse. She came home to Alabama from Brooklyn, New York, once she'd had a surgery that proved to be unsuccessful. When Carolyn saw her sunken body, she burst into tears, holding onto her for at least a half hour. She became her caretaker, giving her baths and cooking for her. She had been taught by the Hospice nurse how to administer Demerol shots to Aunt Dorothy when the pain became unbearable. She gave her all of her other medicines as well.

Later in the evenings, when my Aunt Nanny (Flora) came home from work, she resumed taking care of Dorothy. Several times, my grandfather stopped by to check on things. He said, "Carolyn, you know where the guns are. If anyone comes to that door who ain't spose to be there, you shoot the shit out of them and worry about consequences later." He then turned to his sister/my Aunt Flora and said, "You know, she ain't got good sense. And you know, if I tell her to shoot, she's crazy enough to do it for real. So you need to make sure when you come to the door, you make yourself known."

Knowing that my mother was only seventeen-years-old at the time, he thought telling her to do such a thing was protecting her.

I was deeply saddened at the fact I would never get to meet my Uncle Willie Cee (or any of my uncles), my Aunt Dorothy, or my maternal grandmother, for that matter. My maternal grandmother's name was Inez Maul. She married into the Walker family when she was only fourteen-years-old. A meek and humble woman she was. She earnestly settled into her life as a homemaker, was gung-ho on catering to the ever growing needs of my grandfather. Death seized her when Carolyn was only nine-years-old. In fact, my mother was the one who summoned the paramedics when she passed out near the fireplace the afternoon she died. Many years later she broke down and told me, "Every year for her birthday I would get alone. I looked up towards heaven, and I told her, 'okay mom. It's time for you to come back now. I thought she just left to get some rest. I didn't know she was gone forever.'" It never registered in her head that death was permanent until after her brother/my Uncle Willie Cee was killed when she was fifteen-years-old. So that was two deaths she had to grieve at the same time.

Our grandfather wasn't always a very nice man. Many years after his wife died, he lived with one of his sisters.

When he became angry, he did peculiar things like move into the smokehouse. He even purchased paneling to fix it up to his liking, placing him a mattress on the floor to serve as his bed, and using two big bricks in the yard with a grill atop to cook his meals.

Finally, one day, he decided to leave in September of 1983. He never once looked back for the family he left behind. But not before he gathered all of his tools that he didn't have any use for and took them out in the field. He poured kerosene on them. Then, he set them afire so my aunt, his sister, wouldn't have access to them. He didn't want to feel as if he was doing her any favors. He left, saying as he walked away, "Don't you look for me, and I won't look for you!"

My sister, Sharmeen, told me she stood on the porch, watching with tears flowing down her face as he left with his bag slung over his shoulder. He went about his business starting a new life far away where no one would be able to locate him. It was heartbreaking to learn. I really would have liked to get to know him. Since that wasn't likely, I held onto hope that one day, I would get the chance to track him down until I learned he was no longer receiving benefits from Social Security. It was pretty clear then, that he had passed on. My only hope was he didn't die alone. I hoped wherever he decided to lay his head all of those years, he had at least one person who held his hand in death.

It was an unfortunate account of events when my grandfather abandoned his family. It created a vicious cycle which later spiraled down to his sons, who strayed away from the family after the death of their mother and were never able to be found. She'd been the thread which bounded all of them together. Now, that she was gone, no one was sticking around. They all went their separate ways, seeming to forget that they had any family at all.

The apple didn't fall far from the tree when it came to Carolyn. The wicked spell of abandonment wrapped its arms around her heart. She also abandoned her children and was cold as ice about it. She never once cared about our tears as a result. When we wanted to ask her questions to try and at least understand, she shut down like an engine and pushed her attitude to the forefront. Once we experienced how mean she was, we knew not to ask her any questions. Many days, I smiled on the outside but on the inside, I was crying for answers.

When we moved into our new home, we learned Mrs. Fair, our new mom also had custody of our brother, Jarrett. She decided since she already had him in her care, she may as well get us, too. "I didn't see a need for DHR to put you all up for adoption and you possibly be split up," she said to me, when I was old enough to understand the depth of her words.

My other two sisters Pamela and Sharmeen resided with Aunt Nanny. She lived all but five minutes away from us. So we got the chance to grow up knowing our sisters and our brother. Times we spent with them were precious moments, we always cherished. It absolutely made our day when on weekends, mom allowed us to spend the night with them. Pam tortured us first with stories of a fictitious character she created named, Hatchet Man, who supposedly lived on the back porch. Whenever we aggravated her, she grabbed us and pretended like she was going to take us on the back porch where he was waiting to decapitate us with his hatchet.

When she got tired of filling our heads with tales about the hatchet man, she came up with the mule-dog. He was half mule and half dog. His home was in the barn at Nanny's house. Oftentimes, I heard Pam saying, "Nice mule-dog," as she pretended like she was petting him. I tried to take a peek to see if there was any validity to this so called mule-dog. But for some reason, she never allowed me to see him. There were many lazy summer afternoons when she made me think he was chasing me. It's really pathetic how I never thought to look around while I was running for dear life. I would have clearly seen that there was nothing behind me.

After she had herself a merry ole time laughing at me, she filed and painted our fingernails and toe nails. She made up our faces and bought us juju bees. We felt as if we were on top of the world. Nothing could steal our joy. Nothing could keep us away from our sisters.

Nanny was special, too. When at her house, we could always count on her on a whim to whip us up a nice batch of bread pudding. It didn't have to be a special occasion. She did it because she knew we liked it. For lunch, she made us peanut butter sandwiches with the preserves she made from the pears we picked off the pear tree in her front yard. She spread preserves on our biscuits in the mornings as well. When our bellies were full, we wandered out in the yard to play with her dog, Scotty. At other times, we picked up the figs off the ground that had fallen off the fig tree. We knew that later in the evening, after she had washed them, she was going to give us a handful.

On Friday nights, Nanny allowed us to stay up way past our bedtime. We joined her in the bed. Happy we were to watch episodes of Johnny Carson on the late night show. As a late night snack, she cut us a nice hunk of souse meat with hook cheese and saltine crackers that she'd gotten from Sal's store. I don't remember a time when Nanny ever spanked us. She absolutely adored us, always welcomed us with open arms. She even took us shopping and bought us all kinds of dresses and other goodies. Nanny had plenty of money to treat us whenever she wanted to. But she didn't trust banks. She kept all of her money in a small brown paper bag, locked up in her Chifferobe.

Whenever I became sick while in her care, she concocted a home remedy she had learned of years ago. She spoon fed it to me, assured that whatever the issue was this remedy would cure it for sure.

Things were good until Nanny got sick late one night while Tamara and I were visiting. Her sugar dropped way below the level considered to be safe as she was a diabetic who wasn't always compliant. Pam and Sharmeen were not home to tend to her. Jarrett was not there either. Nanny did not have a landline. She'd always thought if someone wanted to reach her, they could just drop by or wait until they saw her out and about. We had to run in the dark, although we were afraid of what might be lurking in the night, around to the neighbor's house to call mom for help. We prayed we wouldn't get attacked by a possum, armadillo, snake, coyote, or even a deer. Our hearts couldn't help pounding with a rush of adrenaline as we stood knocking on the neighbor's door like we were the chief-of-police.

It was a good thing we put aside our fear since Nanny wound up having to get one of her legs amputated. Gangrene had grown inside of it. Keeping it would poison her instead of helping her. Although she had to get her leg cut off, it didn't make us love her any less. We were quite fascinated with her amputee. The stitch on the front of her stump was sown together in the pattern of a smiley face. Every time she rolled towards me in her wheelchair, it smiled at me. She never wore the prosthesis she was fitted for. She allowed Tamara and me to play with it instead.

Eventually, Nanny moved into a handicapped accessible apartment in Hayneville, Alabama. Since she was now considered handicapped, she wasn't in the position to be as independent as she had previously been. Tamara and I always enjoyed visiting her new apartment. We considered Nanny's place as a mini-resort because we were pretty much free to do whatever we wanted to do. That would have never been the case at home where rules were as common as food.

Housed on the back of the apartment complex was a playground we frequented whenever our hearts desired. We couldn't have been more carefree than we were when we swung on the swing set at our leisure as well as flipped ourselves on the monkey bar. We were having the time of our lives until we started having dealings with a bully who also resided in the apartment complex. He always appeared when we least expected and intimidated us to the point where we didn't know what to do. We informed Nanny, with tears in our eyes, about the many encounters we had with him and contemplated not going back to the playground at all.

"Child, y'all are just as welcomed on that playground as anyone else," Nanny said to us in an effort to soothe away our fear. "Go on out there and play."

We lingered at the door, looking back at her once more as we reluctantly walked out the back door. Sure enough the very one we didn't want to see was there. He started with us immediately. Little did we know, Nanny was watching with the eye of a tiger. She positioned her wheelchair in front of the window so she had a clear view of what was transpiring. We were about to yell out for her the moment the boy reached out to grab one of us. But Nanny was already rolling to our defense.

Ever so gracefully, she rolled up to the back door so she could make eye contact with the boy who was stirring up trouble. She had her stump crossed over her other leg. She told the boy, with one eye closed, the way it always was when she was angry, "Child, I don't know who your mother is, but you are going to die with your shoes on. Mark my words. Don't you got something better to do than pick on girls?" I was reeling with embarrassment. I couldn't believe my ears had heard Nanny say that. I was sure to ask her later on what she meant about the boy was going to die with his shoes on. "Child," she said with a giggle. "That means he's going to die getting into trouble."

It can be concluded what Nanny said to him in the heat of her anger, burning like wood in an incinerator, didn't sit well with that young gentleman. He hastily hopped on his moped, jerking his body as he did so. He placed his helmet on his head and zipped off, making sure to flash Tamara and I a dirty expression as he sped off, kicking up as much gravel and dirt as possible. I knew this was one last attempt to continue bullying us on the sly. But these events were years ahead. We first had to get acquainted in a home where we wouldn't be neglected.

Before it was made official that Mrs. Fair would be our new mom, she first had to endure a visit with us within the walls of DHR. It was a regulation mandated by the Department of Human Resources she could not avoid. We sat together in a room with only a few pieces of furniture and some toys, Tamara and I entertained ourselves with. There was a mirror on the wall. It wasn't just any ordinary mirror. On the other side of the mirror was a DHR caseworker who documented what took place between us and our prospective new mom. They spied on us as if they were members of the CIA, looking for the slightest inkling of something going wrong.

As we played around on the floor, Tamara was adamant about opening the door to the tiny little matchbox room. She had already been instructed not to do so. She decided to push her luck. With a sneaky glare resting upon her little face, Tamara placed her hand on the door and proceeded to twist it.

"Don't open the door." The strange lady who was going to be our mother, sternly said.

Tamara continued to glare at the lady. Suddenly, her eyes became angry. Tamara said to her, "I don't like you because you are nappy headed."

The strange lady, who we knew nothing about said, “I might be nappy headed, but you better not open that door.” We joined her at her house just in time for Thanksgiving. She was our new mother. She lavished us with beautiful clothes and shoes, for when we came to her we only had three dresses we had to share and the panties we had on.

She provided us with sustenance to cure our bloated tummies we had as a result of the severe malnourishment we had been subjected to. We fit in perfectly with mom’s family, who were biologically our family as well. They took us in and our level of regression halted. We got used to the chickens that ran around in the yard like they had a right to be there. I even took the liberty to name the biddies. As always, I refused to listen to mom when she told me the rooster and hen wouldn’t like it if I messed with their babies. I had to learn the hard way when one of them literally pecked me in the behind for doing what mom had advised me not to do.

We also had a dog. Well, he was Nana's dog. His name was Black Boy. At first, we were afraid of him because he was very playful and wanted to jump on you every time anyone came near him. We eventually got to the point where we took him his food, which was always left over scraps. Nana thought it was wasting money to buy dog food.

Everything was okay in our home until mom tried to take us to the bathroom. We were terrified of the bathroom, especially if the door had to be closed. We screamed to the top of our lungs and held onto her legs for dear life. She literally had to peel us off of her to put us in the tub. Something terrible had happened to us in a bathroom, but we couldn't vocalize what it was. No one else was able to tell us either. Maybe it was for the better. Such terrifying memories couldn't have done us a bit of good.

Dolls, ponytails, and mischief

We arose from the warmth of our new bed early on Christmas Morning. Tamara and I ran into the living room to see what awaited us under the Christmas tree. We had never been surrounded by so many gifts before. Our eyes danced with delight as we stood excitedly in our footed pajamas. The first gift I ripped open was the dune buggy. Santa had left it just for me. He left one for Tamara as well, except hers was blue and mine was orange. It was adorned with lights and everything, even came with a remote control. My lips turned up into a smile as I proceeded to run it into the walls. I was even successful in draining the batteries that same day. There were other toys as well under the Christmas tree. But I was interested in Jarrett's police car he had gotten from Santa. It was way cool with its flashing blue lights and sirens. When it crashed into the wall, it flipped over on its own and went the opposite way.

On this Christmas day in 1984, we played and played with all of the goodies we had been graced with. We even had a doll. The first thing we wanted to do was comb the dolls hair and pack it down with grease. Our playtime with our new toys was limited. As much as we wanted to roll around on the floor, amidst the torn wrapping paper, and the debris from the glittery decorations on the Christmas tree, we had to get ready to go to church service.

Mom dressed us in red and white suits. My jacket was white with red stripes. Tamara's was red with white coming down the center. Her jacket buttoned straight down the middle, while mine's buttoned over to the side. Renee, mom's oldest daughter, decorated our twigs on our heads with an array of ribbons and barrettes. They were hardly ponytails. In the midst of the fact, we didn't have much hair, we finally looked as if we belonged to somebody. We no longer looked like the homeless little kids from the third world countries.

When we got to church, we enjoyed hearing mom sing the Christmas song, "Jesus, Jesus, Oh, What a Wonderful Child."

There were other Christmas carols sung as well. While everyone else was rocking and singing along with the choir, Tamara and I sat on the pew visualizing returning home to play once more with our toys. When we exited Unity Baptist Church later that morning, we were both given a brown paper sack that had an orange, an apple, a grapefruit, and a candy cane inside. We smiled brightly, thinking to ourselves that Christmas was the best day ever.

Later on, we had our first Christmas dinner ever. Everything was beyond festive. Mom had really gone out of the way. She not only made sweet potato pies for us, but she made them for several other families within the community. I have to admit that mom made a good potato pie. Many nights, I got up in the night. I tiptoed into the kitchen and cut me an extra piece of that good pie when I didn't think no one else was paying attention. I wasn't selfish. I made sure to cut Tamara a piece as well. That way, if I got in trouble, I could say, "Well, Tamara had a piece, too."

The months came and they went like the seasons of the year. Shortly thereafter, we were enrolled in Sellers Memorial Daycare. We enjoyed riding the blue van every day to what we considered to be school. Our Aunt Nana always made sure we got on the bus safely, and granddad Joe, our foster mother's father, was there to get us off of the bus in the afternoon, making sure to always give us a slice of pie or either a piece of cake as soon as he got us in the house. He allowed us to sit on his knee while he held his pipe in his mouth. We interrogated him like we were high profile Attorney's until mom finally came to his rescue.

As he went to get up out of the chair, we held onto his legs, refusing to let him go until he first gave us both at least two pieces of the bazooka bubble gum he always had in his pocket. We ran to the door behind him as he placed his derby hat on his head, pressed our faces against the door, and watched as he disappeared up the path that separated our house from his. Even though he was not our biological grandfather, he was the only grandfather we had ever known. It was a severe blow to our hearts when he died in 1991.

While Tamara and I were enrolled at Sellers Memorial, we learned a lot of things we were behind on before moving in with mom.

One night, as I lay asleep, my breathing became labored. I made this noise from my lungs that sounded like a whistle. Mom hovered over me, concerned about what was ailing me.

"I believe this child has asthma," she said as she picked my limp body up into her robust arms. She proceeded to rush me to the hospital, only to realize when she got there that she had to wait for a social worker from

DHR to come and sign the release forms granting me permission to receive treatment.

Although I lived in her home, she didn't have legal custody of me. I was a ward of the state. She couldn't make any legal decisions on my behalf. Every little thing regarding my life was at the total discretion of DHR, rulings handed down from the district judge of Lowndes County. They had to be adhered to. There would be serious repercussions to pay otherwise. Since mom couldn't sign the release forms, I suffered longer than I had to. It took a social worker sometimes up to an hour to get there after mom had filled out all of my paperwork. Years later, I learned as a result that I had permanent lung damage that would never be corrected. Even though I have never been a smoker, I've been told that my lungs look like a smoker's lungs.

My new pediatrician, Dr. Albert Holloway, gave mom a prescription to get me a nebulizer. Everything was back on track until I got sick again. It happened again over in the middle of the night. I noticed as the years came and went that my asthma was oftentimes nocturnal.

That particular night, mom dressed me in a pair of yellow frilly pajamas. She put me in the bed with Nana while she got dressed. Once again, she was on her way up the dark road, chauffeuring me to the hospital, praying to God to allow me to breathe freely. Unfortunately, that time, I had to be admitted. The nurse taking care of me removed my yellow pajamas, replacing them with a gown that was opened in the back. I played with the characters on the gown until I tired myself out. The respiratory therapist came to my rescue with a breathing treatment. It was a relief since I had been coughing up phlegm from my lungs and was wheezing quite audibly.

While the mist from the mask evaporated into the air, the nurse rubbed an antiseptic called Betadine, on my arm in search for a vein to stick. I had to have an IV in order to receive the medicine I would need to make me feel better. She sung nursery rhymes to me as she stuck the needle in my arm. This was her way of distracting me from the pain I was about to feel.

"All done, little lady," she said to me and draped her arms around me in a hug when she was finished. She never said so, but I assumed this was a non-vocal apology for creating the boo-boo on my arm.

The next morning, after being admitted, I woke up to several faces glaring back into mine. They all were smiling. Granddad was there. Mama Tee and Uncle H were there as well. They brought me goodies to take my mind off of the needle in my arm. I had been fiddling with it every chance I got; wanted to rip it out of my vein. Renee stayed at the hospital with me while mom ran errands. When I was feeling better, she braided my hair and helped me with my lunch.

In the midst of learning I had asthma, I was still a carefree little girl. I had escaped the horrible conditions of my past and was in a place where I received adequate care and attention. What more could I have asked for? I had dolls, ponytails, and was quite mischievous. But as I traveled through life, I painfully learned I couldn't stay on the boulevard where everything was peachy king. I couldn't pitch my tent only in the sunshine for surely the rain would come. There were some dark roads ahead of me. Hopefully, I would have the strength and the courage to travel to these destinations without giving up.

The story of Nana

Every time I looked into her face, she reminded me of an Indian. Her cheekbones gave way to my thoughts as they were high, and she flaunted long tresses. She specifically reminded me of the Cherokee Indians, except she didn't live in a hut the way I knew Indians to live in, if going by the social studies lesson taught to me in school. There were so many times I wanted to ask her if she was an Indian. Fear kept me from doing so, as she felt that children didn't have the right to question grown-ups about anything. The lady who I talk of name is Mary Walker. I mentioned earlier that we all called her Nana.

Nana was a strict lady. She wasn't down for the "silliness" as she called it. Sometimes, I found her many rules to be quite overbearing. I tried as best as I knew how to play mom against her, simply because as any child would, I wanted to have my way. If I could skirt around handling my responsibilities as a minor, then that was what I was going to do.

When we first became a part of the family, Nana lived in the house with mom, mom's daughter, Renee, and our brother, Jarrett. I quickly adapted to her way of doing things. Experience taught me early on to stay as far away from her living quarters as I could get. For one, it wreaked with the scent of mothballs and Listerine. Besides, if she saw me lurking around like a lost sheep who'd gotten away from his shepherd, I was sure she would summon me to do something, if for nothing more than to empty her bedside commode. I would have rather gotten a whipping than to be caught with that pot in my hand.

Many days, Tamara and I were left in Nana's care while mom worked to keep a roof over our head at the church daycare. As soon as we got off the school bus, we saw her short frame standing at the front door, gazing at us as if we would get lost coming from the bus stop to the house. We knew not to stand idly socializing with anyone for she would surely embarrass us, had no problem at all with coming out to get us with her foot-long switch that she used as her rod of correction.

As we entered the house, we were aware of the routine. It was systematic and never altered. She made sure we did our homework. Sometimes after we completed our homework, she allowed us to play with our cousins Erica and Ashley. They lived across the street from us and became almost like our sisters since they spent many nights with us.

Nana then cooked for us. It wasn't always what we wanted. Whether we wanted it or not, we dared not tell her how much food to put on our plate.

"Nana, that is enough black-eyed peas," I said to her plenty of evenings as I stood watching her pack my plate down with food I didn't like. She continued dipping the cook spoon into the pot until she was satisfied with the amount I had on my plate. She never even looked in my direction as I pleaded with her to be scanty with the peas. I glared at her in disbelief, thinking she was the meanest person in the world as I witnessed sweat pouring out of every pore in her body, including her nose. She paid me no mind. Instead, she walked over to the counter to cut me a piece of cornbread. It was slightly burned on the bottom because she had been nodding in her chair while it was in the oven. I made sure to point that fact out to her. "Oh, child, hush," she said, fanning me away as if I was a fly. "That bread ain't going to hurt you. It will just give you good wind." She handed me my plate and poured me a cup of milk. I knew not to touch it until every drop of my food was gone.

I sighed heavily as I conjured up a crafty plan. I had to make the peas disappear. I sure as heck wasn't going to eat them. I watched Nana out of the corner of my eye until she dozed off again. Carefully and quietly, I tiptoed over to the counter and rolled off a hefty amount of paper towels. I hurried back to my seat. Tamara was snickering.

"Shhhhhh," I mumbled. "You're going to get us caught with all that laughing." I then distributed the paper towels between myself and Tamara. I placed mine in my lap and picked the plate up and began raking the peas onto the paper towel. I was careful not to put them all on the paper towel. That would raise Nana's eyebrows for sure. She knew well it would take me at least forty-five minutes to an hour to eat everything on my plate. She would know I hadn't eaten my food if I came out of the kitchen a moment too early. When that plan didn't work, I scooped up some of my food and put it on my cousin's, Alvin's, plate when he wasn't paying any attention. I know he had to know when he came back from the bathroom that his plate had more food on it. He never said anything. I never spared him as a result.

After dinner, we had to shell purple hurl peas Nana had bought from the vegetable man. It got to be quite a tedious task. I complained to Nana about how my fingers were hurting. She picked up her switch and pointed it at me. "I can make something else hurt, too," she said. I dropped my eyes to the floor and plopped back down in front of my unshelled peas. Eventually, Nana started to fall asleep. This was when Tamara and I grabbed a big arm full of peas and stuffed them in the bottom of the box that had the hurls from the peas we had already shelled. We smiled to ourselves knowing Nana would never figure out what we were up to. When she finally decided to wake up, all the peas were shelled, so she thought. She ushered us off to take our baths. It was bedtime after that. She sat attentively on the edge of our bed while we said our prayers. Then she stood, turned off the lights, walked out of the room, and turned the night light on in the hall. It was just enough light to shine through our room so we wouldn't feel overwhelmed by the darkness.

It wasn't always so easy living with Nana. She had some eccentric ways I just couldn't get down with. If we misbehaved, she made us get down on our knees and call Jesus name repeatedly. Sometimes, this ritual went on for at least an hour. She had a nickname for all of us. Mine was Titty. I asked her, "Nana, why do you call me that?" It was obvious that I was annoyed.

She said, "I call you Titty because you ain't big as one." It was one of those little quirks I could do nothing about because I was the child, and she was the adult. I eventually got over it. Really, I didn't have a choice. Besides, I quickly realized that being called Titty was small potatoes in comparison to when Nana waited until we got into a deep sleep. She entered our room, her cane thudding against the floor, wreaking havoc like a high category tornado, making us arise from our beds to clean up our room.

As I stumbled out of the bed, drunk with sleep, my eyes shifted from the clock on the wall to Nana. I looked at her as if she was nothing short of crazy. She didn't give me a chance to even speak.

"I don't want to hear it," she snapped. "You were supposed to clean this room up earlier and since you didn't do it then, you are about to do it now."

Lady, you are really getting on my last nerve with this crap, I quietly thought. I was careful not to allow her to see me giving her the dirty look. I would certainly, in that case, get a nice dose of her long switch, the same one that she could pop me with way in the kitchen while she sat in her favorite chair in the living room. Of course, she dozed off while sitting in the room supervising us like convicts. Tamara and I took full advantage of that fact. While she was watching Nana to make sure she didn't wake up, I was stuffing clothes in the boxes in the closet. Everything that didn't fit in the boxes I stuck under the bed.

Nana eventually moved into her own house, not even a mile away from us. Even with that small distance, we could not separate ourselves from her discipline and rules. We may as well have strapped on our seatbelts. It was going to be a long ride with Nana. She was the driver. We were the passengers. We realized in the end that she only wanted the best for us.

Here is my story…

Part One: The Boulevard of letdowns and disappointments

My Mother Didn't Want Me

Staring through the Kaleidoscope of innocence

I looked forward to making the long awaited trip to Julia Tutwiler Prison one Saturday out of each month to visit Carolyn. Even though she was an inmate, identified by a number (AIS number) the state of Alabama issued along with a white jumpsuit to serve as every-day-attire, and a cell to be her living quarters for the duration of her sentence, still I always held Carolyn in the highest regard.

She had no say in anything, not even when she got up in the morning or lay down at night to sleep. Yet, in my world, she was like no other I'd ever encountered. She was as beautiful as a sunset illuminating along the sandiest beach in the spring of the year. Her uplifting smile left a feeling of tranquility rustling inside of me like soft fingers through the locks of one resting wearily in a hammock. Just to be in her presence, I likened to a soothing melody descending from the heavens above to irrigate my forlorn existence. Suddenly, all of my miniscule troubles dripped away from my frame just the same as sweat trickling from the pores of one settled amidst the sweltering sun.

As I tenderly gazed into her stunning eyes, my heart skipped a couple of beats. I could envision an unprecedented love interred in those eyes. It was that flawless, what I thought to be unconditional love which gave me the strength I needed to make it from one visitation until the next. Hence, I looked at her as if she was superwoman, adoring her with every fiber of my being and idolizing her as well.

Most of the time, the memories I constructed with beautiful colors of innocence were only a figment of my imagination. It did not stop me from using my heart as a canvas to paint them on. Together, we danced on the moon, riding to a faraway land on a unicorn, the pastel colors of the rainbow eclipsing our way. We sat among a garden of marigolds. She stroked my hair and read fables to me. It was a beautiful masterpiece crafted in my mind. I hung it with love in my heart. As beautiful as I thought it to be, it wasn't the same as having the opportunity to see her in the flesh, to feel her burly arms wrapped tightly around my petite frame, emitting waves of affection from deep within the abyss of her soul. When I was afforded the chance to look upon her face, it was nothing short of heaven on earth.

As the day to visit came nigh, my heart thumped mercilessly in my chest. The smile I wore became more infectious as the hours slowly ticked by. But who was I fooling? I knew I wouldn't be getting any sleep. Tamara and I lay in bed the night before we were to visit her, making tents out of our covers, giggling loudly while telling each other stories. The laughter we shared traveled far beyond the four walls in our room into the hallway and made its way to mom's room. She yelled from her room, "Y'all better cut the snickering out and go your butts to sleep, now. I don't intend to say it again."

We were rebellious little ones. Sleep was the farthest thing from our minds. We continued playing, knowing all too well we may have to be disciplined in the end. We did make an effort to conceal our bouts of laughter. When Tamara was too loud, I put my finger up to my lip, signaling her to quiet it down a notch. She did the same to me, when I was too loud. Eventually, we did fall prey to the mighty forces of sleep.

The next glorious morning, when the sky was exquisite in its form and the sun shone abroad the horizon, I couldn't bring myself to eat breakfast. The house was filled with the delicious aroma of bacon sizzling and eggs frying. I inhaled the scent of mom's Folger's coffee brewing no soon as I left out of my room, chuckled silently as I reminisced on how granddad had always told me, "Chile, you don't want any coffee. Coffee makes you black." Yet, he always had him a cup, most of the time, when I saw him.

The rapid sounds of mom mixing the batter for the pancakes intensified my delightful mood. It was a sound that jolted happiness beyond my wildest dreams. I pitter pattered my way into the kitchen and began to sing along with the gospel artist John P. Kee as he bellowed through the radio sitting atop the counter. Mom never looked up as I slid past her and found my place at the kitchen table. I allowed my feet to dangle while resting my chin in my palms. Mom was doing her thing. I never knew how she could make such a perfect batch of pancakes. I couldn't help noticing I wore the same expression of astonishment on my face when I watched her roll out dough with her rolling pin to make homemade biscuits. Oftentimes, I mimicked mom's swift moves in the kitchen whenever I played house with Tamara.

I continued watching mom with amazement. Although queasiness was fluttering in my stomach, I was certain I was able to eat what was placed before me. Only after a couple of bites, I was full. I sat aimlessly at the table glaring at the leftover food on my plate as if it would magically disappear. Every five minutes I glanced at the oval clock on the wall, hoping it was time for us to hop in the car so we could be on our way. When I discovered only a few minutes had passed, disappointment hovered over me, taunting me like a bully on the playground at school. All I thought of was how much fun I was going to have. Even Jarrett chopping my head off, with his surly and uncalled for words, did not have the capacity to alter my good mood. I did allow myself to think about it. With a menacing glare outlining his face, he shoved me over to the side, "Get your little bony self out of the way," he said as he stormed into the bathroom, slamming and locking the door behind him. I jumped a little, obviously rattled by the thunderous sound it made. But I shook the feeling off and once again, flashed my youthful smile. Any other time, I would have been upset, doing my very best, a snide expression engraved on my face, to assure he got in trouble, but not today. I went to my room and greased my legs. Mom wasn't big on buying lotion. She felt as if some good petroleum Vaseline was capable of shining up anything that was ashy.

An hour or so later, I boarded a white van in Montgomery, Alabama, to be whisked away to Carolyn's home. Instead of being greeted with flowers at the front door, I was greeted with barbwire and correctional officers.

Still, I was exhilarated beyond my wildest dreams. *This is it*, I excitedly thought, hardly able to contain myself. Finally, when the gates swung open I ran into Carolyn's arms, giving her the biggest bear hug I could manage. I was indeed famished for her affection. It was a lucid realization to all who were around me.

After our hug, we wandered over to a table in the courtyard where I jabbered nonstop about everything my mind could conjure. "I got an "A" at school last week. I wrote you a poem last night. We are having spaghetti for dinner this evening. Mom let us join the Girl Scouts."

It did not matter how uneventful the words were that spilled from my lips. As long as I knew she was listening, it was ammunition for me to keep talking. Tamara and I were in competition for her attention. I looped my arm through one of her arms, and Tamara's arm was looped through her other arm. We felt it was our duty to walk with her wherever her feet treaded. She was our biological mother. There was not a thing she could ever do wrong.

There were many times Tamara and I were the only two who felt this way about Carolyn. Our three older siblings were less than enthusiastic to visit the prison. I remember times in between visits when they had not so nice things to say about her. I'll never forget the day when I was on my knees in a chair backed up to the sink washing dishes. I was too short to reach the sink without spilling water all over myself and the floor as well.

Pam, Sharmeen, and Jarrett sat at the kitchen table where they engaged in a heartfelt conversation about Carolyn. I tried hard to tune out the hurtful things they said, but it pierced my heart to the point I burst into tears. Pam looked around from filing her fingernails and gaped at me. She scooted back her chair, stood up, made her way over to me, and wiped the tears from my eyes.

"Tamyra, what's wrong," she asked me.

"I just don't like for y'all to talk about her like that!" I whimpered, afraid to allow my eyes to meet hers. I could feel her looking at me, and I knew her hazel eyes were filled with the glow of sympathy.

On the other hand, Jarrett wasn't hearing my ranting. He stuck to his guns, not caring the least how dangerous the bullets were escaping the chamber. He sighed heavily and said, "Trust me when I tell you, one day you'll understand why we feel the way we feel. Furthermore, you ought not to be wasting any tears on her sorry ass!" Then, with an evil laugh, he said, "She sure isn't wasting any on you."

Pam quickly shushed him as she saw I was becoming more upset. "We shouldn't be talking about her," she said in an attempt to smooth things over. "After all, she is our mother."

"Mother," Jarrett yelled out, pretending like he was shocked. "So who considers a woman who abandoned her children as a mother?"

"Stop it, now," Pam spoke up again. "We may not like the things she does, but she will always be our mother."

I finally looked at Pam, thankful to see that she was defending our mother. She smiled at me in return and wrapped her arms around my shoulder. This infuriated Jarrett even more. He backed away from the table, knocking over his chair as he did so. "She's a coldhearted bitch if you ask me," he spat, making sure to look me in the face as those words fell off of his lips. He walked out of the kitchen, headed to his room. I could hear him saying as he stomped up the hallway, "If she wants to be treated like a mother, she should try acting like one." He then closed himself up in solitude. This was his way of concluding the conversation was over.

Sharmeen never said anything at all, although I knew she was not going to make any apologies for feeling the way she felt. Poor me, I was staring through the Kaleidoscope of innocence where everything was a pattern of beauty. I would soon find out some of the patterns weren't so beautiful. It would be a disappointment creating turbulence in my world for sure.

As the visits with Carolyn came and went, my pleasure to see her never waned. The gleam in my eyes was just as visible as it had always been, never once watered down with a mixture of sadness and anger.

Being frisked by the correctional officers became customary. I assumed the position of stretching out my arms and legs without having being asked to do so. As soon as I saw Carolyn's face, I lit up like a Christmas tree, glowing brightly in a room which had no other light.

Normal conversation became her telling us who all were there for murdering their boyfriends or husbands. She informed us as well of the women who were going with other women within the prison. I knew this was not healthy conversations for our tender ears. But who was I to tell

Carolyn what to say? I found it to be "juicy gossip," like my classmates said at school when they heard something they should not have heard.

When it was time to go, I watched Carolyn and all of the other inmates form a single file line so a head count could be done. They looked like a garden of white Chrysanthemums as they slowly walked back within the walls of the prison. This was their homes. It was a life sentence for some of them.

With a pang of sadness cutting my soul, I waved goodbye over and over again as we loaded the white van which always brought us to the prison. Now it was going to take us home where I regurgitated my memories of that visit until I was allowed to visit her again.

The rearview mirror of disappointment

Carolyn did not stay incarcerated forever. As fate would have it, she got her chance to savor the long lost flavor of freedom once more. She greedily ravished the moment like a wild animal devouring its prey.

The year was 1991. On a day she considered as blessed, she walked out of the prison, leaving behind sordid memories of locked cells and eager inmates who looked upon her with envious eyes as she became a product of their past. I am certain there were things she endured while an inmate at Julia Tutwiler that she never wanted to once more darken the remnants of her mind.

I looked forward to this day. Now that it was here, I was happy to be a part of this milestone. Finally, I'd made it to the avenue of preteen years, it having dangerous curves I could not begin to master. I was eleven-years-old to be exact, feeling as though we had plenty of time to make up for the lost years we missed out on when she was locked up, and even before she was locked up, when still she was missing in action.

After she was set free from behind the walls where it was normal to live in cages, our fairytale existence slowly began to dwindle. There wasn't any fairy dust I could sprinkle in our lives to make things right. I had plans for us. Carolyn had plans as well. Her plans did not coincide with my plans. We weren't going to be the family who lived in the ranch style house with the white picket fence after all. We weren't going to have a pet dog named, Spot, either.

I had imagined how we would plant flowers in the front yard to make our home appear more warm and inviting. There would be a sign on the door that read, "The Walkers." So much for the dream of new beginnings that once made my heart flutter erratically with joy. Instead of blowing each other kisses as we left home for school, we would be shedding tears in the midnight hour, tears that soaked our pillowcases and made our eyes puffy and sad, tears that continued to flow down the youthfulness of our faces because once the old tears were dried, the new set of tears couldn't be contained.

The first time I remembered having to glance into the rearview mirror of disappointment was when Carolyn promised us we would see her for Thanksgiving. Our little hearts couldn't have retained any more happiness than it had already, knowing she was coming for such a special occasion.

Mom had the house lit up with the scent of Thanksgiving dinner cooking. We got up early, anticipating her arrival. Renee, took us to the Thanksgiving Parade in Montgomery, Alabama. We excitedly watched all of the marching bands and the many floats as they passed by where we stood in the crowd. We were on a new level of excitement when our beloved Central High School marching band came through. We even danced along with them when they stopped to do a routine to Bobby Brown's song, "Ain't Nobody Humping Around."

When it was over, it took us a minute to find our way back to the car. Howbeit, once we were sitting in the back seat and had locked ourselves in the safety of our seatbelts, we could not wait to get home. Carolyn would soon be there. We had to hurry up and get there as well.

No soon as we drove up the driveway, Tamara and I practically leapt out of the car before it had time to stop. If Carolyn was already in the house, we wanted to hurriedly jump into her arms. Who could blame us for feeling this way? We had not seen her since her release from prison. We had not heard from her as well. The moment her incarceration was over, so were the letters we had received. Many days, I glanced out the door at the mail lady, hoping she would deliver a letter from Carolyn. It never happened. Although sadness was prevalent, I brushed it off as if she was too busy getting ready to allow us to live with her. "She don't have time to write letters," I concluded.

A few hours passed. Slowly, the ugliness of worry became visible. It invaded our thoughts. Remaining optimistic had become a long shot. The Thanksgiving dinner was set on the kitchen table and it was quite a spread. It was time for the grace and for everybody to dig in. Earlier, I had tried to watch the Macy's Day Parade on television, but I could not enjoy it. Neither did I volunteer to lick the cake batter out of the bowl the way I normally did. Though I wanted to have faith in Carolyn, I constantly looked out the window for her. The least sound I heard, I assumed it was her pulling up in the driveway.

Only moments later, mom brought out the cranberry sauce. Everybody gathered around the table, grabbing each other's hand to say grace. I decided I was not going to eat until Carolyn got there. *Maybe I'll call her. She might be caught in traffic*, I thought. I excused myself and went to grab the rotary phone. I meticulously dialed her number and placed the receiver up to my ear. When I did not receive an answer, I thought again, *She is probably in the store paying for gas. I'll just wait a few more minutes and call her again.* Once I placed the second call, I still didn't receive an answer. I hung up and dialed her number again, and again, and again. I received no answer.

By then, my eyes were filled with tears. I sneaked a glance in the direction of my family, who all stared back with sad eyes. Tamara's eyes were filled with tears as well. Mom looked on with pity. She carried on as if she wanted to say something but looked down instead. I quickly brushed the tears away, refusing to give up hope. She was bound to come. Soon it was 7:30. I was seated in front of the window, waiting and wishing for Carolyn to show up. *Maybe she decided to come late so she could spend the night with us*, I now thought, actually perking up for an hour or so.

Then, it was 9:00 pm. I knew she was not coming. She stood us up, never once placing a call to let us know what happened. Well, I was going to take it upon myself to find out why. With tears flowing nonstop, I once again picked up the receiver to the phone. I dialed her number. No answer I received. I hung up and dialed again and again. She was not answering any of my calls. That only made the pain I felt fester.

I lay in bed later on in the night with Tamara next to me. My heart was as heavy as a set of barbells. No matter how hard I tried, the tears wouldn't stop. Eventually, I fell asleep in the midst of tears and a deep fog of sadness.

The next day, I could not help noticing how Jarrett looked at me with that, "I told you so," expression on his face. I waited for him to throw the brutal punch of saying the words. He never did. He actually tried a little harder to be nice, giving me a pat on the shoulder as he walked out the front door to go play basketball with his friends.

And then anger showed up on the scene!

I didn't hear from Carolyn for at least three months. She avoided me at all cost. I continuously tried to reach her. Every time she refused to answer, I cried again, until one day instead of crying, I noticed I felt angry. I tried hard to keep those feelings at bay, knowing how hard I didn't want my brother to be right. He had warned me about the day I would understand why he, Pam, and Sharmeen felt the way they felt. Even so, I couldn't stop my own not so pleasant thoughts from singing their chorus in my mind. *What the hell is wrong with this lady? She's nothing more than a lowdown cow. I hope she die and go to hell.*

It had never dawned on me until this very moment, why I never addressed Carolyn as mother. It didn't feel natural. No matter how much I thought things were going to work out for us, I couldn't bring myself to call her mother. That special honor was reserved for the one who was truly there for me, the one who had raised her own two daughters and still took me in. That was who mom was. I noticed at times, she cried along with Tamara and I when our hearts were broken because of promises made by Carolyn in which she never had any intentions of keeping.

I've heard the saying, "Time heals all wounds." It proved to be true in my world. As much as I wanted to stay angry with Carolyn, I eventually got over it. My heart was once more carefree like a kid rolling down a hill on a summer's afternoon. I allowed myself to fall victim to the same trap of believing her the next time she promised us something. That time, she assured us she would take us school shopping. I couldn't help believing her. She had a way of making words sound so convincing. I felt I would be a fool if I didn't ride along with her on this pillow of hope. Tamara and I took our baths, and we got dressed. We were seated in the living room to await Carolyn's arrival. We were beyond excited, deciding to shoot the breeze with each other while we waited. I saw Jarrett with my peripheral vision as he entered the living room. He had that, "Here we go again with Carolyn's lies," expression on his face.

I wanted so badly to jump defensive and tell him, "Look, just because you are bitter doesn't mean Tamara and I have to be." Instead, I decided to let the dust settle. I didn't say anything at all. I knew it wouldn't be a good idea. He could snap me in half without much effort. A couple of hours later, I realized again that Carolyn was not coming to take us shopping. She fell back into her same pattern of not answering the phone when I tried to reach out to her.

After that day, alas, I was faced with disappointment time and time again. I remember sitting on the edge of the bed late one evening, crying once more. The reason for my tears were because Carolyn in her latest web of deceit, had promised again she was going to let us live with her. She even went as far as to bring us to Birmingham, showing us the school we would attend when she knew all along, she didn't have any intentions of reuniting with us.

At that low point in my life, I came to the conclusion that Carolyn did not want me. The tears fell harder when that thought escaped the now hollow area in my heart which had housed such high hopes. I had to say the words out loud for it to completely register. Saying it once again created the emotion of anger. That anger invaded my mind. It wanted revenge. It wanted to make me pick up the phone and curse Carolyn out from A to Z, or maybe, I could write her a nasty letter. She would get it for sure, even if she didn't respond.

Where Was My Father?

Was everyone having a dad the latest fad? I too wanted one

The first event I ever considered big in my life was when I won second place in the Spelling Bee Contest while in the fifth grade. I was the typical fifth grader, petite as far as height. I weighed less than 100 pounds. I still had long, thick tresses and at that point in life, often wore ponytails with the cute little multicolored barrettes fastened at the end. Mom hadn't yet processed it with a relaxer the way I saw so many other girl's hair at school and wherever else I went.

My heart still rhythmically fluttered with excitement, if mom would be nice enough to let me have a bang. Such a thing didn't happen often. I knew from experience not to take any privilege for granted. I was still a kid and conducted myself as such, although every now and then, I got the nerve to rise up against authority. Certainly, mom would break me down to my least common denominator. I knew not to press my luck again, at least for a while.

As a child, usually, I was very docile in that I let people convince me to do just about anything, even if it was something I didn't really want to do. I was quite mousy a time or two, would shed tears at the drop of a dime, and allowed myself to be a doormat for the sake of other's not only wiping but stomping their feet on me more times than I care to recollect. When it came to winning the spelling bee, I was a different person. One could say I had an alter ego. My alter ego was not to be downplayed or toyed with when spelling words were involved. Nothing or nobody could take me off of my high because my head was somewhere between the stars and the clouds in the sky.

Mom showed her face at the spelling bee as I stood up front amongst my peers and various instructors from schools throughout the Lowndes County District. I spelled each word administered to me, brimming with confidence, making certain to cut my eyes in mom's direction every now and then. It was something about measuring the breadth of the smile etched upon her full lips that broadened my level of brashness. If that wasn't enough, the fact I got a chance to miss practically a whole day of school definitely sweetened the deal. Nothing was greater than having the unmistakable privilege of riding with Mr. Moore, who was my sixth grade teacher, in his shiny white Volvo.

When it was all over, the first and second place winners of the spelling bee came from my school, respectively. I held onto my trophy as if it was a jackpot. Each time I looked down at it sitting in my lap, I grinned widely like a lucky kid being drafted into the NBA straight out of high school.

It would have been nice to see Carolyn sitting in the audience, her face too glowing with pride the way all the other parents who were there supporting their children were. That was one of those things I had no control over. It bludgeoned my heart, seemingly beyond repair.

I decided to safely tuck away the pain for the time being, refusing to allow sad thoughts to rain on my parade of happiness. That time, I was going to spend basking in the ambiance of my surroundings, a surrounding where I was smiling, relishing in the fact of how I dared to be good at something. No doubt, I would eventually take a nosedive off the mountain of my high, crashing hard into the valley of despondency. Its impact would paralyze my strength, would make me feel I could never go on. But who had time to dwell on such negativity? When fate allowed such misfortune to knock on my door, it would be on my own terms, or so I thought.

The next measure of happiness came to be when close to the end of my final year in elementary school, I was fortunate enough to attend the sixth grade prom. Upon learning there would be a prom, Tamara and I raced each other in the house that afternoon to be the bearer of the good news.

"Guess what, mom?" we asked in unison, pausing to allow what we had said thus far to marinate in mom's head. We glanced at each other. Our silly grins caused our cheeks to expand over the fullness of our faces. I motioned for Tamara to finish telling mom. That seemed to be the cherry on the ending of her day. She wasted no time letting mom know about the prom, an extravagant event hosted by

Mrs. Davis, my fifth grade teacher. Together, we skipped to our room, filling each other's head with dazzling ideas about prom dresses and corsages.

Mom definitely went out of her way to make this event memorable for us. She spared no expense, treating our prom as if it were a red carpet event. Never before did I remember a time when I felt so special. Not only did we have a new dress and shoes from Parisian, we also were afforded the chance to get our hair pressed. We practically ran over to Mrs. Peterson's house so she could run the hot comb through our thick tresses.

Normally, getting our hair pressed was a privilege reserved for Easter Sunday only. So we were not wasting any time skedaddling over to her place where she welcomed us with the same smile we always saw on her face. She even wore this smile at Sunday school when she taught us about the twelve disciples, Shadrach, Meshach, and Abednego (I used to think they were saying Billy goat), the Virgin Mary, and all of the other biblical stories.

Our level of enthusiasm grew once more when we returned home. Mom smiled at us like she had never seen a set of twins more gorgeous in her life. She put baby's breath flowers over the ponytail in the top of our heads while the rest of our hair flowed down our napes, extending almost midways our back. She stood back proudly, hand on hip, admiring her work. It was one of the few times in my life when I actually felt beautiful. Tamara and I walked out to the car that evening, feeling like we were princesses. I pretended mom's car was our awaiting chariot. We slung our hair every chance we got, taking a peek at ourselves in the rearview mirror. I smiled at Tamara. "You look pretty," I said.

"Thank you. You do, too," she responded, reciprocating the compliment I had given to her.

I noticed at the prom how a lot of the girls came through the doors with gentlemen escorting them who were too old to be their brother's as I knew none of them were allowed to have boyfriends. Who else would be escorting them? The wheels in my head started to turn. *Who are they?* I wondered. Then, I heard one girl say, "I love you, dad," as he prepared to leave.

Now I wasn't so green that I hadn't heard the word dad before. I couldn't help feeling a breeze of envy as I witnessed the beauty of a dad and daughter relationship unfolding right before my eyes. I didn't think about it for long though, for I was having myself a ball. It was another one of those thoughts I would have to pull out of my mind's bag at a later date. I did notice the bag of issues to deal with later was getting quite heavy. Soon it would be full and I would have no choice but to give it my full attention, or it would break me down for sure.

It wasn't long before my elementary graduation was the new event to lavish upon. So it wasn't a high school graduation, the commencement in which people usually made a big fuss about. Still, it was my day, a day I was entitled to feel as if I had done something wonderful. Indeed, I had. I felt proud to stand at the town of Whitehall, singing with my classmates, "Whitehall, proudly do we stand. To me you are so grand and bold. With your gallant colors of blue and of gold, and in the future when all of us are gone, and we are far along our way, you'll still be a part of our lives, in times of joy and strife, in darkness and in light, Whitehall we pray."

We had spent many days practicing this song. At times, I heard it in my sleep. It made all the sense in the world for the Whitehall Elementary class of 1991-1992 to feel proud, when finally, at the commencement exercise, we were all in tune. I had to control my urge to laugh out loud when Mr. Moore did his signature hum before we were to start singing. It was an epic moment that I shall never forget as long as there is breath in my body.

Then to get my diploma wrapped up with the cutest little ribbon, was the icing on the cake. If only Carolyn was there to witness it. That thought came across my mind as we exited the stage after receiving our diplomas. Perhaps I wouldn't have felt so bummed, if I had a shiny dad I could show off like most of the girls in my sixth grade class had. The dads were laying it on thick, expressing to their little girls how proud of them they were. As Tamara and I left the building, a few steps behind mom, I was feeling left out. What was so special about them? How come they could have a dad and I couldn't? Was everyone having a dad the latest fad? I, too, wanted one.

Lord, if you hear me, can you just send me a dad, please?

Before summer break was to end, leading to my first year in junior high, I finally got the nerve to ask mom about my dad. I had failed to do so before, assuming since I didn't have a dad, having one must have been a privilege I wasn't deserving of. Maybe I wasn't being as obedient as I should have been. Maybe I needed to work harder to keep my room clean and get along with my sister. Then, maybe I would be able to have a dad.

I tried to be more adept when it came to being a good girl. Regardless of how I was on my P's and Q's, I had no dad to show for it. The disappointment of not having one was taking its toll on me. So now it was time to stop lollygagging and ask mom what the deal was.

She was in the kitchen when I decided to confront her. I peeked around the corner at her before going into the kitchen. I wasn't going to back down. I have to admit, I was nervous. My heart was playing a symphony of anxiousness in my chest. It seemed as if my words were caught in my throat. The urge to vomit right then was imminent.

As I neared mom I completely lost my nerve, pretending I had only come into the kitchen for a cup of milk. I drank the milk I fixed, threw the cup in the sink, and started to leave the kitchen. Upon reaching the doorway, I turned around, sneaking another glance in mom's direction. I wanted to walk out of the door. Instead, my feet led me right back before her.

"Mom," I said, barely above a whisper.

She looked up. "Yes, child?" she responded.

I walked up to her. She was sitting at the table picking collard greens. I cleared my throat and gathered my nerve before I continued talking.

"Wh-wh-why don't I ha-have a dad?" I stuttered. My face was weighted down with sadness. I felt tears wanting to well up in my eyes.

There, before mom's presence, I stood fidgeting and playing with the loose ravels on my shirt to minimize my level of nervousness. She had to know about my dad. If she only told me what his name was, that would be a start. I would graciously accept that piece of information as if it was a kidney to keep me from going into renal failure.

My entire life, I had never heard the slightest detail about him, couldn't help wondering if news of him was some forbidden taboo no one was allowed to talk about. Unfortunately, there wasn't much mom could tell me. I sadly walked back to my room, muttering under my breath. "This doesn't seem fair. Will I ever know him? I only want to know who he is."

As time fluttered by like butterflies in the sky, I was once again able to put this latest blow behind me. It was a good thing I had a resilient spirit because disappointments were coming at me from every angle. I couldn't fold under the pressure of distress. I had lived twelve years so far without a father. Maybe it wasn't such a necessity after all that I should have one.

I rehearsed this lie over and over again just to have the strength I needed to make it from one day until the next. It certainly wasn't the way I truly felt. It pacified me for the time being, until I was placed in a situation where I knew that if I had a dad, he wouldn't have allowed such a thing to happen to me.

I had now started my first year in junior high school. Things were going quite well. The weather was still humid. Even though it was late September, the season had not yet given in to the treacherous chill of fall.

I got off the bus one afternoon in a chipper mood. Finally, mom had started to let Tamara and I cut grass. On this particular day, it was my turn. No soon as I ran in the house, I dropped my backpack on the floor, and changed into a pair of shorts and a sleeveless t-shirt. I ran out of the house and quickly started the lawn mower. I was all smiles once I started to cut the grass, totally blinded by the sweat dripping off my petite frame. It wasn't until I felt Renee nudge me on the shoulder that I realized someone else was outside with me.

"Go in the house now, she said," her voice filled with fright.

"What's wrong?" I asked, my body displaying the disappointment I obviously felt.

"Uncle H is watching you. Go in the house now."

I quickly shut the lawn mower off and glanced over my shoulder. Sure enough, Uncle H had his blood shots eyes fixed in the side rearview mirror of his car, staring me up and down. Suddenly, I could feel my heart beating fast, and I ran to safety.

I don't know how I made it inside of the house because my legs felt like rubber, but I wasn't stopping until I was out of range of Uncle H's roaming eyes. I sat down on the couch, my body trembling with fear. Immediately, my mind drifted back to the year before.

It was a semi warm day in the latter part of March when Tamara and I strolled over to Uncle H's house late one afternoon. He said he had a surprise for us. I don't know about anyone else, but I wasn't one to turn down any surprise offered to me.

The weird thing is, once we got to his house, he wanted me to go outside and get the surprise from under the seat of his car while Tamara stayed in the house with him. I was reluctant and refused to move. I wasn't psychic. Needless to say, I felt that something fishy was about to take place. It was my place to shield my very own twin sister to the best of my ability. That was until Uncle H picked up a brick and acted like he wanted to hit me with it.

I didn't stand around to see if he was going to actually hit me. I ran with all the strength my little legs mustered. I never knew what happened that day. Tamara was very tight-lipped about the situation. But I knew whatever it was, it wasn't good. When she came outside to meet me, she had that same uncomfortable look on her face that she had when she knew one of her teachers would be calling mom to relay to her about some unfavorable behavior she had displayed in class. I knew I wasn't going to get any answers. Finally, I decided to let it go.

Two weeks later, as the shade of morning lifted and welcomed afternoon, Tamara came busting in the house, looking behind as she entered. She acted as if she was running from something that had been chasing her. She was out of breath and crying uncontrollably, the look of panic streaked her eyes.

"What's wrong?" I wanted to know.

"Uncle H tried to put his hands down my dress," she said, almost to the point of hyperventilating.

My mouth flew open in disbelief. Tamara's emotions were transferred onto me. I shared her fear and tears. He had never touched me. I felt bad for my sister but relieved he didn't see fit to put his paws on me.

While trying to process the shocking things Tamara had told me, I felt the urge to vomit. I thought it was quite disgusting for someone as old as Uncle H to be putting his hands all over someone as young as Tamara. I couldn't help wondering if he felt she had done something to warrant him doing such a horrendous and downright disrespectful thing to her. Then, I felt angry. I wanted to beat him within an inch of his life or until he begged for mercy. Whichever one came first. He had to know what he was doing was wrong, if he wanted my sister to remain silent about it. She wasn't even supposed to tell me. It was supposed to be their little secret. The secret had been exposed.

I tried my best to soothe my sister as the tears continued to flow down her face. As I held her in my arms, eventually her breathing returned to a normal pace. I handed her a Kleenex she used to wipe the lingering tears away. There still weren't many words to be shared. I could tell she was embarrassed. She probably felt as if it was her fault she had been handled that way.

It wasn't until a couple of months or so later when I decided to visit Mama Tee, Uncle H's sister, when I realized he had plans for me as well. Mama Tee was in the kitchen when I arrived, welcoming me with a smile.

"Bring those wet lips over here and give me a kiss," she said. I smiled brightly as I walked up to her frame, which had shrunk tremendously in the past couple of years since she now walked with a slight hump in her back.

Uncle H was seated in the living room pretending to be watching television. He summoned me only after a few brief moments of me talking to Mama Tee. I was so scared that I immediately went to him without thinking about it.

"Give your Uncle a hug," he said to me slyly. I leaned over and gave him a hug. I noticed how he held me a little longer than necessary.

When he finally decided to loosen his strong grip, he said, "Now, give your uncle a kiss." I leaned over to kiss him on the cheek. He quickly turned his lips towards me so the kiss landed there instead. I started to back up a little, feeling myself become unnerved.

"Wait," he said. I froze right where I stood. However, I refused to look up at him. Mama Tee had no idea what Uncle H was proposing to do to me in the other room, only a few feet from her.

"Use your tongue," he said.

Finally, I looked up at him. He had a cold glare outlining his features. I slowly backed further away, "I'll see you later, Mama Tee!" I yelled, turning on my heels once I was far away from him to run without him brushing his hand across my rear end.

Tears began to stream down my face as I broke out of my trance. I was still sitting on the couch trembling, too afraid to move. He sat, yet again, one evening in his car, staring through the blinds of my bedroom window. I was wrapped in a towel as I had just gotten out of the shower. The gross feeling that I was being watched disseminated throughout my mind. I looked up, surprised to meet his gaze, same bloodshot eyes as before. He looked as if he'd been drinking. His dirty mind was way beyond the point of stable.

"Tamara, come here!" I screamed, as I ran out of the room.

If only I had a dad. I know he would have protected me. He would have subdued Uncle H, beating him into a bloody pulp. That would serve him right as far as my young eyes could see. He shouldn't have been such a morally depraved pervert.

Tamara and I hadn't told mom what was going on. We thought we could handle it on our own. Since mom didn't know, she sent us spiraling right into his wicked web when one morning we missed the school bus.

"Ask Uncle H to take you to school," she said. She couldn't take us herself because she had to pick up a client and was already pressed for time. Tamara and I looked at each other, dysphoria creeping upon us before we had time to blink.

We held hands while walking over to ask Uncle H if he would take us to school. With nervousness in our steps, we walked up the staircase and stood before him. His attitude was cold. He treated us as if we had done something to him. But he agreed to chauffeur us to school. As he popped the lock on the car, Tamara and I both hopped in the back seat. We sat as close as we possibly could to each other. I felt her pulse as well as smelled the Colgate on her breath. I'm certain she felt my pulse and smelled my minty fresh breath as well.

I couldn't tell which one of us was trembling more. We were that close to each other. Uncle H snapped on his seatbelt and peered at us sitting in the backseat.

"Why are both of you sitting back there?" he spat. His level of discontent had gone in that moment from a one to ten. The veins in his head were visible. Now, I was afraid to look at him at all.

"One of you can sit upfront," he finally said.

Tamara didn't budge, so I eventually crawled over to the other side and got out. I opened the front door of the car and sat down; all the while praying Uncle H wouldn't touch me.

"Lord, if you hear me, can you just send me a dad, please!" were the words that continuously invaded my mind. Thankfully, we made it to school that day without being fondled.

I pretty much yanked Tamara out of the backseat once Uncle H pulled up in front of the school.

"Come on," I managed to say. "We are already late."

As I closed the door, I saw the dissatisfied expression growing more and more with each passing second on Uncle H's face. I read his lips as he muttered a few curse words and pulled away from the curb before we fully had time to get out of the way.

Say goodbye to the dream of ever having a dad

I made it through seventh grade unscathed by the hand life dealt me. I didn't get the cards I always wanted. Still, I could play my hand and be okay. My ability to bounce back kicked in right on time. I went through my highs and lows just the same as anybody else. Some days, I was happy as could be, the preponderance of the evidence was showcased in the way I carried myself. Other days, I had to literally fight off depression.

When it attacked, it was vicious, like a flesh eating bacteria, ripping apart everything within my mind that was vital for my survival. It showed me previews of the worst case scenarios, painted the bleak picture of things not possibly getting better.

By now, Carolyn was a nonfactor. She wasn't coming around at all. She didn't even call anymore. She could've at least pretended to care, so I could have false hope to hold on to. At least then, the tears would have been fewer as I cried myself to sleep so many nights. The last time I had seen her was at a deposition hearing a few months earlier. She didn't seem happy to be there. I was surprised she had even bothered to come. We went before the judge every year to let him know we were satisfied in our foster home, and not one time had she bothered to show her face. Even when DHR volunteered to buy her a bus ticket to see us, she refused.

I still wanted her, needed her. Yes, even loved her. It was becoming more evident how she didn't have time for me in the least. She had a new life to tend to. The way she carried herself, I would be a distraction to what she considered the desires of her heart.

As much as I wanted a dad, sadly, I still did not have one of those either. No one to call me his beautiful princess, no masculine figure to shield me, or go to special lengths to be assured I was okay.

Though my road had been bumpy, I survived my monotone blues. They had a tendency of serenading me at the most inopportune moments, but I wasn't going to sing its chorus of self-pity. A new chapter in my life was about to be constructed when mom decided to let Tamara and I join the Mighty Lions Marching Band. I was going to ride the bandwagon of a fresh start for as long as I could be a passenger. We both wanted to play the saxophone, deciding after much coercion to play the clarinet instead.

Band practice was a fun challenge. I knew the band director carried a no nonsense aura about himself. He would not tolerate slack from anyone in the band. He was brilliant, to put it simply, but made everyone aware he wasn't down with the childishness.

I knew not to play with him when one day in the gymnasium, the principal was having a rather difficult time getting order with the students. No matter how much he told them to settle down, they kept on talking and playing.

Mr. Pugh, the band director, stood up from his seat. He slowly walked over to the podium and just stood there, looking around the gymnasium. He didn't have to say one word. Yet, everyone became quiet as a church mouse. You could hear a pen drop in the place.

Then, there was the time when he was teaching his music class. There was this particular student who continuously disrupted the class. Mr. Pugh had already given him the look twice. He did not take heed to the warning. The third time he spoke out was the straw that broke the camel's back.

Mr. Pugh stood up from behind his desk. He carefully walked over to the student, never uttering one word. He picked up the desk with him in it and carried him out of the classroom, sitting him just outside the door. He gave the young man a blank stare, walked back into the classroom, closed the door as if nothing had happened, and carried on with class.

I sat there with my mouth wide open, almost shaking in my chair, praying I never rubbed him the wrong way. Just to hear him call my name to answer a question would cause me to cower down in my seat, becoming quite the damsel in distress.

I knew I needed to work hard to be successful in the band. But I felt as if I had a place where I belonged. As hard as it sometimes was, I did my best to keep up with all of the seasoned members of the band. It wasn't so easy for me to learn the lines and spaces. The lines were EGBDF, which the band director assured me were easier for me to learn if I said the phrase, "**E**very **g**ood **b**oy **d**oes **f**ine." He knew exactly what he was talking about. I soon caught on. The same rule of thumb applied when it came to the spaces, which consisted of the letters ACEG, "**A**ll **c**ows **e**at **g**rass."

Band practice wasn't the time to think you were going to relax and kick it with friends who caught the late bus. Mr. Pugh brought the blood, sweat, and tears, never showing the slightest bit of sympathy.

We had to march from the school to Mount Moriah Baptist Church. Then, we had to make the painful journey back. Oftentimes, I seemed to lag behind until one day, I heard Mr. Pugh approaching me from behind.

"Get those legs up, Walker," he gruffly said. "Speed it up, Walker. Christmas will be here soon."

I was too scared to say anything, or to even let a single tear roll down my face. As painful as it was, I attempted to speed up my pace, cursing him under my breath the whole time.

My Aunt Flora (Nanny) had told me about the wonders of Epsom Salt, when I was only a couple of years younger. At the time, I laughed at her story, thinking it was ridiculous. Now, the joke was on me because I was seriously contemplating taking a dive in some of that good ole Epsom Salt once I was home, safe from the madness Mr. Pugh composed right along with his music.

The time came when the practice sessions were more extensive and excruciatingly painful as we were preparing for our annual trip to the Mardi Gras. Mr. Pugh was determined we would be the best we could be while marching in a mass number of parades in Mobile, Alabama.

Sometimes, sessions carried on to after eight at night. Despite the pain, I smiled and bared it.

Only recently, my father, Mr. Emmett, had finally decided he would meet Tamara and me. I wondered what it would be like to finally see his eyes looking deeply into mine for the first time. Those thoughts I brought with me to school and band practice as well.

One afternoon, we had just put together our instruments and were walking out the band room to practice our formation. As I walked out, I noticed Mr. Pugh chatting with mom. *What is she doing here? Band practice won't be over for at least a few more hours*, I thought, my eyebrows raised.

I stood there watching, along with Tamara. A few seeming to never end minutes later, Mr. Pugh walked towards us. He refused to make eye contact with me or my sister.

"Walkers," he said. "Go put your instruments up and get your belongings." He walked back into the band room, never saying another word, still not making eye contact. Whatever was wrong, I knew mom had shared it.

By the time Tamara and I were seated in the car with mom, my curiosity was way beyond the norm. There had to be a reason she came to get us from band practice so early. I was determined to find out.

While Tamara sat in the back, I was in the front. She had the same perplexed expression plastered on her face. I knew without a doubt something was definitely wrong. Mom spoke up before I had time to say anything.

"Girls, I'm afraid I have some bad news. I know you were looking forward to meeting your father, but that's not going to happen. I hate to have to tell you this, but he died last night."

"He what?" I asked. I knew I had to have heard her wrong. How could that be? He hadn't upheld his end of the bargain. We were supposed to meet him soon. We were supposed to finally have the chance to be his daughters, and he would be our father. It was all mapped out in my mind. I had carefully constructed it with much thought.

Tamara didn't say anything at all. She sat in a daze, sadness swimming in her eyes. I didn't know how to feel. I wanted to cry, but my anger was stronger than my need to shed tears. I had to work really hard to keep control of my erratic breathing.

Only a few months prior to our father's passing, we sat in the car with mom one Saturday afternoon. The traffic was backed up because of a funeral procession. I was reading a novel so I didn't pay it much attention. Tamara was noticeably irritated. She wanted to get home so she could talk to her boyfriend on the phone.

"Girls, Mom said, interrupting my reading. "You know that is your brother's funeral procession on your father's side." Only then did I look up from reading my novel. I didn't even know I had any siblings on my father's side, and definitely not one who had passed away. Now not only would I be denied the opportunity to get to know him, I wouldn't get to know my father either.

The following Saturday, we headed with heavy hearts to our father's funeral. I only wanted to go because I would finally have the chance to see his face. Maybe there would be a way I could see the resemblance between him and myself. We entered the church wearing cream colored two-piece suits. Our hair was cut short in the top and was long in the back.

Soon as I walked in, I caught a glimpse of my father's face. His body was stretched out in front of the church, where devotion is usually led.

"So, that's my daddy," I said to myself, feeling my legs wanting to give way. I didn't have the strength to walk up to the casket, so I motioned for my social worker and Tamara to sit on the first available pew. Together, we sat there in silence while Mrs. Logan, our social worker, went to retrieve an obituary for both of us.

I thumbed through the program but wasn't really interested in reading how he was a good husband to his wife and a good father to his children that he accepted with no problem. I didn't even want to know about what a devout Christian he was and how he was such a good deacon.

I flipped the program over and glared at the picture on the front. He had been a deputy in his younger years. He was down on one knee with his law enforcement uniform on, a big broad smile on his face. The same exact smile I had on my face on my school day pictures. I thought, *A deputy, huh? Wonder why no one ever arrested his ass for being a deadbeat father? He's got some nerve to be smiling all big as if he was a good person. How dare he fucking die without keeping his word to us? I hate him. I hate him. I swear I hate him. I hope he burns in hell.*

Mr. Emmett, lay peacefully in his light blue casket. He was buried in a black suit with white gloves. One of his hands rested on top of the other one. He looked as if he was lying down to take an afternoon siesta.

His daughters, my half-sisters, were overcome with emotion. As was his sister and nieces and nephews. As they walked around viewing his body, some of them took single flowers out of the arrangements and laid them across his chest. His sister, the one who had been going on and on about how he wasn't our father, fainted. Her fainting was followed by screams from other members of the family. I buried my face in my hands. I couldn't see how I could be at a funeral and not have one ounce of sympathy for the deceased.

When I walked by to view his body, I was sure to look at his face extra hard, desiring to know how many of his features I had. Finally, I turned to the family, my family…shaking all of the hands of those who were on the front pew, those who he loved and was proud to claim as his own.

When I grasped his wife's hand, she looked at me strangely as if she knew me but couldn't put her finger on how. I thought, *Lady, your husband is my father*. I walked slowly back to my designated seat, peering over my shoulder once more to sneak one more glance at his corpse.

The funeral directors had already let the lid down on the casket. They proceeded up the aisle with his body. I sat down in my seat, continuing to watch, feeling cheated, feeling bitter, and feeling there was no way possible I would bounce back from this heartbreak.

While all of the deacons and deaconess were standing up to the front of the church going on and on about how honorable he was, I wanted to stand and tell the world how he abandoned two twin girls, and didn't give a damn about it.

Depression Rocked My World

Dark clouds hung over my soul

As a child, I always thought the clouds in the sky were beautiful. One of God's greatest works of art. Even He said that it was good when He constructed them on the second day of creation. I found myself looking up at the clouds in awe, the irises in my eyes tented with the glow of fascination as they loomed over the fullness of the earth.

They reminded me of huge cotton balls. I would give anything if I could walk on top of them, maybe even slept on top of them since they looked to be very soft. I was certain I would have sweet dreams, probably wouldn't ever want to come down.

It was strange how something I thought to be so beautiful changed within a matter of moments to be so ugly. When the thunder yielded its mighty roar and the lightning flashed with madness across the sky, I no longer considered the clouds to be beautiful. I didn't fancy their presence within my company.

When the storm was on its way, the clouds welcomed it by turning dark and gray. They made me feel gloomy inside. I hid myself in my room, not wanting to see the overwhelming darkness the clouds brought over the sculpture of the earth. This same scenario applied when it came to how I was feeling after the death of my father. Dark clouds hung over my soul.

I found myself not really wanting to talk to anyone about the level of pain I was feeling. No one would understand.

They probably would say, "Get over it already, girl. You didn't even know the man."

It has been said often that the truth hurts. Sadly, my truth regarding not knowing my father made that statement so much more than just a hypothesis. I didn't know the person who planted his seed in my mom's uterus. It was the most embarrassing thing ever to have to go to his funeral to meet him. He wasn't able to talk to me. He didn't even know I was there. Besides, had he cared about me, he would have been a father to me before he passed. It wasn't my fault I was born. I wasn't there holding the candlelight when he and my mother were doing their thing. So why did I have to feel the pain of rejection? They enjoyed the activity to get me here but were slack when it came to dealing with the consequences of the activity.

They never seemed to lose any sleep over their decision to abandon me as if I was the garbage sitting on the street corner waiting to be picked up. It was quite the opposite for me. So many nights, I kicked it with insomnia. Sleep wasn't coming my way, even if I paid it to.

With the passing of one day and the dawning of a new one, I sat in my room. It was my safe haven away from eyes filled with concern. My shoulders were slumped with desolation. Tears fell wherever they landed.

My mind took me on an excursion of deep depression. I could cut it with a knife and have servings for months to come. The bottom line was, I loathed myself with a passion, didn't want to see my face in the mirror. Something surely had to be wrong with me. *Am I ugly*? I thought, definitely in the arms of self-pity. I allowed my mind to drift back to things of yesteryears. The tears continued to fall from my face. Willingly, I walked down the path of what I would like to call, dark moments.

The first thing I thought about was how Uncle H had gotten away with putting his filthy hands all over me. It got to the point where Tamara and I finally got the courage to tell mom what was going on. She listened carefully and immediately called DHR (Department of Human Resources). It was something she had to report right away. As a result, our social worker came to the home to interrogate us about the events stemming from Uncle H's lewd behavior. When it was all said and done, it was determined to be insufficient evidence. It was our word against his. The fact he didn't get punished made him feel as if he hadn't done anything wrong at all. He used it against us. The old fart went around the neighborhood telling as many people as he could get to listen about how Tamara and I were liars, ungrateful little heifers who should not be trusted. Many days after that, he brought freeze cups for the kids a lady in the community made out of Kool-Aid, making sure to always leave Tamara and I out.

Perhaps, it wouldn't have been so bad if Uncle H had been the only person who tried us in the worst way possible. This was not the case. There was another guy who got off on messing with young girls. One day he saw me walking. He waved his hand at me.

"Come here, girl," he whispered. I trusted him. There was no reason for me not to take heed to his request. I walked up to him, standing only inches away from his face. I felt his breath on the tip of my nose, which was filled with the stench of nicotine and beer. He moved to the side so I could accompany him.

"Why don't you go in the kitchen and get yourself a Popsicle," he murmured, almost too low. "But you have to eat it over here because your mom might not want you to have one."

As I slid passed his sweaty body, his eyes were calculating the circumference of my rear end. I tried my best to disregard his roaming eyes as I retrieved the Popsicle from the freezer and sat down to the kitchen table.

"You don't have to sit in there," he whispered in a raspy tone, motioning for me to come into the living room with him. He stood in the doorway, looking me up and down, beaming to the point of no return with lust.

Uneasiness reached out for me without warning. With the pace of a tortoise, I walked over to the opposite couch from where he sat.

"Come sit on my lap," he went on. "You see the money on that table?" he asked me. "Well, that's for you. Why don't you lean over and get it?"

No one had ever given me money. So, of course, I thought I was pretty special. That was until I leaned over and this man allowed his hand to touch me on my bottom. The fact I had on a sundress made it so much easier for him to grope me as he pleased.

I jumped out of his lap as if I had been sitting in a hot seat, dropping the half-eaten Popsicle to the floor. My heart pounded immensely. Now, I only wanted to leave. I tripped over the coffee table, stubbing my toe, trying to get away.

"Don't you want the money?" he repeated, unbothered by the look of fear on my face. He had his hands up as if he was saying, "What's the deal with you?" That alone made me know even more I needed to get away from him, quickly. He didn't give up his quest to have me so easily. He stood up, rushing to the door before I had time to touch the knob. He placed his body in front, blocking my way of escape.

"You can make up to five dollars a week, if you do whatever I ask you to do."

"Please, let me go," I pleaded, my voice completely choked up with tears. It didn't dawn on me until years later how he had propositioned me to be his whore.

He slipped through the cracks of justice as well, getting away with it, just the same as Uncle H had. My mind continued roaming. The tears flowed still. That time, I allowed my mind to reroute me to the summer before I became an eighth grader. I watched with disappointment as mom packed her bags. She had to leave the state. Tamara and I could not go with her because the judge presiding over our case did not permit us to go.

Carolyn was in Birmingham, Alabama. She promised us she would come to get us and allow us to spend time with her while mom was away. Those plans fell through, just the same as all of the other plans she made.

In the end, we had to go to the United Methodist Children's home in Selma, Alabama. As it turned out, it wasn't so bad. There were plenty of teens around our age who kept us company. Tamara and I actually enjoyed ourselves until I almost drowned in the swimming pool at the facility.

I left out of the cottage Tamara and I resided in late one evening. I was accompanied by Tamara, two guys, and another girl who lived in the cottage. I knew I couldn't swim but had made up in my mind to stay in the shallow end of the pool. When we arrived at the pool, there were several other teens from other cottages on the campus already in the pool. One particular guy named Quintin Brown, who I had been eyeing ever since seeing him outside of his cottage with a couple of his friends, was also in the pool. Obviously, he had noticed me as well because no soon as I was in the pool, he began to play with me the way teens play when they have a crush on each other. He splashed me with water. I laughed hard but splashed him back. He swam over to me and picked me up, dunking me before I realized what he was about to do.

I went down to the bottom of the pool and miraculously floated back to the top. Before I had time to run to safety, Dewayne, one of the guys from the cottage I stayed in, picked me up and dunked me again. Neither one had a clue that I didn't know how to swim as I floated down to the bottom of the pool a second time. They were simply having fun. They meant no harm whatsoever.

When I came back up, I screamed and kicked like a wild woman. From that moment on, I was not myself. I shook uncontrollably. When I tried to speak, my words would not come out. I didn't have any control over my reflexes. The supervisor from my cottage along with several other people, grabbed me out of the pool. They hovered over me, trying their best to calm me down. As the evening turned into early night, I had to be rushed to the hospital. None of their efforts to calm me down had worked. When no one was paying attention, Tamara sneaked on the phone and called mom to alert her about what was going on.

"Mom, something is wrong with Tamyra! She's not acting right," she said, totally torn apart. Her voice quivered uncontrollably as she told mom the heartbreaking news regarding my condition.

It was all mom needed to hear to come rushing to my side. "I've got to go see about my child," she said to her daughter, Renee.

"Well, I'm coming with you," Renee said. They hopped in the car and were on the way. It took all of the strength she could muster not to scream when she saw me. I was definitely not myself. Instead of upsetting me any further, she walked over and grabbed me in her arms. "I'm here, baby," she said as she gently rocked me. "Momma is here."

Although I was supposed to stay at the children's Home for a few more days, mom took me back home with her that night. Then, suddenly, I received an impromptu call from Carolyn a few days later. I thought she was going to come get us at last, so we could create beautiful memories to last a lifetime. Sadly, that was the farthest thing from her mind. She only called to get information about what had happened to me. She had no problem with trying to identify possible negligence from someone else when she was the most negligent of all.

Depression hovered over me as if it was my bosom buddy. It befriended me, like it really had my best interest at heart. I took hold of its hand, walking with it wherever it decided to lead me.

You're worthless. Who do you think will ever want you? Your mother and father didn't even want you. Your life is not even worth living.

All of those things the depression whispered to my mind. It was quite cruel with its analysis regarding the invalidity of my life.

I bowed my head, totally and utterly ashamed for having the nerve to ever think I deserved to be loved. I then begin to say it to myself: "You're worthless, Tamyra. Nobody wants you, Tamyra. Your own mother and father didn't even want you, Tamyra. Your life is not worth living, Tamyra."

After reciting the anthem of low self-esteem, I was comforted with more tears streaming down my face. They were so numerous. I drank them as water.

That night, I crept out of bed. I looked over at Tamara. She was sleeping soundly. We both had our own bedrooms, but we refused to sleep alone. We had to have each other. Her mere presence, I considered to be my sleeping pill.

I tiptoed up the hallway, careful not to wake anyone. In fact, I peeked in all of the bedrooms to make sure everyone was sleeping. When I knew the coast was clear, I tiptoed into the kitchen. I opened the silverware drawer and took out a knife, the one mom mostly used for cutting up potatoes and collard greens. It had ridges on it. It would be perfect to end my life.

I carefully placed the knife up to my wrist. I pushed it into my skin, trembling at the thought of how painful it was going to be. I pushed it a little harder, trembling even more. The tears were still on the scene as was depression. It was my cheerleader, wooing me to follow through with the plan.

But then I saw my reflection in the cupboard. I couldn't do it. I quickly dropped the knife into the sink as if it was fire and had burned my hand. I ran out of the kitchen like someone was after me. I jumped into bed and cuddled as closely as I could to Tamara. Her warmth would ease the melancholy lyrics playing in my mind.

The following days, I battled with the emotion of shame. I couldn't believe I had actually put a knife up to my wrist. I knew I was in a serious funk. I didn't know it was called depression.

Once I learned the clinical definition to the word depression, my mind once more took me on a trip to the avenue of the past. It was the year 1990. We all were getting ready to go to mom's retirement celebration. She had worked at the daycare center at the church and was finally closing that chapter in her life. Tamara and I were quite excited. We knew there would be cake and ice cream. We couldn't wait to indulge. Just as we were walking out the door with Renee leading us, a car pulled up in the yard.

My oldest sister, Pamela, stepped out of the passenger seat. She was obviously upset. Tears were flowing down her face. I watched her approach the front door, so torn apart that she could barely walk. What had her so bothered was that my other sister had shot herself in the stomach. She used my Aunt Flora's gun to do so. As the gun went off it startled my aunt.

"What was that," she asked, trying her best to figure out what was transpiring in her very own house.

"I shot myself," my sister weakly responded.

The police and paramedics were contacted. She was, at that very moment, being rushed to Vaughan Regional Hospital in Selma, Alabama, everyone hoping she would pull through. Her reason for shooting herself was that she was depressed.

I don't think the reality of what had happened sunk in with me right away. Tamara, on the other hand, was so nervous and upset that she immediately began to vomit. In just a matter of moments, our world had been totally flipped upside down. No one had given depression an invitation to R.S.V.P. Yet, it was in our lives. It overcrowded our space before we fully had time to access the situation.

When we arrived to the hospital, Tamara and I were not allowed in the intensive care unit. The rule was, you had to be sixteen years of age to visit. We were only ten-years-old. I didn't know how to feel. I wanted so badly to see my sister. I wanted to know was this what depression did to you? If it made you feel so low that you would take your own life, then it was the most heartless thing ever and I wanted no part of it. This was exactly what I had allowed depression to do to me. It was a silent killer among us, evil to say the least.

Silver Lining

Behind every dark cloud there is a silver lining. I heard this quote of optimism falling like poetic lyrics from the lips of many. I didn't doubt it was true, just didn't believe it was applicable to me and my situation. Yet, I held out my hand for the smallest seed of hope. If such a thing was true, I wanted the silver lining to sprout in my life, rescuing me from my daily blues. It wasn't healthy how I continuously harped on situations I had no control over. I knew this to be true. My issue was that I didn't know how to let it go and move forward with my life, a life which had the potential to still bud out with stems of greatness, a life that wasn't over until God reached out his hand and whispered, "Come home with me, my child."

After realizing how depression had caused one of my sisters to attempt to take her life the way I was going to do when I was standing in the kitchen with that knife up to my wrist, I knew I needed serious help. I wanted to be better, tried with all my might to make it be just that.

I was left with the thought of how I was going to do it. It burned like an inferno within my soul. If it was the last thing I did, I was going to put Carolyn and Mr. Emmett out of my mind.

I turned my attention back to the band. Mr. Pugh hadn't changed a lick. He was still tough as nails. I welcomed the toughness. That bit of discomfort and pain would keep my mind from dwelling on the pain of my life I felt behind closed doors when I was alone with my thoughts that always spoke solemnly to my mind. When that didn't work, I had a psychiatrist named, Dr. Clinton Smith who I was seeing, who was more than willing to help me.

As all of this played out in my life, I couldn't help remembering when I was nothing more than a little girl, who desired with everything to dance the dance of mellowness. Whenever I scraped my knee, mom always put some form of ointment on it. She put a Band-Aid over it. The ointment shielded the wound from infection. It always made me feel better. It wasn't long before my tears dried up. Once more, I was playing hopscotch in the sun. I wondered why there wasn't any such ointment for life's woes and misfortunes. You just had to grin and bear it, all the while showing no one any sign of weakness. For certain, you were dissected in their minds. They had all kinds of queries and analyses of your situation, even with their own issues having them doubled over in pain.

I passed the eighth grade later that month with flying colors, couldn't help cheering up knowing I was going to be officially in high school, at last. High school was the place where you got the utmost respect from peers. You were considered to be one of the big dogs, all because you were in high school. At least, that was how I always looked at things.

There was nothing worse than being in Junior high, where it seemed as if everybody looked down on you, like you were a piece of lint on their freshly ironed shirt needing to be flicked off. You didn't know where anything was, had to rely on the upperclassmen to steer you in the right direction. Sometimes, they looked at you funny as if you had a lot of nerve to ask them anything.

I wasn't going to have to deal with that anymore. I had graduated on to bigger and better things. While I knew I would never be a bully, I relished the idea that I was going to be one of the big kids. I would be the one the novice came to for advice.

Becoming a high school student had been the most grown up thing I had done since being able to partake in communion for the first time at church. Maybe it felt good to appear to be in charge of something at school, since I wasn't in charge of anything at home.

Two weeks into the start of the new school year, I had my first boyfriend, although our relationship only lasted for about two-and-a-half to three weeks. I remember when our eyes first locked. I blushed wildly. My heart fluttered to the tune of infatuation. My eyes swam with adoration. A smile erupted across my face. Maybe this was the silver lining I so desperately needed.

He was much taller than I was and sported a high top fade. He walked me to my classes before he went to his own, carrying my books as well. We both had classes on top of the hill. His was before mine. We always made sure to grab each other hand as we walked past each other. I couldn't help thinking, *Look at Tamyra getting her groove on.*

I thought everything was fine until one day, he sent another guy he knew to tell me he didn't want to talk to me anymore. It stung deeply. It was a pain I never really got over. He stayed in my heart throughout my years of high school, even though the day after our breakup, he became cold as ice to me. He treated me as if I had leprosy and he had to stay as far away from me as possible to keep from getting infected.

I allowed his unfavorable behavior to affect my self-esteem. There were days I locked myself in one of the stalls in the girl's restroom and cried my eyes out, trying desperately to figure out what I had done to him. I couldn't even look him in the face as I slid back into my seat in class after one of my crying episodes.

It was an uphill journey for me to be focused in any class I had with him. Suddenly, the guy who I had liked so much, intimidated me. I felt it necessary to show him, in a subtle way every chance I got, that I indeed was good enough.

Eventually, I did move on. Someone had actually wanted me, even if it was only for a brief period of time. That had to mean something. *Maybe I wasn't ugly after all*, I thought. *Or maybe I was, in fact, the ugly duckling who at last had transformed into the beautiful swan.*

Only a brief while later, I was back in touch with Quintin who had dunked me in the swimming pool when I almost drowned. He was still a resident at United Methodist Children's Home. Long had things returned back to normal for me since my near death experience. His whole reason for dunking me, in the first place, was that he had a major crush on me. I was feeling him, too. So, we tried to indulge in a relationship. It didn't last long. Our relationship was strictly talking to each other over the phone. Even with talking on the phone, I had to be off at a certain time. He desired to be able to touch the assets. That couldn't happen if he didn't even get the chance to see me (the assets). I considered our break-up to be a minor blow.

Again, things began to look up once I was granted an opportunity to be a part of the Junior Reserve Officer Training Corps (JROTC) program at school, under the tutelage of Sergeant Major Deese. He was another one who could be as gentle as a mother cradling her child, when necessary. He didn't play the radio when it came to being less than organized within the squads, platoons, company, or battalion, for that matter. He issued out demerits with gladness in his heart, if it came to that. I do admit I received my fair share of demerits, mostly for not wearing the color socks I was supposed to wear with my uniform.

My platoon was called, Delta. I felt something special having the chance to march with my squad. The feeling that I was important rocked my soul like a canoe on top of the tidal waves in the ocean.

I wanted to join the JROTC when I was in the eighth grade. I was disappointed when I learned I had to be in at least the ninth grade before I could. Now that I'd finally gotten the chance to participate, I wasn't going to blow it. Eager I was to show off all of my military moves when I got home.

I was at easing all over the place, about facing, parade resting, and saluting everyone who came my way. Also, I would stand in a full-length mirror, admiring myself in my uniform. I smiled hard at the image that starred back. I was beautiful. I was someone special. Maybe now I could fathom the idea of loving myself, at least a little.

I went as far as to become a part of the drill team. On special occasions, the drill team wore red berets. We had ropes attached to our shirts. I thought I was really something when my rank was promoted from Private First class to that of Corporal. I even had ribbons I'd earned to decorate my shirt, placed on the opposite side from my name badge. It did my heart good to see mom smiling proudly at me every Wednesday when I left out of the house all decked out in my uniform. What was even better was that I learned how to shoot a rifle.

Regardless of what I did, happiness didn't last for me. Happiness, in my world, was like sand through the hourglass. The sand would only remain for a short period of time. I couldn't even enjoy the time I had for constantly thinking of how bummed I would feel when it was over. I would look upon what used to be my fate with eyes smoldered with sadness.

I always reverted back to being depressed. As hard as I tried to believe I was somebody, I still felt worthless. Carolyn's abandonment always, no matter what I was doing, found its way back into my mind. It taunted me with the painful fact of how she wasn't there for me the way she should have been. It was like a tape recorder constantly playing over and over in my mind. I couldn't understand. I was still feeling the blues about Mr. Emmett as well. A counselor informed me that I should write out my feelings towards him in the form of a letter. I did just that, hoping I could have some relief from the stabbing pain in my heart. But to no avail. I felt like it was a silly thing to do. I tore up the letter before I even finished writing it.

Even though I was too young to have children, I never imagined I could ever walk away from them, not caring in the least about their well-being. I wanted to be around to see them grow up, to see them excel and come into their own. It would warm my heart for them to reach out and grab hold to the reins of independence, riding its torrential curves to success, regardless of how hard it became.

Sickness Strikes

The kiss of death

I puzzled my brain trying to figure out the answers to the Geometry problems I had in math class. I'd barely conquered Algebra without feeling as if my brain was going to explode from knowledge that just didn't want to stick. Geometry wasn't a joke.

How the heck am I supposed to figure this out? I quietly pondered while simultaneously scratching my head in confusion. I made every effort to solve the problems before me, knowing deep within the chance of doing so was less than slim to zero. Soon, I gave up on the notion of getting any of the answers correct and started writing a story that I was going to make sure had a happy ending.

Who the hell supposed to understand what a Pythagorean theory is anyway? I brusquely thought, needing a way to clear my conscience. I knew well my full attention was supposed to be on my math assignment. I simply couldn't deal with it. My attitude was, "If I get in trouble, so be it!"

As far as writing, I was glad I had the gift. I learned when I was only ten-years-old that I could write. Fortunately for me, I had been taking full advantage of it ever since I knew I could make characters come to life on my paper. I wrote when I was happy. I wrote when I was confused. I wrote when I was sad. Whatever emotion I ever felt, it was deemed worthy for me to write about.

Writing was the only thing possessing the power to take the edge off of what I considered to be my problems in life, problems that seemed to always be at the equator of my thoughts, even when I was doing well. They were also problems having the capacity to alter my behavior. They had a tendency of making me act ways I wouldn't normally act.

Though I was only a teenager, I'd become quite knowledgeable of the fact life was an up and down rollercoaster of daily events. As long as I kept gazing sadly out of the window of depression, the view never changed to my liking. I desperately needed my confidence to be awakened in my soul. I needed it to tell me to rise up from the bowels of defeat and make myself known. For it was true when all falls apart, that all comes together. I simply had to get my mind right. Nothing else would do.

But I was so afraid. The fear made me feel as if I could vomit up my stomach contents, even if I hadn't put anything in it. This was definitely one of those times when it seemed easier to stay in the rut rather than to move forward. I never realized before that I was the crab in the bottom of the bucket, holding my own self down.

I embraced being a sophomore in school as if it was my salvation, and it alone had the infinite power to make me whole. I had to admit, it was quite rewarding to no longer wear the shoes of the rookie of the high school clan. As far as I could tell, I had worn them well. Now the soles were ripping. They needed to be replaced with new ones that would lead me down a path of new opportunities, opportunities that would induct me into the world of maturity, force me to grow into the garments I needed to wear at this point in life.

Too bad mom didn't consider me to be mature enough to do the things so many of the girls at my school were doing. I still had a bedtime, not to mention a curfew, which was to be in the house at the stroke of dusk. This was never a rule we had a problem with breaking because I rarely had any friends. Furthermore, Tamara and I weren't really allowed to go anywhere either, unless it had something to do with church.

Going to church wasn't negotiable. Church was like our second home. We had to go regardless of whether we wanted to or not. There was no way around it, no need to try and pull any punches.

Back in the day, when we first became part of the family, Tamara and I enjoyed going to church. We'd never heard such a thing as a choir singing or seeing people fellowship with one another after service had officially ended.

There were also the annual revivals we attended, not just at our church, but churches all over the community, as well as Vacation Bible School during the summer months.

There were programs where Tamara and I had the chance to recite a speech/poem. It felt good to receive applause after we were done. Nothing proved to be better than when we had the chance to participate in a skit, or when I got the chance to stand in front of the church and tell what I learned in Sunday school that morning. I didn't always pay attention to Mrs. Peterson, the Sunday school teacher. Even so, I always made sure I allowed just a small portion of the lesson to sink in my ears and find its way to my heart.

As I became older, church wasn't so fun for me anymore. I was very impressionable, swayed by the opinions of my peers.

"Why y'all mom always make y'all go to church?" asked many of the girls we wanted to befriend.

Sadly, I allowed their disdain for church to make me ashamed of something I really enjoyed. *Maybe church is not so good,* I thought, suddenly angered that we had to go all the time. I tried my luck with questioning mom about it once. Just as quickly as I gathered the nerve to do such a daring thing, she shut me down.

"The girls at school moms don't make them go to church," I murmured, under my breath.

"Well, I tell you what," mom said, her voice slightly elevated. "You go and live with those girls because as long as you are in my house, you are going to do what I tell you to do, and in this house, we go to the house of the Lord. Now unless you want me to knock your eyes out of your head, you had better stop rolling them."

I knew then, to drop the discussion, as well as my attitude. I didn't comprehend exactly how serious mom was about church until one Sunday, she made me wear my sneakers with my dress.

I knew I was supposed to get together my stockings, slip, and shoes the night before. I was good at procrastinating. The next morning, I searched relentlessly for my church shoes. To no avail, I couldn't find them. I felt a slight sense of relief thinking mom would excuse me from services since I had no shoes to wear.

"Girl, you are going to church," she sternly said.

"But, mom," I refuted.

"Tamyra, I don't want to hear it," she continued, practically raising the roof on the house with her loud boisterous voice. "Get those sneakers and put them on your feet and get out to the car now."

Up until the year 1995, we attended Unity Baptist Church, under the leadership of the late Reverend Leroy Jenkins. Unity Baptist was located in Whitehall as well. Right before we were to turn fifteen, mom took us out of that church. We joined, Helping Hand Bible Ministry Church in Selma, Alabama, becoming the sheep of Pastor Ralph Edward Sr.'s flock.

Services at Helping Hand were a lot more radical than I had ever seen in my life. I had witnessed people, "Get happy," in church as mom called it. The ushers rushed to whoever was happy side and fanned them until the spirit passed over. Here, at this new church, they took, "Getting happy," to an all new level.

The first time I saw someone fall out in the spirit, I sat up to the edge of my seat with my eyes bucked. "What in the Sam hill is going on," I whispered low enough where no one heard me.

What was even worst is no one else was alarmed. One of the ushers grabbed a sheet out of the closet in the sanctuary and covered up the lady who had fallen out. *Okay*, I thought, *so y'all going to just let the lady lie on the floor like that and not help her up.*

There came the day when I saw someone get so engrossed in the spirit that they took off running around the church. It was as if whoever it was were searing in flames, and running was all they could do to be free from the massive burns that would come about. Mom was giving me the look, so I knew not to laugh the way I wanted to. I looked down in an attempt to stifle what would be an infectious bout of giggles.

Some of the church members spoke in other tongues. That had to be the creepiest part of it all. "What in the world are they saying?" I asked Tamara, as I nudged her in the side. She was just as clueless as I was. To add to my dismay, there was also an altar call.

This was where the pastor laid hands on you with holy oil. I noticed how it seemed as if everyone he touched fell out, convulsing as they hit the floor. When it was my turn, I held down all of my weight. One of the deacons stood behind me to catch me, I guess, when I fell.

"Put your hands up, daughter," Pastor said to me. I obeyed him, but my thoughts raced at the speed of lightning. *I don't know who he thinks he is. Mannnnn, I ain't got time for this. I don't care how loud he yell, I'm not going to fall. I'm just not fixing to fall and shake all over the place like it's something wrong with me. So, he might as well skip me and find somebody else to lay his holy hands on.*

When I attended Unity Baptist Church, I always knew when Reverend Jenkins was about to finish preaching. The pianist sat at the piano playing music as he sweated profusely and everything he said from that point on, sounded like he was singing. Some of the church members stood up in their pews, waving their hands and telling him to, "Preach, pastor." At last, he said, after wiping a bucket of sweat off of him with the towel hung around his neck, "The doors of the church are open!"

No matter how sleepy I had previously been, when it got to this part of the sermon, I suddenly perked up, growing more and more excited as I knew it would soon be over. Inside, I was mentally doing the funky chicken as I thought of what I was going to do after church.

This didn't take place at my new church. You never knew when Pastor Edwards was going to be finished preaching. There were no hints given out to let me know it was coming to an end. Many days, I sat on the pew, rolling my eyes up in the top of my head. "Will you hurry up, please, for goodness sake? It don't take all of that," I said to myself.

The only good thing I considered about the church, at this given time, was the fact we had a nursing home ministry. After church, we had the chance to visit the elderly. This made my day, as my Aunt Nanny was a resident at the nursing home of choice. Mom took us to see Nanny throughout the week, when she had time. It was an added bonus when we saw her on Sundays, too.

Nanny's health had deteriorated even more. She was no longer in the position where she could live on her own. Before a bed in a nursing home was found, she stayed with her sister, Mary (Nana), for a couple of days. To say it was a disaster, was an understatement.

Nanny woke up in the middle of the night. When she did, she was in an uproar, taking all of the drawers out of the dresser and knocking things over, all the while shouting angrily as if someone had done something to her. She barricaded herself in the bedroom, sliding the dresser in front of the room door to keep Nana from coming in.

During the day, she rolled around in the kitchen in her wheelchair, messing with everything she got her hands on, including the eyes on the stove. If anyone tried to redirect her behavior, she became very combative. I stood back, shocked, watching Nanny, my heart breaking with each passing second. I didn't recognize her. The Nanny I knew would never act this way. I felt sad that she was troubled and couldn't begin to relax.

Little did I know she had a condition called, Alzheimer's disease. Alzheimer's was a form of dementia. It affected the brain which, at times, caused its victims to have behavioral problems. The staff at a nursing facility knew how to handle her when she had one of her episodes.

Most of the time, when we entered the nursing home, Nanny was asleep in her wheelchair. She was parked in the sitting room with several other residents. There was one particular lady who was also a resident, who made it her business to tell me her life story whenever I came to visit Nanny. I started tiptoeing past her whenever I saw her seated in the sitting room. I didn't want to be rude, but if I had to listen to her tell me how much she liked a big plate of rice with tons and tons of butter on it one more time, I felt as if I was going to puke.

As far as Nanny, it took her cursing mom out one good time for her to realize she shouldn't wake Nanny up when she was sleeping. When she wasn't asleep, she was confused, sometimes forgetting she was even in a nursing home.

"Why don't y'all go back there and get you something to eat out of the freezer?" she said.

I looked at her crazily, thinking, "Okay, Nanny, what's up for real?"

"Don't look at me like that," she replied, obviously offended that I was staring at her in the tone of voice I had on my face. "It's all mine. I went grocery shopping and y'all are more than welcomed to anything back there in that freezer," she continued her quest to get us to have something to eat.

Almost instantly, the light bulb in her brain popped on. She realized she was in a nursing home. Such realization altered her attitude. I literally could see the wheels in her head turning as she looked over to one of the residents sitting next to her and angrily said, "I can't believe that bitch had the nerve to put me in a nursing home." The resident she relayed that information to only moaned in response.

There was the constant battle she had with the nurses and CNA's at the nursing home, when it came to her being compliant with taking her meds. They gave her the nickname chicken, because she was like the mother hen at the facility, keeping everyone in check.

"Mrs. Walker," one of the CNA's softly spoke, "Are you going to eat your lunch today?" she asked.

"I don't want that mess," Nanny responded. "Bring me some milk and bread, child!" Because of Nanny, the facility allowed every Friday evening to be milk and bread bash day for the residents. Whereas the dining room was skimpy plenty of days, on Fridays it was filled to capacity.

Once I got over the initial shock of Nanny's behavior, it became kind of funny. I jeered her on; wanting her to say things I knew wasn't true. She truly believed it was the truth, and hey, I didn't think there was anything wrong with me being entertained in the process.

"Now, what happened again, Nanny?" I asked her while about to fall over in my chair laughing.

"Stop it, Tamyra," mom interjected. "You are not supposed to be encouraging her. You know that."

Eventually, Nanny took ill. Mom brought us to Vaughn Regional Medical Center to visit her, where she lay barely breathing in intensive care. The nurses were lenient and decided to let us see her even though we were supposed to be sixteen.

Slowly, I walked over to the bed, careful not to upset any of the medical equipment she was hooked up to. Alarms were blaring. I noticed her heartrate was steadily dropping. I placed my hand under the cover, wanting to hold her hand, quickly snatching it back when I realized she was ice cold. I looked upon her face with tears in my own eyes. She had her mouth opened as she breathed. Her respirations were few.

I watched closely as the apnea episodes increased, listening to the dreaded sound of the rattle in her throat, which made it sound like she had a terrible cold. I looked over at mom and saw her with her hand on Nanny's forehead, silently praying. That was all the confirmation I needed to know I was losing my Nanny. In a matter of minutes, she would expire. Her body would transform back to the dust of the earth and I would harbor a broken heart that would cause me to regress as far as my depression was concerned.

It finally happened at about three that afternoon. Nanny's heart rate dropped quite fast. When it got to 35 beats per minute, I excused myself. I couldn't stand there and watch her die. I rushed downstairs, waiting for mom to come out of the parking deck with the car. Before I could buckle myself in the seatbelt, Nanny's nurse came through the doubled doors. She had that look on her face. Still, I had to hear the words.

"I'm sorry," she said. "Ms. Walker just passed."

Tamara and I both began to hit the back of the seats with our fist. The tears fell repeatedly.

Having to tell Nana her sister was gone, was beyond painful. The sadness emulated in her face was too much.

"Well, I guess there is nobody left but me now, Lord," she said as she burst into tears.

I didn't know what to say. I stood over her lift chair where she sat, massaging her shoulders as she cried. The kiss of death was not one I longed for. It wasn't fair how I had to lose my Nanny. I couldn't help feeling sorry for myself, wondering why it seemed as if I always had to lose.

Like a mighty force asthma invaded my world

I got hit by a car when I was fourteen-years-old. It happened during the summer months of 1994. Tamara and I were eager to attend 4-H camp that summer, so eager, in fact, I forgot to look both ways as I crossed the street to retrieve the applications for camp.

As the car was upon me, I stopped wide-eyed in the middle of the street, waiting for my fate. When it made contact with me, it swoop me up into the air. I landed on top of the car, rolling onto the hood, and then falling onto the ground. The impact was so forceful; it knocked one of my K-Swiss's off of my feet.

For a moment, it seemed as if time stood still. Everything was mute. I didn't know if I was dead or alive until I heard mom screaming, "Oh, my God, my baby, my baby!" I tried my best to stand up so she would know I was ok. The last thing I wanted was for her to think the situation was worse than it actually was. It took a while for her to calm down. Even when she saw that I was ok, she couldn't stop crying. Several onlookers had called 911 on my behalf. The ambulance was in route. However, mom decided at last to transport me to Baptist South Hospital, after she'd finally gotten the strength to calm down. I felt sorry for the lady who had hit me. She immediately jumped out of the car. She ran over to me, grabbed me in her arms, hugging me tightly. "Why didn't you look both ways? I am so sorry. I am soooo sorry. Please, forgive me." Her words became repetitive and then inaudible as her crying intensified.

I was fortunate to have escaped death again, though I was dinged up pretty badly. Some of my peers thought they should tease me once they saw all of the bandages I wore as a result of getting hit. One of them said,

"Oh, yeah girl, you was flying, but then you ran out of gas, and that's why you landed on top of the car." Another asked me, "How does it feel to know how to fly?" The taunting and teasing quickly became annoying. I cursed all of the ones making fun of me out in my head. Outwardly, I smiled and giggled right along with them, pretending that I thought what they said was funny.

It was after this incident with the car that my asthma really decided to give me a run for my money.

Later, the same year, I got really sick when I went on a trip with the band. It acted a fool too when we went to Dayton, Ohio for the Walker/Gresham family reunion. My asthma always had a tendency of showing out whenever I spent the night in unfamiliar places. It was always getting in the way, not wanting to allow me to have even the slightest bit of fun. I decided to give the asthma a name, Cassie. I'll never forget when I had to be carried out of a Girl Scout sleepover at the elementary school I attended because over in the night, Cassie decided she wanted to rage.

My chest was heaving, the wheezing was unbearably loud. Howbeit, no one was able to arouse me out of my sleep. I wouldn't have been so upset if I hadn't looked forward to this night for weeks. I even brought my breathing machine with me, taking precaution, knowing mom wasn't going to let me out of her sight without it.

I didn't think I would have to use it. I hadn't a clue I would have any trouble at all with my breathing. But Cassie had other plans. I didn't come to until I was placed in mom's car and we were heading home. Tears sprung to my eyes as we drove away. Disappointment made its way to my side. My sister was sad, too, when I left. She sat on the same pallet I had been laying on, letting tears drop into her ice cream as I was carried away.

Now that I was a teen, here Cassie had once again showed up uninvited, altering my plans of having a good time. Really, what I wanted to say was, "Cassie you lowdown, Bitch!" In the end, I decided against it, trying instead to get control of my asthma. It was truly spiraling out of control.

As time passed, it got to the point where I was hospitalized every month, sometimes twice a month for way over a year. This ordeal was still going on when I turned seventeen-years-old. My worst episode to date happened in April of 1997.

That day, I remember the sky being a light shade of blue. It was a beautiful day God had created. He was gracious enough to open my eyes to let me be a part of it. There were a lot of things I could have been doing. To the contrary, I was in the ER, wheezing up a storm, my chest tight, and my shoulders slumped. I tried my best to inhale and exhale while chopping up every other word coming out of my mouth. As I waited on the triage nurse to call my name, I felt hot tears forming in the corner of my eyes.

"How unfair," I mumbled to myself, using the palm of my hand to quickly brush the tears away.

Shortly thereafter, I was rolled in a wheelchair to trauma one. Several nurses proceeded to hook me up to the necessary equipment, allowing them to monitor me closely. I wasn't moving much air at all, didn't even flinch as I felt my skin being broken with a needle.

"I need a bag of saline," I vaguely heard someone say.

"We need a portable chest x-ray," another voice chimed in. I watched in awe as someone else tied a big blue tourniquet around my arm in search of a good vein to stick so she could put my blood in a tube and take it with her. Then, there was the cold stethoscope placed against my chest. I could feel someone putting a mask over my face. I yanked the mask off and threw it on the floor, because it made me feel like I was suffocating.

"I can't breathe, I can't breathe," I gasped.

"Try to calm down," the nurse said as she appeared by my side.

"But, I can't breathe. I swear, I can't breathe," I continued.

"You're going to be ok," the nurse continued to soothe me, giving me a reassuring pat.

The breathing treatments continued every hour. In addition to the breathing treatments causing my speech to be slurred, there were now several pumps on my IV pole I had to drag around wherever I went.

As the evening commenced to turn into night, I noticed my chest was still tight, though I was slightly better. My blood pressure had stabilized; that was until the next morning, when the patient care tech approached me with a basin of warm water.

"Miss Walker," she said, "I'm going to give you a bath."

"Oh, no, you're not," I objected, almost snatching the IV out of my arm. "I'm not helpless. I can bathe myself."

"Did I do something wrong?" the patient care tech asked me. Her mood had suddenly changed from cheerful to that of annoyance.

"Look, lady," I snapped. "I can bathe myself."

I honestly didn't try to be mean, but I had never heard of such a thing as someone giving me a bath when I could clearly do it myself. Only a short while later, Dr. Scott arrived. "So, how is your breathing," he asked, reaching for his shiny Littman tucked neatly in his lab jacket.

I briefly surveyed him, starting from his head, traveling down to his feet as I had never seen him before. He was the new doctor on the block. I decided right away that I liked him. He reminded me of the civil rights leader Malcolm X. I especially liked how he did not count me out because I was a teenager. He allowed me to have input in my care plan. For that, I had the utmost respect for him. I had the pleasure of seeing him every day for the remainder of that week.

When week two of my hospitalization arrived, Dr. Holloway was on call, making hospital visits.

"So, you're here again, Miss Walker," he murmured, in his deep voice I had grown accustomed to hearing over the years he had been my doctor. Before I responded, he had his stethoscope up to my chest ordering me to breathe in and out. The wheezes were still on the scene, stubborn as ever, refusing to be brought under submission.

He replied, "We're going to keep doing what we're doing," and he walked out the door. The next day, after the same routine, he said again, “We’re going to keep doing what we’re doing.” Again, he walked out the door.

My roommate, who had Sickle Cell Anemia, was getting to go home. I was happy for her but sad at the same time, because now I would be alone. We had gotten along so well, telling each other about our lives away from the hospital throughout the nights when we were restless and could not go to sleep. We both turned our noses up at the food on our trays and ordered the foodservice worker to take it away most of the time before we even took one bite. I did not know what I would do now since she was going home, was not sure if we would stay in touch. I sighed heavily, forcing a smile on my face as she packed up her belongings. Before completely exiting my room, Dr. Holloway turned around and looked at me. “I want you to stay in this bed as much as possible,” he demanded.

The next day, after listening to my chest, I saw a few furrows arise in his head, and he didn’t say anything as he walked out the door. I did notice, however, his steps were rushed. The wheezing was worse despite the fact I was on a countless number of IV drips. As he nearly ran out of my room, my mind drifted back to a few hours before when it was the middle of the night. I awakened to find several nurses standing over me. They all displayed the same worried expression on their faces. Such solemn expressions scared me. So, I said the first thing coming to mind, which was, "I need to go to the bathroom." I didn't expect one of the nurses to literally help me to the bathroom. She held onto me with a firm grip as I walked back to bed, and then, when I was once again lying against the sheets, she tucked me in and readjusted my pillows. I knew something was definitely wrong, but I refused to dwell on it, was not sure if I even wanted to know. Eventually, I fell back asleep.

A few hours later, I received a visit from another doctor, one I happened not to like too well and who I had a mind on several occasions to "Tell a piece of my mind." He was the rudest person I had ever encountered in my life. As he came closer to the bed, he hastily said to me, "Turn over. I need to talk to you." I was cuddled up with my teddy bear I had gotten as a "get well soon" gift. Without any regard to my feelings, he yanked my teddy bear away from me and tossed him on the other bed in the semi-private hospital room.

"Why am I not getting any better?" I asked in response to his curt attitude. The resulting look he gave me was unbearable. I quickly lowered my eyes to the floor to avoid his glower. "You're not getting better, Miss Walker, because you have bad asthma, and you're going to die," he stated in the most hateful tone I'd ever heard from a doctor.

I couldn't believe he said that to me, although it wasn't the first time he had said something so horrible and downright out of line. Earlier in the year, I had been in his office for a routine visit. After listening to my lungs, he took off his stethoscope and said, “I don’t understand why you are alive. I have never heard anyone sound as badly as you do, and they’re not on a ventilator or in your case, dead.” He even told mom that she should look for her black dress for my funeral because I wasn’t going to live long. I just glared at him in response. I knew how flip my mouth could be. At a time when I wanted to spew venomous words, I was thankful mom had always instilled in me how it was never acceptable to disrespect adults. That did not stop my thoughts from getting the very best of me. I cursed him out a dozen times or more in my mind.

Now because I had relapsed, it was back to continuous breathing treatments. Before I had time to wrap my mind around what was taking place, suddenly out of nowhere, mom materialized by my side. She sat on the bed with me, something she had never done before. She rested her arm on my lower leg and stared at me hard. I could not read her expression. There was definitely something eerie about it.

A few moments later, my sister Sharmeen appeared. She came into the room and crawled into the bed with me. I caught Tamara peering around the corner at me before she actually came into the room. The day before when my sister, Pamela, came to visit me, she said she could definitely tell that there was a shift in my condition. I was sitting outside in the hallway with several other patients as the weather was bad. This was protocol when a tornado was supposed to be underway.

After Tamara came in my hospital room, a few minutes later, Carolyn came shuffling through the door. She was crying hysterically as she walked over to me and placed a teddy bear in my arms. By now, mist from the mask was getting into my eyes, but I never stopped glaring at Carolyn. It took her quite some time to get her emotions under control.

When Dr. Holloway left the room that morning, he called mom and told her she needed to come to the hospital right away. By the time she got to the hospital, he caught her at the elevator and gave her the bleak news about my condition. "Mrs. Fair, I don't think she's going to make it this time," he said. "I've been increasing her meds daily, and she's not getting any better. I'm not going to give up on my girl, though," he assured her.

Mom listened intently. Her heart was breaking. But she couldn't allow herself to give into the emotions she was feeling. She had to be strong for me. She had to believe that the God she served would heal my body regardless of the prognosis she'd just heard.

After hearing such sad news about my fate, mom, in return, called Sharmeen. She informed her of what was going on before coming in the room and sitting on the bed with me. Tamara overheard Sharmeen discussing the matter with one of her friends. She stood in the doorway of the apartment crying her own tears, torn apart at the idea she could possibly lose her twin sister.

Sharmeen decided to call Carolyn. She was in an uproar. "Tamyra, is really sick!" she yelled at her through the phone. "The doctor doesn't think she is going to make it. If you care anything about her, you need to get to this hospital right away." Thus, this was the reason Carolyn walked into the room all broken up. Her conscience obviously was letting her have it. Even though she'd given me the teddy bear her boyfriend had bought for her for Valentine's Day, that wasn't enough. Less than an hour later, after she arrived, she left and went to the gift shop. She came back with several "get well soon" balloons, flowers, candy, and a get well soon card. She placed it all on the bedside table before me, hoping to see the slightest hint in my eyes that all was well.

Over the next few days, I saw several doctors, including a gastroenterologist who thought I needed to have a Barium Swallow. Once in the x-ray room, the tech told me to drink the contents in the cup he had given me. I took one swallow, and for the remainder of the time, I stood there peering inside the cup. The taste was so awful that I guess I felt like I just needed to look at it. I tried to take another swallow when prompted to do so, but my lips just quivered. As soon as I put the cup up to my mouth, I gagged and said, "I'm sorry, sir, I just can't do it."

A couple more days passed away, becoming a part of the past. I was doped up on so much medication. I literally felt like ants were crawling through my face. Being in the hospital bed had drained me of all of my energy. So as I sat in the recliner adjacent to the bed, once again, I cried. Those were tears of defeat. I felt very much defeated as I reached up in an attempt to hit myself in the face. This was my way of making the ants I thought were nesting there fall out.

Later on, when I had no choice, I got back into bed. As I got myself settled under the covers, I suddenly sat upright, grabbing hold of the rails on the bed, and noticed I was hyperventilating.

"Are you, all right?" I heard the lady carrying my lunch tray ask me. What I was feeling, at the moment, was the most ridiculous notion ever and therefore, I decided not to answer her for fear I would be called crazy. I continued sitting there, declining to eat lunch, holding onto the bedrails still with as firm of a grip as I could muster. I felt as if I was about to float out of the bed and holding on, was all I could do. By now, I had worked myself into a sweat. I looked over at mom, and I asked her with a shaky voice, "Why is this happening to me?" It didn't help that I was also suffering from dysphagia (difficulty swallowing).

The normal shakes I had from the breathing treatments were more like epileptic episodes. My slurred speech was almost inaudible. The first male nurse I had during this hospitalization looked at me with sympathy as he changed the empty bag of IV fluids on my pole. He leaned over me and whispered encouraging words to me. I never looked up to meet his gaze. I was disgusted and bloated from all the steroids being pumped into my veins. My face looked like that of the Pillsbury doughboy, and I refused to look in the mirror. But when I was alone, I put my Kirk Franklin CD into my boom box. I stuck my ear buds in my ears and listened to track one over and over again. "Savior, more than life to me", the words to that song lifted me up, made me take my eyes off of my situation.

Finally, the day for me to be discharged, two weeks and two days later came. Even then, I still had a slight wheeze. Dr. Scott was back on call. He wanted me to stay an extra day. But I wasn't having it. The asthma specialist had assured me that I could go home. At last, Dr. Scott gave in. I knew the only reason I was discharged was so I could get ready to board a plane the following Monday to go to another hospital in Denver, Colorado. As I stood to pull up my pants, I noticed I could not button them. Those were the same pants I had worn when I was admitted. I was so happy to be leaving the hospital until I couldn't even fathom the idea of griping about it. I packed up all my get well gifts, including about seventeen cards and more than a dozen balloons that were on their own floating all over the room. I said goodbye to all of the nurses who had taken good care of me, and I was on my way.

Several days after I was discharged, the get well gifts were still pouring in. I even got a visit from Mr. Seaborn, the Superintendent of the Lowndes County School System. Seeing him made me think back to when I was in the hospital. I looked up one day and saw my school principal Mr. Perry glaring at me. He waited patiently for the Respiratory Therapist to put away the tubing for my breathing treatments before he entered the room. The pulse ox on my finger noted my oxygen level was 97 percent, which was good. My heartrate, however, was elevated. He walked over to me and assured me that all of my classmates were thinking of me and that everyone was rooting for me to get better.

The next day as I awaken from a nap, I looked over and saw the Sergeant Major from the ROTC at school. He had come to see me as well. He sat in the chair, watching me, but he was careful not to disturb me from sleep. We both smiled when we looked each other in the face.

Mr. Blocker, my seventh grade math teacher came to see me too. He stood over me with a get well card in his hand. I smiled to myself as I remembered being in his class. His most famous words were, "I want to see the white of your eyes," and of course, "Miss Walker, you're getting a mommy letter."

Also, on that day I learned that I was on the prayer list at several of the churches in my community. It felt good to be graced with so much love, although I wished it could have been under different circumstances. The cherry on the cake was that Carolyn, had made her way back down to see me the day before I was to leave for Denver. I don't know where the outpour of tears came from, but she hugged me tightly when she got ready to go back to Birmingham. With a shaky voice, she told me she would keep in contact with me, and she may even come to Denver to see me. I never heard the words, "I love you." The thought of her coming to Denver to see me was exciting. I knew deep within it was just a figment of her imagination, if not an outright lie.

National Jewish Medical and Research Center

One day, shy of a week later of being discharged from Baptist South hospital, my social worker and I arrived at Dannelly Field Airport in Montgomery, Alabama, just before 7:30 in the morning. As we prepared to leave on our flight, I had a wide range of emotions running around inside of me. This was the first time I was ever boarding a plane. I had heard about the turbulence which sometimes occurred on planes, even the fatal crashes. I was never one to be pessimistic, but what was I to think? There by my side was mom, Tamara, Pastor Edwards, Cousin Lillian, and Niaikia, a friend from school. They were all there to see me off. Pastor Edwards ordered us all to hold hands as he prayed for my safe arrival to my destination. Afterwards, I hugged everyone twice and slowly walked away to get on the plane. I turned around a few times on my way to the plane, and each time, I waved again to the ones I loved most.

It took about forty-five minutes for me and my social worker to arrive in Atlanta, Georgia. We got off the tiny matchbox airplane we were on to board another plane at least three times bigger. When the plane left the runway, I dropped my headset on the floor as I felt something in my ears. I swatted at them several times before I finally looked over and asked Mrs. Mamie Jackson, the social worker that was accompanying me, “Can you see if there is something in my ear?”

She smiled and replied, "Relax, Tamyra. Your ears are popping."

"Oh," I said, forcing a halfhearted smile. I placed my headset back over my ears and thumbed through the magazines mom bought for me. The one thing I found to be surprising was once we were in the clouds, it felt as if I was sitting in my living room at home. I gazed out of the window at the beauty of the clouds, imagined what it would be like if I could sit on them.

As we neared the airport in Denver, Colorado, the flight attendant's voice came alive over the speaker. She ordered anyone who was standing up to return to their seats and for us to all put on our seatbelts. I even had to turn off my portable CD player. A shuttle waited for us once we had exited the plane and retrieved our luggage from baggage claim. I was sure to take in the many sites of this big city. I was speechless. The reality of my situation was finally setting in.

Here I was, only seventeen-years-old. I was in this strange place I had never been to before. My social worker was only there with me for about three days, and then, I was all alone. Throughout my stay at the hospital, whenever I became anxious, I went to the window in my room. Although it wasn't snowing at the hospital, I could see snow on the mountains miles and miles away. I thought of my twin sister. I later learned that she was thinking of me as well.

The staff at National Jewish Medical and Research Center greeted me with smiles when I entered the hospital. The nurse over the day program immediately stuck a stethoscope up to my back and proceeded to listen to my breathing. The physician decided she, too, wanted to listen to me breathe. They used a stethoscope having two heads on it. I had never seen anything like it before.

After the admittance process was over, I waited patiently to be issued one of the easy access gowns you always have to wear in hospitals. I was both surprised and elated when I was never issued one. This hospital was more like a dormitory. The part resembling an actual hospital was located on the second floor.

I had fun my first day at the hospital getting to know everyone. Unfortunately, I had to stay on the second floor my first night. I could not have anything to eat or drink after midnight since the next morning I was going to have a twenty-four hour PH probe study to assess how much acid I was producing and to see if it was coming up my esophagus. I did not see what this procedure had to do with my asthma. My physicians were certain they would obtain information from this study aiding them in determining why my asthma was so bad. I thought I would be relaxed when it was time for the procedure to be done. Those thoughts were rendered null and void when I saw exactly what was going to be done. I held my breath when the technician stuck a tube up my nose. As the discomfort from holding my breath became evident, I reached up and yanked the tube out of my nose before the technician had time to tape it in place. I sat up on the table glaring wildly and breathing hard. "Can we please not do that again?" I asked.

"Calm down, honey," I heard someone whispering in my ear. "Would you like me to hold your hand until it is over?"

I sat there a few more moments, scared out of my mind. I knew the procedure had to be done. After rationalizing with myself that everything was going to be okay, I reluctantly gave the nurse my hand. She, in return, smiled at me and gave my hand a tiny squeeze.

Those twenty-four hours had to be the worst twenty-four hours of my life. Every time I swallowed, I felt the tube down my throat. Having to carry around the computerized box keeping track of everything was a little too much. Whenever I ate something, I had to press "eat" on the computer box. The little tube loved getting caught on bread. As a result, I felt like I was choking. After breakfast I fasted for the rest of the day. Whenever I took medication, I had to press "medication" on the box. Even when I wanted to sleep, I had to press the little man on the box that said "lying down" and vice versa when I was sitting up.

The nurse assigned to me was very friendly. She took every precaution to make sure I was as comfortable as possible. She even came to visit me every two hours. The last time she came to my room, she sat on the edge of the bed with me, and she said, "Why don't you try to get some sleep, sweetie? Every time I come in here, you've got those pretty little eyes open."

I just knew I was going to have the opportunity to enjoy the day room the next day as I saw several other teens around my age. I was anxious to get to know them. But there were more tests having to be done. Knowing this put a serious damper on my mood. I contemplated not cooperating. Howbeit, I went along with the flow. I sat in the giant box that looked like an ice cube. I sealed my lips around the giant mouth piece sticking up out of the bottom of the ice cube look alike. I put my hands up to my face as instructed and panted like a dog when asked to do so. I breathed into my lungs through a nebulizer some medicine that was actually supposed to induce an asthma attack, just so my team of healthcare providers could know exactly how bad my asthma was.

I attended the boring asthma education classes, even though I nodded through most of them. I attended group sessions and talked about my feelings regarding having asthma. I watched other patients around my age get highly upset when they learned they were going to be put on a big burst of Prednisone. Some of them even rolled around on the floor, kicking, and screaming. I wasn't quite as dramatic when I received the news that I was going to be taking about 40 mgs of Prednisone every other day.

That wasn't where the treatment ended. I swallowed my pride every day, and I blew into this tube called a peak flow meter three times a day. I allowed nurses to put clips on my nose and have me to breathe into a mouthpiece attached to the end of a computer. If I blew all the bricks down on the screen or all the leaves off the trees, my lung capacity was great. I never could get past the second tree of leaves or the third row of bricks.

I was then introduced to a new gadget called the aero-chamber. It was a device I was supposed to stick my inhaler in. Whenever I had to use the inhaler, I was supposed to press it into the aero-chamber, and then suck the medicine out of it so I wouldn't lose any of the medicine.

I even kept my cool when one of my peers stuck a fake rat under the lid of my dinner tray one evening. He conveniently stifled his laughter until I actually removed the lid. When I saw the rat, sitting right next to my mashed potatoes, I screamed, throwing the whole tray on the floor.

I took the lid and hit at the rat I thought was real. All the while, the guy who put it there was laughing so hard until he turned red in the face.

"What are you laughing at?" I shouted.

"It's fake, girl. I got you good," he said in between bouts of laughter.

Everyone else was laughing as well. I personally didn't see what was so funny. But I chose not to get angry. That famous quote, "Revenge is a dish best served cold," came to mind instead. I spent the next couple of days devising a plan to get him back. One day I just took off running for no reason. I acted like it was something seriously wrong. The guy who'd stuck the rat under my dinner tray followed suit. But then he fell right smack on his face trying to get away. He laid there on the floor like a blog of goo, looking confused. I burst out laughing and asked him, "How does it feel to be made a fool out of?" He looked at me with embarrassment written all over his face. He wanted to be mad, but realized that he couldn't be. I was merely getting him back like I had purposed in my heart to do.

I have to admit, my time at National Jewish wasn't all bad. One of the parents, who opted to stay at the hospital with his son, had a habit of going out to Wendy's every Friday night and getting all of us Chocolate Frosties. I got the chance to make arts and crafts whenever I wanted to. The activities director, Mr. Wardell, took all of us (patients) out of the facility quite frequently. My first week there, he took us to see the movie, Anaconda. At other times, we went to the mall and to the zoo. The days came and went quite fast. I smiled bigger than I had ever smiled since becoming a patient at the hospital when one day the mail carrier brought me a stack of letters my classmates in my 4th period English class had sent to me. The next day, I received a card from Clifford Jackson, another classmate, who I had known the majority of my life. I liked the words in the card. His personal words were what stuck in my mind.

“Tamyra, things are just not the same here without you. Hurry up and get well soon so you can come home,” is what I saw scrawled at the bottom of the card. Under those words was his signature. If ever there were such a thing as someone’s heart melting, I think mine was like butter when I saw those words. CJ (Clifford) was an alright person when he wasn’t aggravating me, but I never would have guessed he was sentimental. I made sure to tape that card to my bulletin board, after I showed it to all of the staff.

A few days later, I received a letter from Tacorya Crenshaw, one of my church members. It was equally as touching as the card I had gotten from CJ. The gist of the letter was that at every free moment I had, I should declare I was healed in Jesus’ name.

Five-and-a-half-weeks later, I was ready to board another plane and head back to sweet home Alabama. Fortunately, for me, mom was with me now. I got off the elevator one afternoon. There she stood with a big and bright smile plastered across her face.

"Mom," I screamed, simultaneously running into her arms. We embraced for several moments. She showed me the pictures Tamara had taken at the Junior Prom. I felt a pang of sadness knowing I had missed out on such a special event. But I safely tucked those sad feelings away as I didn't want anything to ruin how happy I was to see mom.

"Tamyra, I have some bad news," Mom said once we were sitting, facing each other in my bedroom. Immediately, I felt the strength I had drain from my body as I prepared myself to hear what mom would tell me.

"We buried somebody at home while you were away…"

"Who was it, mom?" I interrupted. I could feel my heart wanting to escape through my chest.

Mom studied my face for a second as if she was considering not telling me after all.

"Please, mom, tell me."

My voice came out more like a shrill. I put my hands under my legs to keep them from trembling so badly.

"Donte," she finally responded.

My eyes widened as I stood and sat back down again. "Donte Hyde!" I screamed. "No, mom, that can't be true. I just saw him, mom. I swear I just saw him."

"Yes, baby, I'm afraid it's true."

Once again, I stood and then, I sat down again. For a few, seeming to never end moments I, was mute.

"Mom," I said with trembling lips. My voice got caught in my throat. I swallowed hard and tried again to express my thoughts. "I saw him a couple of days before I left for Denver. He was walking up the street. I was weak from all of the medicine I had to take at the hospital. It was hot outside. I could barely make it, and I felt like I was going to pass out because it was so hot. When he saw me, he stopped. Suddenly, he came rushing down in the yard. He grabbed me by the hand and asked me if I needed any help. He was nice enough to walk me back to the house. He wouldn't leave me until he knew I was going to be all right. That's the last memory I have of him. Now, you're telling me he is gone…" My voice trailed off. Mom only nodded her head as she brushed tears out of the corner of her eyes.

"But… but… but he was too young, mom," I blurted out as I felt my own tears falling down my face. I realized, as I tried to swallow this pill of reality, how precious life was. I had survived a terrible crisis, even when my own primary physician had doubts in his mind I would. I didn't know if it was fair for me to still be walking around. I did know I was blessed. It was clear to me now why mom was waving her hands and giving praises to God my last few days in Baptist Hospital.

At that point, I had enough strength to get out of the bed and walk around. My doctor had urged me to walk as much as possible so I could regain my strength. Mom watched with gladness in her eyes. When I walked back to the room, she had her hands extended. This was normal behavior for mom. So I wasn't surprised. I had no idea it was because of me. She was grateful the bad report the doctor had given her was repealed by God.

Sickness had definitely struck in my life. Despite how bad it was, I made it. There was no reason for me to ever feel so bad about myself or to hate myself. I should've loved myself just the same as God loved me when he spared my life. In the midst of it all, I was a wounded teenager. I still didn't think I was worthy of anyone's love.

A Future So Bright

Senior at last

When I emerged from the comfort of the bed, my first day as a senior in high school, I was greeted with a rush of elation as my feet thudded heavily against the floor. Exhilaration graced my world with such great magnitude, taking dominion of all within me and altering it beyond my wildest dreams. I was as jovial as an unsupervised kid in a candy store who had just been given his weekly allowance to splurge at will. Regrettably, I'd already had several false alarms when I awakened throughout the night, thinking it was time for me to arise and prepare myself for the day at hand.

"At last, I'm a senior," I squealed. The indescribable feeling of nervousness mixed with excitement unfolded in my mind. I kicked away the covers, scrambling like a wild person, ready to jump into my freshly ironed jeans and shirt I had gingerly laid out on the back of the chair in the living room while the evening was still young. I was ready to grab my backpack, head out the door, sprint up to the bus stop, and engage in small talk with my neighbors until the bus came to whisk me away to school. I would then be welcomed by my classmates, who also were seething with a massive amount of enthusiasm.

To my dismay, this series of events had only been a pipedream. As I sat upright on the side of the bed, I noticed a piercing pang of disillusionment stabbing me like an icepick through a block of ice when I discovered how night was still on duty conducting its shift.

I walked over to the window, looking with sad eyes at the darkness towering over the sky. Everything was still except my pulse beating rapidly with anticipation. "If it was something I didn't want to do, the hours would have quickly passed by," I groaned with a tone of aggravation as I sauntered back over to the bed and plopped down with much attitude.

What was even worst was every time my sleep was interrupted, it took me nearly thirty minutes to drift back off. Now that it was a quarter to six in the morning, I beamed with a deep sense of amusement as I stretched and yawned noisily. Imagine how tickled pink I was when I was sure it wasn't another false alarm.

As I pulled the handmade quilt on my bed up over the pillows, I allowed my mind to take me on an excursion where it enlightened me with sneak peeks of what would probably take place on the first day of school. Daydreaming had always been one of my favorite pastimes. I was known to do it at any given moment, would sometimes get in trouble when it caused me to not do things I knew to do. I did not have much time to daydream this particular morning or I would miss the bus, didn't think I could handle having such an adversity on the first day of school.

I dazzled like a lavishly dressed ruby in the finest jewelry store as I rushed to the bathroom to wash my face. I never remembered a time before when I was so fixated on getting to school. I hummed a tune of merriment while brushing my teeth. Finally, I was going to be considered the cream of the crop. In my mind's eye, there was no greater honor to bestow.

I entered Central High School that humid morning in August of 1997 with the stride of entitlement in my steps. The sidewalks, leading up to the school, were packed with a congregation of teens grinning and showing off their new Jordan's, Air Force Ones, and trendy outfits they'd been fortunate to get for back to school. They hurried through all of the doors standing open for them. Some of them shoved their way through. Eager they were to reconnect with their long lost friends who they hadn't had any form of contact with since the last day of the previous school term.

As I sashayed up the long hallway, I heard the squeals of highly energized girls as they leaped into the arms of their boyfriends. I shuffled past the guidance counselor's office, the lockers, and the girls and boys restrooms in high spirits. It didn't take me long to notice how all of the lack of confidence I exhibited in earlier years of high school seemed to have melted away like butter spread on waffles.

I didn't feel the need to dastardly tread behind anyone else the way I normally had as if I needed them to first appear confident before my own confidence came out of hibernation. I held my head up high, even when I passed by the cliques who were always considered to be popular. They had the usual, "Don't-talk-to-me-because-I-am-better-than-you," glare displayed on their faces. I knew I didn't fit in with that crowd and I was glad I had finally gotten the courage to stop trying. I would just be myself the way mom had always told me I should be. So as I passed by them I hit them with the, "Don't-talk-to-me-because-I-don't-have-time-to-deal-with-stuck-up-wannabe's, glare.

Apparently, all of my other classmates reciprocated my feelings of superiority. We took our rightful place, which was at the center of everyone's attention. One would think we had practiced how it was going to be throughout the summer. We gave each other high-fives, chatted with those we considered friends, and acted the same as we had seen the other seniors act in previous years before we finally had the chance to sit on the throne.

This was the day I'd waited so long for. But if I was to be completely honest, if it wasn't for my overinflated ego needing to be stroked immensely, this day was no different from any other first day of school I'd attended, except now I was a senior. I'd only reached the final milestone in high school before I began another phase on my journey. For the life of me, I didn't understand why I felt as if confetti should be raining down from the clouds.

It wasn't just that I assumed I would be the head honcho, the reason I was so excited about the first day of school. Only a few months before, I had missed a large portion of my junior year of high school because of my impromptu visit to National Jewish Medical and Research Center in Denver, Colorado. It was a very trialing time in my life. So many days while I was going through my bout of sickness,

I thought it for sure would be the death of me, and I would never be able to live the life I imagined I would live. Now since I was able to be at school, instead of lying in a hospital bed, it was proof of how I was doing so much better. To be honest, I was happy to finally be among my peers. I danced joyously, relieved and happy my asthma was finally under control and wouldn't affect my senior year. At least this was what I thought. Little did I know, I would wind up being a homebound student before Christmas break.

I adjusted to my senior year in high school with no problem, felt it was cool if I skipped a few classes here and there the way I saw so many others do. This was the one way I could be tried-and-true, so I assumed. I soon discovered, after hiding out in the girl's bathroom, that cutting class wasn't my cup of tea. While everyone else was getting away with it, I was the one to get caught because I didn't know how to be cool. The thought of how upset mom would be if she knew I was cutting class and how she would have no reservations at all about breaking out her good ole switch if I didn't get my act together, kept me at least halfway in check.

The last thing I wanted or needed was for her to show her face at the school because I was acting unruly. She wasn't going to be showing up just to talk. Even though I was seventeen-years-old, she constantly reminded me that I would still get my butt tore out of the frame, if I deserved it. As long as I lived in her house and she had to care for me, I was not too old to be corrected.

The day came when it was time for me to take my senior portraits. It was hard for me to conceive this was really happening for me. I had always been a photogenic person, ready to smile heartily whenever anyone dared to hold a camera up in front of me. Now having the chance to capture my smile in photos for no other reason than it was a ritual for seniors about to graduate from high school was more than I could stand. I couldn't wait to pick out my outfits for this special event.

"These pictures have to be perfect." I giggled as I thought of the many poses I would strike. I don't think I had been more thrilled except for when I got the notice from school stating I had passed the exit exam while I was still a junior. I remembered that joyous day as if it had just occurred. Tamara tore into the house that afternoon from school. I lay in bed gazing out the window at the bus as it passed by. Sickness had caused me to miss joining my sister in being present on the teacher's roster. I rolled my eyes in exasperation as I heard her stampeding up the hallway like a herd of horses towards my bedroom. Quickly, I closed my eyes, deciding right then to pretend like I was asleep. She stood over me like a warden waving the paper in her hand.

"Look what I got," she panted, out of breath.

"What is it?" I asked with my eyes still closed.

My heart was racing from the breathing treatment I had recently taken. I was trying with no success to relax.

"We passed!" Tamara then shouted. "We passed the exit exam! All three parts! On the first try!"

By now, my eyes were widened in sheer amazement. I clearly remembered a smart aleck teacher telling Tamara and I with a smirk, "You two are going to be crying when you get those results." I sure wished at that moment I could've been waving that little paper in front of her face. "What you got to say now teacher dearest," I probably would say. I forgot about how I was just sulking and jumped out of the bed, snatching the proof out of Tamara's hand.

"Oh, my, God!" I shrieked as I read it for myself and proceeded to dance all over the room. I paid no mind to the fact I was standing barefoot on the floor. This was a careless mistake I would pay for later on in the night when I felt Cassie wanting to cut up. I was still on cloud nine when mom drove up from work. I met her at the car before she had time to get out and shoved the letter in her face.

"Ugh, girl, have you lost your mind?" she fussed. "You better get your behind in the house and get some shoes on your feet now. You know if the wind blow hard, you will be sounding like a six o'clock train."

Now, I was wise enough to know a photo shoot is not nearly as important as it was for me to pass the exit exam.

If I hadn't passed the exit exam, there wouldn't have been a need for me to engage in the photo shoot. That little diploma, encased in the green folder, would have never been mine, an everlasting trophy as an award for crossing a finish line in my life. The joy in my heart from both events brought many smiles to my face.

Relapse

Just as sure as the sun shines upon the face of the Earth, there will come a time when the gusty winds will raise up its voice to be heard. Its mighty roar will bring the sun under subjection. Even with the sun's power to bring about warmth to even the darkest areas of the world, it will have no choice but to pack up its rays and bid farewell.

The same rule of thumb applies when my asthma went into remission. I was doing really well and didn't hear any of the annoying wheezes I had gotten so used to hearing throughout the years. Even when I was so called "doing my best" they would still be there, never fully exiting the premises of my respiratory system. If I did well all day long without any incidence, I was sure to have some kind of issue during the night, if nothing more than a coughing spell leading up to some tightness in my chest.

I felt fortunate how I wasn't going through any of that drama at this point in time of my life. The going to see the doctor every two weeks was a thing of the past. Carrying around two and three inhalers at a time was obsolete also. In fact, I was doing so well, I had even taken it upon myself to discontinue some of the meds I was supposed to be taking on a daily basis.

"What's the point?" I rationalized.

"I'm feeling better. I don't even wheeze anymore. This Prednisone doesn't do anything but make me swell up anyway. I'm not taking this shit anymore." And I didn't. Whenever mom asked me if I had taken my medication, I had no reservation about lying to her. But the truth always came out.

Unbeknownst to me, the medications I stopped taking were preventative meds. They kept the asthma attacks far away from me and from ruling my life the way they had done for a big part of my childhood and into my teens. Up unto this point, it didn't matter what I wanted to do. If Cassie (my asthma) wasn't down for it, I could just hang it up, and put my hopes for a little normalcy in my pocket and leave it there.

Because I had to have things my way, I wound up having another run-in with Cassie, who had been sitting patiently on the sidelines of my life waiting to again have her chance. When she rose up, she wasn't nice about it. As a matter of fact, she put me back in the hospital for a few days. I couldn't help feeling defeated while I lay in the hospital bed in a solemn mood, holding my head in my chin and wishing for better days. This being sick foolishness was for the birds. It could not be the outcome of my senior year. I had things to do, places to go, and people to see. None of it could be taken care of with me lying in the hospital with an IV in my arm and a nasal cannula stuck in my nostrils. The vomiting as a side effect of the excessive breathing treatments was not fun in the least.

"Miss Walker, you are overmedicated, that's the reason you keep vomiting," my doctor had told me when making rounds. "We're going to lay off the Solu-Medrol and cut back the breathing treatments, and hopefully, you'll feel better tomorrow," she continued. In response, I lowered the bed to a comfortable position, attempting to fall asleep.

When I was discharged, Cassie decided to stick around for a while. I did manage to get better. I was able to join my sister and classmates back at school. That was until the next month when I was admitted again to the hospital, and the next month after that. It got so I was again missing too many days out of school. There were times, when I wasn't in the hospital, if it was raining outside, mom wouldn't allow me to go to school.

"Tamyra," she said in that authoritarian voice of hers, "Go on and get back in the bed. It's raining cats and dogs out there. I'm not fixing to be in the ER with you all night."

Eventually, the school and the Board of Education put their heads together and decided to make me a homebound student. Otherwise, I would be retained. So now there was no more going to school for me. While my sister was getting up extra early to get to the bus stop on time, I was still in bed watching with eyes filled with envy.

That was until I got addicted to *Young and the Restless* and *Days of Our Lives*. Sitting in front of the television during those two hours, made up for my not being able to go to school. I lived to see 11:00 a.m., Monday through Friday. I fixed me a big bowl of Frosted Flakes and plopped down in front of the television, ready to tune into the life of Victor and Nicki. When *Young and the Restless went* off at 12:00, I waited patiently for *Days of Our Lives* to come on at 12:30 p.m. I was obsessed with watching Sami and Lucas's antics, would get angry with them and call them all kinds of names as if they could hear me.

The cliffhangers at the end of the week drove me into a maddening rage. I can't count how many times I said I wasn't going to watch it anymore which turned out to be a lie I could have saved. I knew full well I would be in the same spot on the couch the next day when *Days of Our Lives* came on.

Graduation

On May 23, 1998, at approximately 8:30 in the morning, I graduated from Central High School with honors, despite the many odds I had faced. Pomp and circumstances was being played by the band as I marched into my graduation.

"Tamyra, get on the right foot. Please, don't mess up the formation," I had to keep telling myself. To say it was hot was an understatement. Fans were blowing everywhere in the gymnasium and the bleachers were filled to capacity. I was now eighteen-years-old, about to receive my diploma, and still alive.

Only a couple months prior to this day, I had to have surgery due to the acid reflux I learned I had at National Jewish Medical and Research Center. The surgery took place only a few days after I attended my senior prom. I remember so well because I had to take the hairpins out of my hair. I couldn't have my nail polish on my fingers either. This was depressing to me because I was certain I would enjoy my nails and hairdo way past prom.

Right before I was rolled out of my hospital room at Children's hospital in Birmingham, Alabama, to go to surgery, someone told me, "If you have on underwear, you have to take them off." I opened my eyes and glared at the lady who said that to me.

"Why?" I groggily asked. "I'm having surgery on my stomach, not my panties."

I woke up again while I was lying on the table in surgery. The room was extremely cold. I could see scalpels and all sorts of cutting devices everywhere. As the surgeon looked into my eyes, he said, "Put her out now." Immediately, I felt a mask over my face. A voice told me to breathe in and out. I didn't remember anything else until I was in recovery uttering inaudible phrases here and there.

The ride home from Children's Hospital was a rough ride. My stomach hurt badly from the incisions I had as a result of the surgery. I thought on all these things while the speaker at my graduation was speaking. I thumbed over the program. The words, "A journey of a thousand miles must begin with one single step," stayed on my mind.

Those months I had been a homebound student wasn't all easy. Mrs. Cosby, who had also been my Algebra teacher in eighth grade, only came to the house twice a week. She was always nice, going to special lengths to ensure I understood the assignments I had to turn in. Still, at times, I found staying focused to be a formidable task.

It didn't help that I was also going through another bout of depression. There were some so-called high and mighty individuals at the school who went out of their way to make certain I wasn't allowed to accompany my class on our senior trip to Orlando, Florida.

"I don't think she should be allowed to come. If she is not well enough to come to school like everybody else, she shouldn't come on the senior trip either," one person said.

"Well, it's not her fault that she is sickly," someone else chimed in. "It would be kind of heartless to deny her the opportunity to have fun with her class just because she has an illness she didn't ask to have."

This was the debate that was up in the air regarding my fate. God worked it out in my favor though, and I joined my class at Grad Night at Magic Kingdom. As long as my asthma specialist didn't deem the trip to be excessively strenuous, and I had a family member to accompany me in the event I got sick, I could go.

I couldn't help thinking on all of that while at my graduation and how much fun I'd had. I was sure to take lots of pictures. That was a moment in my life I knew I would want to look back on.

While sitting in my designated seat, I also smiled at how I had just attended Class Night the night before. It was a great time in my life, a time when my depression and feelings of worthlessness were on ice. I knew, as always, they would make an appearance when I least expected it.

But the present events taking place in my world were a nice distraction.

With the biggest grin ever, I grasped the principal's hand as I was handed my diploma.

"Well done." I heard someone say as I exited the stage, abruptly blinded by the array of camera lights flashing in my face. I was careful not to trip over my own feet while walking down the stairs since I was wearing heels. *It seems as if all eyes are on me*, I thought as I gave into the bleak feeling of shyness washing over me.

I smiled even harder as I sat back down in my perspective seat while the remainder of my classmates received their diplomas. When it was all over, I walked out into the sunlight to mingle with my family who were waiting proudly for me. My sister, Sharmeen, cried when I left the building. She had my niece Breonna, who was three-years-old at the time, sitting on her hip as she wiped tears from her eyes. My other sister, Pamela, flashed me the prettiest smile I had ever seen in my life.

Once out in the early afternoon heat, I bumped into my pastor and his first lady. There were also other people from my church who had come to see me graduate. Even so, I still felt as if a piece of the puzzle was missing. For one, my brother, Jarrett, was not there. He had been incarcerated in the state of Florida since I was sixteen-years-old. I wanted him to be there, felt as if I needed him to be there. We didn't always see eye-to-eye. However, I knew he would have been proud of me. I imagined he would have hugged me tightly, nodding his head at me, signifying his approval.

Carolyn wasn't there either. That was simply by choice. My graduation from high school wasn't an important enough event for her to grace me with her presence. It was a pill I found myself gagging on as I tried my best to swallow it. What was even more depressing was that there was nothing I could do about it, but move on with my life.

A New Lease on Life

Upward Bound

Our deepest fear is not that we are inadequate. Our deepest fear is that we are powerful beyond measure. It is our light, not our darkness that most frightens us. We ask ourselves, who am I to be brilliant, gorgeous, talented, fabulous? Actually, who are you not to be? Your playing small does not serve the world. There is nothing enlightened about shrinking so that other people won't feel insecure around you. We are all meant to shine, as children do. We were born to make manifest the glory of God that is within us. It's not just in some of us; it's in everyone. And as we let our own light shine, we unconsciously give other people permission to do the same. As we are liberated from our own fear, our presence automatically liberates others.

Throughout my tenure as a living vessel, I've discovered the above quote by, Marianne Williamson, taken from her 1992 book, "A Return to Love," has always been one to facilitate the need for growth in my heart. I perceive it to be plausible in every aspect of the words. Whenever I hear it recited, an abundance of motivation is always ensued. If for only a moment, its words bare the infinite power to whip me out of my melancholy state of mind. They take away the uncomfortable feeling resembling the blistering cold of winter, replacing it with the welcoming sunlight of spring where everything blooms with the beauty of anticipation. If only I would allow those encouraging words to marinate deeply within my wounds, it would be the first-aid needed to fashion me for greatness. My suffrage would consequently be extinct. Proudly, I would be deemed a pillar of strength.

The deep dark secret I tried to keep under wraps was unveiled at last. It could no longer be hidden away like an illegitimate child conceived in an extramarital affair. The undistorted truth was, I needed all the motivation I could get. I needed it to release unto me its vigor that would be like liquid Drano to my mind.

Now, I don't have the credentials of a shrink, but I've come to realize how a mass number of people don't like to recognize his/her own flaws. It makes them look despairingly into the mirror of reality. The image glaring back shows them not to be the perfect individuals they wanted everyone to believe they were. For some, that revelation is a brutal blow to their ego they find hard to recover from.

My reality was my mind had been known to be clogged with some pretty unhealthy things. In return, it held me captive, far away from the potential to bear the ripened fruit of success. One thing I did know, there was no way I could sit idly and watch my life slip through my fingers as if it had no meaning. I had to hold on to hope as if it was a defibrillator to keep my heart from flat lining, embark on the next chapter of my life with a zealous mentality, and proclaim myself to be all I was predestined to be way before God proposed to breathe into me the breath of life.

Since I'd graduated from high school, it was a profitable time to move on to bigger and better things. The day was young. There was much to be done before the sun came down off its throne. But despite my ability to discern such a straightforward fact, it was much easier said than done. I had to literally prune my mind of the weeds of discouragement growing wildly and unkempt in my mental garden. They had become the focal point, covering up everything God said was good.

I conveyed earlier that no matter what avenue I found myself on along the tempestuous journey I treaded, depression and low self-esteem were sure to tag along. One would think they were security guards posted up to keep me safe. Instead of protecting me, they sprinkled seeds of self-hate in my life's soil.

The acts of self-hate multiplied. They gave life to feelings of worthlessness and hopelessness. As I paddled along the way, I had become quite the pitiful one. I failed to realize I didn't have to be at that point. I don't know if any of you have heard of the saying, "I had to fake the funk." Well, I got pretty good at faking. I verbalized what was expected of me, acted the way I assumed would be tolerable for all who were on the outside looking in, smiled, even when it seemed as if I would need a can of WD-40 to loosen the muscles in my face so they would move the right way. I even gave advice to others about what they should do regarding their situations in order to reap a favorable outcome. It was then, with great shame, I glared into the windowpane of hypocrisy, for my own emotional status was a war zone I couldn't begin to handle.

When the chips were down, I had to keep reassuring myself, "Tamyra, don't be so hard on yourself. You just graduated from high school. You are as good as anyone else. You can achieve whatever you put your mind to."

As hard as I tried, the words I said in a desperate plea to awaken my self-worth out of the bowels of defeat, seemed to go in one ear and straight out the other. The seeds I planted didn't fall on good soil.

Thinking on that reminded me of the Parable of the Sower (Matthew 13:1-9). I've read those Scriptures many times. I took them to apply to myself even though I was the one who attempted to speak goodness into my own life. I heard the words I spoke blaring like a trumpet in my conscience. Therefore, I should listen and take heed to what was being said.

Many nights, it seemed as if the lightning of self-loathing flashed mercilessly. I was afraid, lying in a fetal position upon my bed, trying perilously to ward off the aftermath of it all. It didn't help that the thunder roared viciously as well. I felt as if I had to hide myself the same as a kid playing hide-and-go-seek with a group of his friends. I found the lightning and thunder to be an evil duo seeking to destroy what had taken years to construct, sometimes seemingly with not enough building materials to secure the foundation.

In the midst of it all, God had his hand on me. He didn't allow the fiercely brewing storm to harm me. Yes, it whipped against the walls of my flesh so that I thought I would fall apart. As hard as I found it to be, I picked myself up and I went on, even though at times, I walked with a limp. I kept telling myself, "Weeping may endure for a night, but joy comes in the morning." This was a Scripture found in the 30th book of Psalms I'd also become acquainted with when I was only a tot. It still had special meaning to me. Even when I wasn't certain of the words, I would say them over and over again.

It wasn't farfetched to grasp the thought of joy coming my way. Whenever it decided to visit, it was going to jumpstart my heart, give it the spark needed to reach out, and grab exactly what was in store for me. What better way to start my quest for a new lease on life than to attend Upward Bound the summer of 1998?

Upward Bound wrote its first entry in the journal of my life in the wake of my junior year of high school. It all came to be on the campus of Alabama State University.

Initially, I went to the University on Saturday mornings to take classes. I was only sixteen-years-old at the time, partially felt out of place because I was amidst a boiling pot of personalities.

While I was bubbly and loved to smile, I noticed how some of the Upward Bound participants got quite upset if you even had the nerve to speak to them. They considered it to be disrespectful for you to speak to them, unless you knew them personally.

One guy, named Lawrence, who I eventually became cordial with, actually got so angry with someone that he broke the case in which the fire extinguisher was kept, all because someone looked at him a little too long.

My eyes widened as I witnessed the glass shattering and blood trickling down his fist that he held in the tightest grip. *I know dang well this didn't just happen,* I thought while inadvertently rubbing my eyes as if they were filled with sleep. I flattened my body up against the wall to assure none of the glass came my way.

As I stood there with my respirations doing their own thing. I tried to shake off the sight of what I had seen like a gruesome nightmare torturing me in the middle of the night with no light shining in my room except the glow of the stars nestled high above in the sky.

One thing was very clear. I could never get used to such rampant behavior. Therefore, it took quite some time for me to adjust to being around other people who I knew nothing about. I found myself shying away from mostly everyone, refusing to even attempt to make friends until I noticed some of my classmates from high school were also a part of the Upward Bound Program.

Slowly then, I began to loosen up and actually enjoyed the program and all it had to offer. I thought it was the coolest thing in the world that we received a stipend for coming to class. It wasn't much, but it was enough for me to waste on nonsense, which I did every time I received one.

As I took a retrospective walk down memory lane, I smiled coyly when my mind stumbled upon the time I attended the Kwanzaa Program put on by the Upward Bound staff. I remembered wearing a black pantsuit mom had bought me from Parisians. I was sure to drape an

African sash across my shoulder in commemoration of the African heritage.

As I caught a glimpse of my frame in the full length mirror hanging on the back of the door in my bedroom, for just a split moment, the feeling that I was beautiful metastasized like cancer invading my soul.

For that occasion, mom allowed me to get my hair done, and I thought I was the bomb.com with my waterfall ponytail. It came to me as a surprise how some celebrated Kwanzaa as opposed to celebrating Christmas. But instead of being critical, I kept an open mind. I could hear mom speaking ever so gently in my ear, "Tamyra, everything in life is not going to be to your liking. But that doesn't mean it is wrong. Remember always how passionate you are about people listening to you. This is a great time for you to practice the Golden Rule… Do unto others as you would have them to do unto you."

Truth of the matter was, I couldn't argue with what mom said. As usual, she was right. Even when I didn't like the taste of the truth, it was like medicine to a sick body. If I took it the way I should, everything ailing me would resolve itself.

Things were a little different when I attended Upward Bound the summer following my high school graduation. Whereas I had only been going on Saturdays, now that it was summer, I would have the chance to stay on campus.

I had already been accepted into Alabama State University as an incoming freshman. So the classes I took while in Upward Bound for the summer would count towards my Bachelor's degree. I couldn't have been more delighted than when Tamara and I were issued our key to our very own room in the CJ Dunn Tower dormitory. I held my composure until I was alone in the privacy and confines of the room assigned to me. When I heard the door click close, I looked around my space, expelling a nervous giggle and began to imagine how I would set things up on my desk and along the shelves above my bed. "Things are going to be great," I said aloud. I had to say the words to convince myself.

We had a curfew, of course, as we weren't considered to be part of the regular population on campus. But who cared about all of that? I certainly didn't. I was going to do exactly what I wanted to do, in the manner I wanted to do it. Mom wasn't there to stop me. That was all I found to be of importance.

Trouble in Paradise

I don't know why, but it always seemed as if no matter how much I was enjoying myself, there would be something to come along to dispense havoc. It would rip off my peace of mind, leaving me feeling barren inside and clutching insanely at the torn pieces of my existence that once made me whole. Whenever I thought of it the poem,

Nothing Gold Can Stay, by Robert Frost, comes to mind. He had to be feeling some kind of way when he recorded those words… *Nature's first green is gold, her hardest hue to hold. Her early leaf's a flower; But only so an hour. Then leaf subsides to leaf. So Eden sank to grief, so dawn goes down to day. Nothing gold can stay…*

The original high I felt of knowing I was on a college campus eventually wore off like perfume splashed about a woman's neck at the ending of the day. The highs and lows brought me down so that, at times, I thought my place was on the ground looking up. Every day I dragged myself out of the comfort of my bed to attend classes, forcing a weak smile whenever someone looked upon my face as I passed them on campus in the mornings and afternoons as well.

I don't know the reason why I felt I had to disguise how I really felt. Behind closed doors; when no one could witness my fate accept the four walls, my emotions were cruel to me. They let me have it, raw and uncut. They showed no compassion whatsoever. I cried openly for only a few scraps of sympathy, for I thought the lashings of torment I received were a bit too much. If only it would shield me, allow me to have a little peace, I would be ever so grateful.

At the ending of the day when I was finished with class, as soon as I entered the room, I changed into a pair of gym shorts. It was time for the mask to come off. I could no longer hide how I really felt. I fell across the bed with tears descending heavily down my face. I didn't even bother to wipe them away. I lay there, soaked in my own bad feelings, depression beating me as hard as it could. I tried to refocus my attention on the conversations I'd had with my pastor only a year or so before. He always had an open door policy. Whenever I needed to talk, I went to him. Regardless of how long the conversations lasted, he always listened with an attentive and caring ear. While I ranted about this and that, he flipped through the pages of his

Bible. He was sure to respond to what I said to him, so I wouldn't feel like he was ignoring me.

The Scriptures he shared in the midst of him counseling me were always fitting to my situation. "Let me tell you something, Tee," he said to me as soothing as he could. "The devil knows what great things lie within you. He does not want you to have what God has ordained for you to have. If he can get in your mind, he feels as if he has hit a homerun, and it'll be easy for him to steal your soul."

I sat before my pastor, twilling my fingers nervously, as quiet as a kid being read a bedtime story. I dared not interrupt. I knew the things he said to me were the truth. In case there was any doubt in mind, he always referenced the Bible.

"I don't want you to take my word for it," he continued. "I'm going to show you so there won't be a need for you to feel misled." He showed me John 10:10 in the King James Version of the Bible. I read the words with conviction: *The thief cometh not, but for to steal, and to kill, and to destroy: I am come that they might have life, and that they might have it more abundantly.*

After reading the Scripture, I allowed silence to sing to me a song while the words submerged beneath the surface of my mind. Pastor Edwards was silent as well for a brief moment. Then, he carried on. "You can defeat the devil, Tee. God gave you the authority to do so. But you have to be prepared…"

Again, he flipped through his Bible until he came upon Ephesians 6:11. Once there, he handed the Bible to me and ordered me to read. I hesitated before reaching out to grab the Bible. He nodded his head, signaling to me that it was okay. I grabbed hold of the Bible and sat it in my lap, proceeded to read the scripture silently.

"Read it aloud, Tee," my pastor interrupted.

"Put on the whole armor of God that ye may be able to stand against the wiles of the devil," I read in a submissive tone. "What are wiles?" I then asked, confused.

"Wiles are nothing more than tricks! It's what the devil uses to lure you in," he responded.

Before the ending of each session, we always prayed together. When it was all over, I felt renewed in my mind, body, and soul. I felt like I could go on. I just knew in my heart everything was going to be okay.

Now, if I could feel so enlightened at the moment, I don't understand why I didn't remember everything my pastor had diligently taught me. I allowed the devil to come into my mind like a thief in the night. I allowed him to cause disarray when I had the sovereignty to demand him to flee back to the pits of hell from where he came.

Trouble came knocking once more when one hot afternoon after class, a group of girls who attended Upward Bound with us, came to me and Tamara's room door. The earsplitting banging on the door jolted me out of my trance. I sat up and brushed my hair back with my fingers before I hopped off my twin bed and pranced over to the door. Tamara was sitting at her desk on her side of the room. She had her eyes fixed on the door as well. We were eager to know who was coming to visit us.

"Who is it?" I yelled in my southern drawl.

Before anyone had a chance to answer, I had already opened the door. Three of the girls stayed in a room on the third floor. The other girl stayed in the room adjacent to mine. Most of the time, she wasn't there because she had taken residency in the room with the other girls on the third floor. I knew all of them well. A couple had attended high school with me, so our connection wasn't only based on Upward Bound.

"What's going on?" I asked, chipper to say the least.

Having someone to talk to besides Tamara worked wonders on my mood. It didn't dawn on me until all of the girls started speaking at once that they weren't there to shoot the breeze. I put my hands up, signaling that we couldn't all talk at once. My sign language must have been understood because everyone became quiet. I stood there, staring at each one of their faces, wondering what in the world was going on. Before I had time to speak on the matter, one of the girls spoke up.

"Which one of y'all stole my money?" she asked. Her voice dripped with attitude.

"What money?" I responded, my eyes augmented with disbelief.

"Oh, don't try to play dumb," she snapped.

She had her hands on her hip and was yoking her neck. I could tell she was putting on a show for the other girls who stood in the background as if they were her do-girls. Such theatrics let me know, right away, I needed to get defensive and be theatrical myself.

Instantly, my hands balled up into a fist as I stood there eyeing each and every one of them. I could already feel the pattern of my breathing shifting from that of calmness. I wasn't going to hit either one of them as long as they didn't hit me, even though the urge to do so was imminent.

By then, Tamara had risen to her feet. She joined me at the door. Her facial expression told me she was aggravated beyond measure. When she spoke, I was certain.

"First of all," she retorted, the tone of her voice elevated, "Who do you think you're talking to like that?"

"I'm talking to you," the girl fired back.

I knew then, there was about to be trouble in paradise.

"I asked which one of you stole my money?" she repeated her first question.

I guess she thought she was tough as nails and we would fold like a shirt just because she was so-called going off.

All of the girls peered inside our room as if they had a right to do so. I couldn't believe they were accusing us of such a heinous act, especially the girls I'd graduated from high school with only a few weeks before.

When we were at school, attending classes together and eating lunch together in the lunch room, they all appeared to be cool with me. We never had any issues. At times, we laughed together, shared a few jokes here and there, and I even helped them with a few writing assignments since I had the gift of writing. Now since someone new was in the picture, they didn't seem to be concerned about me and my sister anymore. It was as if our worth had dropped like the Dow Jones stock market. They had the audacity to be standing in our doorway snickering under their breaths as if something was really funny.

I continued to stand there, disappointed, my eyes shifting from one girl to the next. I could feel myself wanting to cry. The tears lie dormant in my eyes. If I blinked one time, it would be over with. I literally willed myself not to do so.

Please don't cry now, Tamyra. This is definitely not the time. They are already laughing at you. If you cry, they will really think you are weak. You can't cry. Please, don't cry.

My thoughts wanted to besiege me. I felt them jostling around inside of me needing to be heard. Finally, I spoke up, thankful my voice wasn't choked up with the tears I wanted to let fall.

"I don't have your money. Why would you think…"

"Well, who else took it then?"

I was rudely interrupted by one of the other girls. She walked into the room without permission. One by one, the others followed suit.

"I tell you one damn thing," my sister snarled. "All of you better get the hell out of our room now!"

"Or what?" the girl whose money supposedly had been stolen, allowed her voice to be heard again.

Slowly, my hands began to shake to the beat of melodrama. Anger brewed inside of me like the winds blowing when a storm was coming to town. I felt violated in every way possible. Never in a million years would I have had the gall to barge into someone else's room, slinging accusations left and right with no proof to back them up. I would have expected to get my butt tore up. It was downright disrespectful, if nothing else.

Everyone now spoke again at once. I couldn't get a word in as they all shouted in different tones at me and my sister. I backed away and watched in what seemed like slow motion at the drama unfolding in the spot my sister and I laid down at night to have sweet dreams. I tried unsuccessfully again to speak my mind. My words once more fell on deaf ears. Without uttering another word, I turned on my heels and stormed out of the room. Their erroneous behavior was more than I could bear.

"Where do you think you're going?" I heard someone yell as I practically ran out of the room. I never responded. Instead, I looked down at my feet as I made my getaway. At all cost, I avoided the elevator because I knew there would be other people getting on and off. The last thing I wanted or needed was for someone else to see me so rattled. It was bad enough the intruders in my room had seen me that way. I felt bad leaving my sister all alone, but I felt I was about to lose total control. My heart was beating perpetually in my chest as I shoved open the door to the staircase leading down to the first floor. When I was alone in the basement, I paced the floors, breathing erratically. I had my hands up to my head, silently praying I could pull myself together.

"I can't believe they are doing this. They got a lot of nerve," I kept saying, as my steps became repetitive.

Then, as if someone had injected me with a needle alerting my senses to what was transpiring, I got the strength to storm back up the stairs. In hindsight, I should have never left my sister to handle the situation on her own. I knew I wouldn't have appreciated it if she had left me.

When I exited the staircase on the second floor, I heard them all yelling in unison. The yells became overbearingly loud as I stood in front of the suite leading to our room. None of them were backing down from each other as I made my way to our room door. No one paid me any mind when I screamed as loudly as I could, ordering the girls to leave our room right then. They briefly looked at me, dismissed my attempt to bring about peace to our living quarters, and then, went back to having it out with my sister. My heart was still doing its thing as it beat rhythmically to the commotion playing like a hymn in olden days. I was so outdone and livid that I failed to realize how I wasn't breathing at all. As I tried to gain composure, I took three deep breaths. Suddenly, the voices halted, and all eyes were on me. Tamara rushed over to my side.

"What's wrong, Tamyra," she asked, her tone of voice filled with panic as my eyes rolled up into the top of my head. I passed out in the middle of the floor, convulsing all at once.

Belly of the beast

You may not control all the events that happen to you, but you can decide not to be reduced by them. This inspirational quote is the brainchild of none other than Dr. Maya Angelou. Ever since I was a little girl, I have always admired her. She reminded me of what I had the potential to be, as she was a renowned writer, something I aspired to be at some point in my life, and I was determined to get there, one way or another.

When I read her book, *I Know Why the Caged Bird Sings*, I found it to be uplifting. I could rest assured knowing if she overcame obstacles in life when the odds were stacked against her, so could I. At one point or another, I fell off the wagon, found myself regressing instead of progressing. I fell deeply into a pit of self-destruction.

Depression once more reached out for me. We became intimate as always, and I was lured off the path I should walk. The Scripture, 1st Corinthians 15:58, comes to the surface when I think of how I was supposed to be. *Therefore, my beloved brethren, be ye steadfast, unmovable, always abounding in the work of the Lord, forasmuch as ye know that your labor is not in vain in the Lord.*

If only I'd had the mentality of the goat from the gospel song I'd often heard as a kid, I would've been okay. The song was called, "Shake It Off and Pack It Under Your

Feet." One of my favorite gospel groups, the Williams Brothers, were the ones who sung it. It told the story of a prized goat who fell into a well. His owner, who was a farmer, tried with no success to rescue him with a rope. When he saw it wouldn't work, he eventually gave up and decided to give the goat a decent burial by shoveling dirt into the well. However, when he checked on the goat, he noticed it was still alive and that it shook off the dirt and packed it under his feet. The farmer then continued to throw dirt into the well until the goat was high enough to scamper free on dry land.

Although a lot of people consider goats to be stubborn animals, in this case, the goat's stubbornness could be reframed as ambition in that he had an innate desire to live. He refused to give up hope, decided to use whatever came his way to reap the results that he really wanted.

It took some time for me. It wasn't until my eyes stumbled upon the above quote by Maya Angelou that I was moved to rise up out of the gutter of depression wanting so desperately to consume me. It was time for me to pack up its many bags of misery and sit them on the street corner of my existence, for those simple words by Maya Angelou had shed a bright light of optimism into my mental house. I was so high, I felt I could hold the weight of the world on my shoulders without breaking a sweat. Howbeit, throughout the course of living life and being trampled over by its ups and downs, I allowed my motivation to be burglarized. Everyone else around me always seemed to be so happy. I felt out of place like the neighborhood bum would feel in an Armani suit. Whatever the spell was lingering in their lives, it wasn't coming near me. I concealed it as best as I knew, masquerading like I was auditioning for a part in a Broadway play. Truthfully speaking, the floods of desolation were so turbulent, it uprooted everything in me that should have been anchored.

I know some of you are wondering what happened after I passed out in the middle of the floor. Well, here goes. It came as no surprise how the same girls who were all up in my face accusing me of stealing, ran like a murderer approaching them in a rat infested alley when I passed out. I'd had a panic attack. My sister immediately phoned mom following the incident, and she was on her way to take me to see Dr. Holloway. Even though I had turned eighteen-years-old, I still was under the care of my pediatrician. If no one else knew what to do in that most relevant crisis, he definitely knew.

By the time we made it to his office, I seemed to have been okay. My tears were dried up on my face, although my hair was ruffled from where I had been lying on the floor. My appearance was the least of my worries as I impatiently tapped my finger against my leg. I sat on the examining table, waiting for the doctor to show his face. The irony of the situation is while I sat there, broken inside,

I wore a shirt stating I was, *Too blessed to be stressed.* I didn't doubt it for one second. I truly was blessed. I was alive. My stomach was full, and I had clothes on my back. Despite the overflow of blessings, stress was the story of my life.

While continuing to wait, I knew I didn't want to explain to Dr. Holloway what had happened only an hour or so before. I was beyond embarrassed and wanted to disappear off the face of the earth. Suddenly, I saw the doorknob twisting and froze. I held my breath as the door creaked open. Dr. Holloway had his eyes fixed on me as he entered the tiny room, wearing a blue lab jacket instead of the usual white most other doctors wore. His stethoscope slapped against his chest as he turned to fasten the door.

"What happened?" he quizzed, walking up to me and placing his brawny hand on my shoulder.

My eyes fell to the floor, and I quivered in my seat as the emotion of discomfort was beyond chilly. I was trying to gather my thoughts. It was necessary that I relayed everything to him exactly as it had occurred. I peered up at his face. His expression was soft. It comforted me. It told me whatever the problem was, he would be there for me. He wouldn't look at me differently. He would still be my doctor and devise the perfect regimen of care for me because that was what a good doctor was supposed to do for his patient.

As I sat there looking in his face I couldn't help refocusing my attention on the time when I was younger. In fact, I was about six-years-old. I was sick and he was in the process of admitting me to the hospital. I walked up to him so short of breath that I stopped only a few steps away from him and slumped over, with my hands resting on my knees. Knowing that I was short of breath he picked me up and sat me on his knee. He allowed me to lay my head over on his shoulder and coached me with calming my breathing. He was trained to be my doctor. The fact that he was also being compassionate towards me branded my heart in a special kind of way. So, of course he would care about what I was going through now. I'd only gotten older. But I was still, "his girl," as he'd always called me.

Relief washed over me as I felt my shoulders begin to relax. Finally, I opened my mouth to speak. The unthinkable happened again. I fell off the examination table, convulsing violently. Dr. Holloway grabbed me by the shoulders and gently eased me down to the floor, so I wouldn't hurt myself. He stepped over me and twisted the knob on the door. I heard him as he told mom, "I'm going to get her a shot to calm her down."

Mom sat on the edge of her seat with a perplexed expression woven into her face. I managed to calm down when I felt the coolness of the medicine from the syringe injected into my hip. Dr. Holloway kneeled down next to me until the shaking had completely stopped.

I wasn't aware of what was going on, why out of nowhere I would fall out and shake all over the place as if I had lost my natural born mind.

"You had a panic attack," Dr. Holloway informed me once I was calm again. "Don't worry about it. It's more common than you think," he furthered his dialogue after witnessing the disturbed glower I wore like mascara. He picked up my chart and began skimming the pages. It was so big from my many visits that it had to be broken down twice. But of all my visits the present situation was one I didn't want to be recorded in my chart. I had never gotten so angry that I had resulted to having a panic attack. I couldn't understand why it was happening now. I didn't want to think about it anymore. I just wanted to pick up the mental remote control and fast forward past this part of my life. Alas, that could never happen, and I later learned that sometimes when you fast forward, you miss things pertinent to survival. Sure, this was not a good time for me.

It didn't feel good. It didn't look good. Still, I had to go through it. I couldn't cushion all of life's blows. Some of them, I had to feel.

Those pages in my life's story could not be left blank. They told a story of hope being born, even when I felt like I was in the midst of the belly of the beast, and it would reach the eyes of many going through similar situations. They would have the courage to stand up and take hold of the reins of their lives. They would feel the dry rot of pain vacating the premises of their self-worth and it would be a feeling no one could mimic unless they, too, had gotten to the point where they felt it as well. It would then occur to them that they should lift their hands and with the fruit of their lips, thank God for allowing them to overcome.

It Gets Worse Before it Gets Better

A cry for help

Long before I realized there was such a television channel as Lifetime, I had watched movies where the plot often resulted in someone being a crazed maniac. The characters got away with doing a countless number of things before getting caught. I would be sitting on the edge of my seat, popcorn and soda in hand, rooting for the one cast member who was able to point out their deranged issues long before anyone else did. But unfortunately, the crazy character was very skillful in making the one who was on to their antics seem to be the bad guy, if he/she didn't cause that person to mysteriously disappear for snooping in the first place.

Finally, close to the end of the movie, everyone else recognized what should have been known early on after discovering a few bodies mutilated beyond recognition and scattered in various places. If the villainous characters didn't wind up in jail or dead, they were thrown into a mental institution to, hopefully, get help with their issues. The end credits rolled, and that would be the end of the story.

When I thought of any form of mental institution, I saw and heard in my head, cells being locked. I envisioned patients on padded beds wearing strait jackets while a psychiatrist observed the behavior through a tiny window carved in the middle of a steel door. I imagined pills being shoved into the patient's mouths against their will as they screamed and kicked wildly, trying their best to keep from swallowing the pills. If that didn't suffice, they were strapped down and injected with something that would surely calm them down, often making them appear to be zombie-like.

I didn't deny that I had issues like everyone else, but I wasn't crazy by a longshot. I wasn't schizophrenic! I wasn't plagued with an antisocial disorder where I had no regard for anyone/or anything other than myself. I didn't even consider myself to be bipolar, which according to my perception, was on the bottom of the totem pole as far as mental illness was concerned. I might've been OCD, and to be honest, I wasn't even ashamed to own that.

Whatever happened to hearing voices before being deemed fit to enter a mental institution? Or at the very least, weren't you supposed to be a serial killer who killed because they had mommy issues or someone at some point treated them unjustly, and on a whim they decided to go on a killing spree to prove a point?

It seemed that was the way it always panned out on the Monday night movies I watched with mom and Tamara. How in the world did anyone ever dare think for a half of a split second, I needed to be populated with the mentally insane? My terminology for them, when I was younger, was looney tunes. I never expected someone to think I was a looney tune.

This was how I wound up on the path in my life where it seemed there was no light reflected to guide me safely along the way, and the twists and turns in the path were like a maze I couldn't meander my way through.

After having two panic attacks in the same day, I felt numb inside and shaken to the point where I wouldn't be able to make a comeback. My lack of friendships and bad feelings about myself had always made me feel there was something wrong with me. Many times, I tried to overcompensate for my own unfavorable thoughts. I did everything to prove to everybody else how great of a person I was.

I didn't want anyone else to feel about me the way I felt about myself. I could front like everything was okay, if no one else knew what the deal was. They wouldn't be able to remind me of my issues and I would simply cover them up. If I had to spread myself thin to disguise the truth, I would gladly do so.

When all else failed, I tried to think happy thoughts the way my counselors had always taught me to do throughout the years. But I had been spinning my wheels in vain. All I saw was myself on the floor shaking and so forth. It didn't happen while I was alone. Other people had seen me reacting in such a way. The petrified expressions of all who witnessed it was the worst part of this shenanigan. No matter what I was up against, I felt that form of behavior was intolerable. I had a reputation to uphold. Sadly, I was putting a dent in it by acting that way.

At the time when all of this transpired, I was eighteen-years-old, still a baby in the eyes of many. The only ailment I had known myself to have in those eighteen years was asthma. I hated having asthma with a passion, how it always came along uninvited or when I least expected it and wrecked my life. But I would have rather had a breathing tube down my throat or taken a big dose of Prednisone everyday as opposed to having a panic attack.

Though I tried, I couldn't divert my attention from how I wasn't able to stop myself from shaking, which very well mimicked a grand mal seizure. Under the circumstances, and wondering what everyone who saw me having the panic attack thought of me, I stressed myself to the point of where I had a full blown asthma attack. What started out as minimal tightness in my chest, turned into my being admitted to the hospital before the new week had time to be born.

On what would have been the last day of my hospitalization, Dr. Holloway walked into my room on 5 North with his stethoscope in hand, ready to listen to me breathe. He stopped dead in his tracks when he found me sitting up in the bed, crying my eyes out. It should have been the least of my concerns, but I was modest about him seeing me cry. Immediately, I lowered my eyes to the floor, grabbing the crumpled tissues I had piled up next to me, and dabbed at the still flowing tears.

"I'm sorry you're upset, Ms. Walker," Dr. Holloway muttered as he gained the strength needed to continue walking towards me.

"I'm okay," I mumbled, my voice cracking.

"No, you're not," he responded while placing the bell of the stethoscope up to my chest and ordering me to take a deep breath. I noticed that I trembled as I breathed in and out. I sniffed and sneaked a glance in his direction. As quick as I tried to be, he caught me looking at him.

"You want to tell me what's wrong?" he asked, at last, while sitting on the edge of the bed with me.

I shook my head despondently and again, lowered my eyes to the floor. I knew my cracking voice would make saying anything else to him a difficult task. So even when I wanted to lay all my issues out on the table to be observed as if they were in a museum, I held my lips together instead.

Ever so gently, Dr. Holloway placed his hand on my shoulder, lightly squeezing in an effort to comfort me. While the unsettling feeling of humiliation made its way to the surface, I listened to the hands on the clock as the seconds ticked by. *Surely, he has other patients to see*, I thought, feeling even more uncomfortable to say the least. As if my guardian angel, he sat there a few more minutes, giving me the opportunity to change my mind. I thought nonstop about telling him what was wrong, but I couldn't bring myself to do so. Every time I opened my mouth, I quickly lost courage. The words needing to be expressed for some reason or another would not come.

"Well," Dr. Holloway finally said with a sigh as he stood, "I'm going to have a psychiatrist to stop by and see you today. You need to talk to someone." He said those words in a matter-of-fact tone. He wasn't asking my permission to do so the way I preferred him to do.

I merely nodded my head, refusing to look up until I heard the door close, and I knew I was alone. I placed both my hands over my face and sobbed bitterly. One would think I'd just watched the burial of a close family member as I tried to figure out how I would go on without him/her in my life.

Eventually, I became exhausted. I climbed out of the bed and walked barefoot across the floor. I gazed pathetically in the mirror at my image. I then turned on the faucet and splashed water on my face. My eyes were above and beyond puffy. I looked like a raccoon, for crying out loud.

Once I'd dried the water, I dragged myself and the IV pole back to the bed. My dinner sat on the bedside table. It was cold by now. I lifted the lid and the first thing I saw was cauliflower looking back at me. I grimaced as I felt the need to puke. I refused to even glance at anymore of the meal as I placed the top back on the tray and fell soundly asleep.

What I didn't expect was to wake up a couple of hours later with a guy who wore thin-framed glasses hovering over me as if he was hungry, and I was his meal of choice. If the chiming of the IV pump hadn't alerted me, there is no telling what he would have done to me. *Am I dreaming*, I thought…knowing full well I wasn't when I felt his cold hand graze across mine. Out of reflex, I yanked my hand away.

"Who are you?" I asked, reaching for the call light so I could let the nurse know my IV pump was saying I had an air bubble in the line.

"I didn't mean to frighten you," he said apologetically, while pushing his glasses further up his pointed nose.

"Who are you?" I asked again in response.

My voice was now seasoned with irritation. *Fuck you mean you didn't try to scare me*? I silently thought. Then, it dawned on me that he had to be the psychiatrists Dr. Holloway had sent to talk to me. Immediately, I felt remorseful, wishing I hadn't been curt with my choice of words.

"Ugh, sir, I didn't mean to be rude," I chivalrously whispered, offering up my own version of an apology.

He nodded his acceptance, sat down in the chair next to the bed, and said, "Let's talk."

"Talk about what?" I quizzed as if I didn't know what he was referring to. He didn't say anything, just stared at me with a, *You know what I'm talking about,* expression carved upon his middle-aged face.

"I really don't know where to begin," I said at last with a sigh, figuring he wouldn't budge to leave, if I didn't fess up.

"How about you start from the beginning," he interjected, now sitting back in the chair and crossing his never seeming to end legs. He grabbed a pen from his shirt pocket and flipped open a notepad that he carried in a brown leather notepad holder.

"All I know is I feel sad most of the time," I managed to say, shrugging my shoulders.

I neglected to tell him about the panic attacks. I felt that was privileged information he didn't have to know about. Besides, if I revealed to him about the panic attacks, I would be forced to once more relive the dreaded events I so desperately wanted to forget. I'd seen the images enough to last a lifetime. That was definitely one time I didn't want to harp on things I had no control over.

"I can tell you have had a rough time," he said at the ending of our conversation, "But trials are all a part of this thing called life, and I can assure you that you will be okay." Do you believe that things will be okay?" he asked, surveying the worry lines adorning my otherwise clear face.

"I want them to be," I admitted, interchangeably feeling defeated and aggravated. "Well, if you sincerely feel that way, you'll get there if only you do what I ask of you. You've got to think enough of yourself to get the help you need to ensure that everything will be okay. To do otherwise would be the ruination of yourself."

By then, he'd closed his notepad and replaced his ballpoint pen back in his shirt pocket. Without saying anymore to me, he stood up, and left. I watched him as he walked out the door and disappeared up the hallway. As he turned the corner, nearing the elevator, I threw my head back against the pillows. I had a lot to think about and not nearly enough time to think about it. I wanted to get to a point in my life where my past would no longer dictate my future. I wanted change. But would becoming a temporary patient at Meadhaven be the hallmark of change I needed?

Meadhaven

As I walked into the building facing the bumper to bumper traffic on the East South Boulevard, I felt as if my feet weighed a ton. I could barely get them to transition the way I needed them to. Nervousness settled its hooks deeply into my flesh, leaving me to feel a wave of nausea as it made me think I wanted to keel over right then. I clung to mom as if I was a little girl trying to escape the wrath of the bogyman as we approached the nurse's station. She could protect me because even though I was close to being nineteen-years-old, still, she was my mom. It was a mom's job to protect her child at all times, especially when she had a justifiable cause to be scared.

“There’s no need to be afraid, Tamyra,” she whispered in my ear as she handed my duffle bag with all of my personal belongings to the lady sitting behind the desk. The medium built lady who wore her hair slicked back into a bun and whose complexion was caramel in color, offered me a smile. Her lips were covered in the reddest shade of lipstick I had ever seen. She had piles of mascara caked up above her eyes as she extended to me her freshly manicured hand. Reluctantly, I grabbed her hand, and she gave it a firm shake.

“Everything is going to turn out the way it should,” she assured me in a voice deeper than I thought she should have. Then, as if she could read my mind, she laughed amusingly and said, “I know what you are thinking. My voice is too deep, right? I’ve heard so many people say that.” I didn’t respond, just stood there thinking, *Look, lady, you said it. You’re not about to incriminate me.*

I continued clinging to mom, trying my best to swallow the lump appearing to obstruct my airway. I took a moment to look around the place, relaxing a little when I saw a bookshelf filled to capacity with novels of all genres I could possibly think of. Even if I wasn't willing to admit it then, I knew those books would be a great pastime for me. My being a bookworm wasn't a phase I would eventually grow out of. I still enjoyed the peace there was to gain from reading years later, after I discovered it was a hobby.

As I continued skimming the place, my eyes fell upon a stout woman pacing back and forth in what I learned was the dayroom. She seemed to be in a trance and methodically counted the squares on the floor. I could tell she was under the influence of medication. She mumbled softly to herself while continuing to count the tiny squares on the freshly mopped linoleum.

Any inkling of comfort I had begun to feel, hastily flew out the window at that point. I became nervous all over again. *Why did I agree to come to this place? I should have told that nerdy freak I didn't want to come. What makes him think this was the place for me? He should have kept his nose out of my damn business.* My thoughts relentlessly spoke to me. They seared my mind with the flames of bleakness. I had nothing to extinguish the flames.

While I was freaking out, mom signed papers on my behalf since I wasn't of age to do it myself. A young man, who looked to be mid-twenties, emerged from out of nowhere. "I'll be showing you to your room," he said, motioning for me to follow him. I looked back at mom, my vision now blurred with tears.

"Are you going to come with me?" I asked, almost pleading. I could see her eyes watering as well. She maintained her composure and smiled instead.

"No, baby, I will see you in a couple of days, okay. Now go on with the nice young man. I promise you are going to be okay."

Slowly, I began to walk away from mom. Only a few steps later, I turned on my heels and ran back into her arms. "I love you, mom," I blurted out, squeezing her like I had squeezed my teddy bear a many of nights when I'd had a nightmare. Just to feel her arms around me seemed to have been all the therapy I needed. I wished everyone else could see that as well. All I needed was my mom to love me. I knew she did love me without any doubt in mind. She'd proved it throughout the years when she took care of me after my biological mother wouldn't. "I love you, too," she assured me, allowing the confirmation to slip from her lips. She planted a wet kiss on my ear. We embraced for a few more seconds. Finally, I let go.

"Well, this is it," the young guy said, once we were standing in my room.

"Thank you," I murmured while walking to the door to see him out. I hoped he picked up on the hint that I wanted him to leave me in solitude. Regrettably, that wasn't the case.

"First things first," he cheerfully said as he pulled the chair away from the desk and sat down as if we were long lost friends catching up on the latest gossip.

"I just want to lay down," I whined, a slight tinge of insubordination wanting to flare up in my voice. He paid me no mind and instead reached out to grab my bag.

"I have to see what you have in your bag," he stammered, peering up briefly to note the expression I had on my face.

"Why?" I asked, squinting my eyes in confusion. I quickly leaned forward and picked my bag up off the bed, slung it across my shoulder, and looked back at him to see what he would say next.

"It's routine," he went on. "Don't be offended," he offered as comfort. "Everyone who comes through these doors as a patient has to go through this."

"But why," I snapped, not ready to give in yet. To say my mood was foul was an understatement. I was outraged. Really, I wasn't angry with him. I was mad at my situation. I needed someone to take it out on. Unfortunately for him, he was the perfect bait.

"You mean to tell me," I fumbled on, pausing for only a split second, "you have to approve of what I wear? You must think you're my daddy or something?"

Without giving him a chance to speak, I began throwing everything in the bag on the bed so he could see. "There you have it," I retorted sarcastically.

"I'm going to have to lock this belt up, and I'll need you to take your shoestrings out of your shoes and give them to me as well." He looked at me again to see what my response would be. Of course I was outraged.

"Look here, motherfucker. It'll be a cold day in hell before I give you my shoestrings!" I yelled. "How am I supposed to tie up my shoes without shoestrings? If you want some shoestrings, I suggest you go and buy your own."

Once those last words escaped my lips, I sat down on the edge of the bed and folded my arms across my chest, showing him I wasn't to be toyed with because I was known to be defiant.

"Please, Ms. Walker, don't make this harder than it has to be," the young man said with a sigh. I could see him rubbing his temples with my peripheral vision. I admit, I felt slightly bad knowing I was giving him the brunt end of my attitude for no apparent reason at all.

"Fine," I said, "Here, take it! Do you want my socks, too, or is it okay for me to have them?"

"That won't be necessary," he replied, walking towards the door with my belt and shoestrings in his hand. He backed up a couple of steps. "What is that around your neck?" he asked, pointing at the gold rope I wore with the tassels at the end.

"Oh, this is my rope I received at graduation. It signifies that I graduated with honors." Regardless of how bad I was feeling, I couldn't help smiling a little as I reflected back on graduation. He dropped his head, seemingly almost ashamed to let the next words slip out of his mouth.

"I'm so sorry, Ms. Walker, but I will have to lock that up as well."

I didn't respond at all. I yanked the rope from around my neck and handed it to him. I followed him to the door as he exited the room and slammed the door before he had the chance to say anything else. I then plopped down on the floor and began to cry. "This is fucking inhumane," I said amidst the tears.

I must have fallen asleep and thought I was dreaming when I woke up and noticed the other bed in the room was now occupied, in that it had an overnight suitcase sitting on top of it, and a few other tote bags as well. I pulled the curtains apart, a little surprised it was still daylight outside. At last, I jumped out of bed, smoothed the wrinkles out of my clothes and tiptoed to the door. Just as I prepared myself to peek into the hallway, a Caucasian girl, who looked to be about twenty-one-years-old, walked into the room. Our eyes locked instantly. She extended her hand to me.

"Hi," she said cheerfully. I couldn't keep the furrows hidden in my forehead.

Why does she seem to be happy to be here? I asked myself while shaking her hand.

"This is my son, Brandon," she proudly announced, turning to the side, so I had a better view of the little boy sitting on her hip. He smiled at me, and I was prompted to smile back as I reached out to tickle his chin.

"It must be visiting hours?" I asked knowingly, meaning it more so as a statement than a question. I knew it was selfish for me to feel the way I felt, but I secretly wished mom could have come back to visit me. It was hard not to feel envious seeing my new roommate with her family as her mother had just walked into the room. I was all alone.

"This is going to be a long night," I mumbled to myself, walking back over to the window to watch all of the patients mingling with their family and friends.

Life is not a crystal stair

When I was a pupil in junior high school, I became very acquainted with a prolific writer by the name of Langston Hughes. While sitting in English class, I noticed he came up in various discussions where I listened intently. I had never been a fan of Shakespeare and couldn't understand half of it, thought it was the most tedious thing ever. I assumed it was going to be the same mumbo jumbo when it came to Langston Hughes and what he had to convey.

To the contrary, I found that I always enjoyed his poetic pieces, a lot of them obviously stemming from his own life's issues. Oftentimes, his phrases seemed to grab me and say, "Hey, listen up child, these words are for you." I especially felt that way when it came to his poem entitled, "Mother to Son." I even went as far as to print it out and kept it as a sacred memento. I could almost see the worn expression of being tired plastered on young Langston mom's face when she uttered the words, "Well, son, I'll tell you: Life for me ain't been no crystal stair. It's had tacks in it, and splinters, and boards torn up, and places with no carpet on the floor – Bare. But all the time I'se been a-climbin' on, and reachin' landin's and turnin corners, and sometimes goin in the dark where there ain't been no light…"

I very well related to those words. No, I wasn't a mother, but I'd also walked across the rickety boards of strife, thought a many of times they would cave in as I tried to make it to safety.

In the little time I'd been at Meadhaven, I'd grown accustomed. I had gotten somewhat used to how some of the staff eavesdropped on conversations I engaged in with other residents. I also got use to watching them as they materialized in my doorway every fifteen minutes to jot down on their little chart what I was doing.

"Y'all can give it a rest," I snapped after the first few days. Their persistence irked me more than I realized. Quite frankly, I got tired of hearing them shuffling the papers on their clip boards, especially at night when I at least tried to get some sleep. I huffed loudly, trying to be intimidating. "I don't care how many times you come to this damn door," I continued griping. "You won't see me with a knife up to my throat. I guess that's what you want to see, huh?"

As the days passed away and were laid to rest in their final resting place, more and more rooms started to fill up with other patients who all had their own issues to deal with. While our problems may have not originated from the same circumstance, we all had one thing in common. We allowed our issues to get ahead of us. Consequently, the issues wound up handling us instead of us handling them. They hampered our ability to lead the lives which had been outlined on our life's blueprint. God was the architect who designed the blueprint for us. It was never his intention for us to falter along the way. He wanted us to lean and depend on him…to trust him to make everything all right, even when it seemed as if that wasn't possible.

When I was a child, I was told the biblical parable about how God divided the Red Sea so his people could walk across on dryland for the sake of not being defeated by Pharoah and his army. I was also told how he turned water into wine and how he took two fish and five barley loaves and fed over five thousand hungry souls. If he could do such things, then our issues were no match for Him. Unfortunately, we treated our issues as if they were more powerful than God, allowing them to back us into a corner and keep us hostage.

As a patient at Meadhaven, I learned about the varying issues of the other patients in the daily group sessions I attended. Initially, I'd been against the idea of sharing so many intimate details about myself in front of a group of strangers I didn't know from Adam. As I listened to some of the others, who weren't afraid to spill the beans, I clearly saw how I wasn't the only one who went through ups and downs. It wasn't my place to be judgmental, just the same as they couldn't be judgmental towards me. If everything had been okay, none of us would have been there to begin with. We all weighed the same, regardless of what issue we had on the balance beam of life because we were all in the same place seeking help.

As I pondered on such prophecies, once more the poem by Langston Hughes dropped into my spirit. I especially liked the part when his mother said, "So, boy, don't you turn back. Don't you set down on the steps 'Cause you find it's kinder hard. Don't you fall now – For I'se still goin', honey, I'se still climbin, And life for me ain't been no crystal stair."

I'm remised to say that life had not been a crystal stair for me either or a bowl of cherries. I couldn't, as the songwriter said, "Live and laugh at it all." But I could survive. It was in me to do so.

Wolf in sheep's clothing

I'm sure a lot of you have read or at one time or another, heard the story about Little Red Riding Hood. In my days of youth, it happened to be one of my favorite stories. When given the chance to pick out a nice story to read at the doctor's office or even at the library, you could bet your bottom dollar I was going to pick Little Red Riding Hood. I couldn't wait to once more read about her and her basket of baked goods.

Although the story piqued my interest in that I found it to be amusing, at the same time, it also depicted a valuable meaning I was supposed to be able to grasp in the midst of the entertainment. In the heart of the story, Little Red Riding Hood found herself in a rather sticky situation when she came in contact with the wolf who disguised himself so he could get close enough to use her for his gain.

Every time I read the story, I always had ill feelings towards the wolf, felt that he was totally out of line to go as far as he did for the sake of deceiving Little Red Riding Hood. As much as I hated that scene in the story, it wound up applying to my life and my current situation as well. I, too, was put in the midst of a deceptive individual who wanted what he wanted and would go to deep lengths to be assured that he had it.

By the time I became a patient at Meadhaven, I was way over the Golden books, including *Little Red Riding Hood* as I wasn't a child anymore. As opposed to being fascinated by children's books, I found myself attached to this one particular person who was also a patient at Meadhaven. At first glance, I wasn't interested in him the least. As far as I was concerned, he could take all of his so-called fancy compliments that he directed towards me and shove them where the sun didn't shine. It was hard not to feel some type of way towards him. He was old enough to be my father. In fact, he had a daughter who was a couple of years older than I was. She had children of her own. At that point in my life, I could barely take care of myself. I wouldn't have begun to know what to do if I had been responsible for another life outside of my own. To be honest, I probably would have ruined him/her. I already had a damaged spirit and warped existence. What could I have possibly invested into a child at that point in time?

This guy, who resided with me at Meadhaven for the time being, went far and beyond what I considered to be normal to gain access to my attention.

"I think you are really cute," he said to me, one day while we were in activities, a sly grin dripping from his face like saliva from a dog greedily awaiting his lunch. Our assignment was to cut clippings out of the magazines and newspapers we had before us so we could create a collage that depicted what we thought to be our strongest and weakest characteristics.

Fortunately for me, that assignment was right up my alley. I had always enjoyed doing creative things such as that. The man bothering me at such a time when I was lost in the world of creativity, made me feel as if I was being pestered. I likened him to a fly constantly buzzing in my ear while I was trying to sleep at night. I tried hard, as nicely as I could, to pretend I hadn't heard the compliment this man had freely given to me. But he was persistent. He continued making small talk with me every day until I finally decided to hold a decent conversation with him, a conversation that didn't start with hello or end with goodbye.

"Whew," he said jokingly, when I responded to his usual greeting. "I thought I was wasting time even talking to you. I wasn't going to give up until I knew for sure," he went on with a slight smile.

Whatever, I thought. I dare not let him see I was feeling this way about him. Regardless of the rationalizations I juggled within my mind, I thought it was wrong for me to feel the way I felt. Maybe he was simply being nice after all. The least I could do was return the favor.

The ill feelings I had towards him did not last. They came and went like the seasons of the year. Eventually, we got to the point where it was easy to think we were conjoined at the hip. Everywhere he went, I wanted to be there. I wanted to be in the same air as the smoke that emitted from his cigarettes. When he expelled it from his lungs, I wanted to be there to breathe in its toxins. I later learned, he wasn't the person he presented himself to be. The trauma from the blow was a major setback. Usually my mental radar would have been blaring like a smoke detector when I was about to be caught up in a situation I had no business being in. Can you believe in this case it didn't even go off? Maybe the batteries were dead. There were many days I wished I had listened to the psychiatrist who wore the thin-framed glasses.

You see, outside of attending group sessions, I also had to have a weekly visit with the psychiatrist. As I sat down in the plush chair in his office, I determined that he conducted himself in the same manner as he had the day I first met him when I lay pitifully in the hospital, dark billowing clouds of despair distorting my ability to see the silhouette of the sun rising. The verdict said I would get through this, but I'd already allowed the shackles of depression to entrap me and to sing to me the blues like I had front row tickets to a B.B. King concert.

"Girl, you ain't going to make it, might as well throw in the towel now cause life just ain't fair. It has failed you so. You're better off in your grave. At least then, you won't feel the pain!"

I created the lyrics to this pitiful song. For years I sung it from my heart. I didn't miss a beat. In every scenario, I always saw the cup as half empty rather than half full. Even if the cup was empty the truth was that it was refillable.

"So I see you're finally adjusting to things," the psychiatrist said to me in a queer tone of voice. I nodded my head, agreeing with what he said, deciding after much thought that I needed to elaborate.

"Yes, I am. It's a good feeling knowing that I am not alone. I didn't have anyone to talk to at home. Everyone was always too busy to listen. They were in their own world. I didn't want to bother them with my issues because I honestly didn't feel as if they would understand or be able to relate. So I kept it all inside. I'm so glad I don't have to do that here. I can be honest without the overwhelming feeling of being judged."

After allowing those words to flow off my lips like a song, the psychiatrist spoke.

"Well, I am glad you are gaining something from the group sessions. I have to warn you, though, Miss Walker," he went on. "It's natural to be concerned about others who are going through issues. But you need to focus on yourself. Otherwise, you won't get as much out of this as you need to get. You can be compassionate, just don't get caught up."

Up until that very moment, I had listened to everything he said. I turned everything off, especially my ability to listen as if it was a radio when he told me I shouldn't be concerned about others. At least that was the way I took it. I couldn't understand his logic. Wasn't it because he was concerned the reason I was even a patient at Meadhaven? If that was the case, why was it such an issue for me to be concerned about the other patients, specifically the guy who I had been paying close attention to for a few days at that point?

Little did I know, the psychiatrist knew exactly what he was talking about. He wasn't trying to steer me in the wrong direction, the way I wanted to believe he was. He was a doctor. He had witnessed more in his career than I had in my whole life. I don't know what made me think I didn't have to listen to him. Maybe it was the sinister undertone in his words, or maybe it was simply the fact I wanted to have my way. Either way, not listening was a detrimental mistake. The very one I wanted to get close to wasn't all he projected himself to be. He wasn't even close.

Knowing now what I should have known then, there is a particular Scripture I feel the need to share. It comes from Matthew 7:15 and the words are: *Beware of false prophets, who come to you in sheep's clothing but inwardly are ravenous wolves.* No other words were needed to describe the guy I met at Meadhaven. I assumed he had my best interest at heart. He was nothing more than a wolf in sheep's clothing. It wasn't in his nature to only want nice conversations with me. In addition to wanting sobriety over his alcoholism, he also wanted me in his web, to plaster me up against his mental wall as an accomplishment he'd achieved.

The Carousel Never Stops Turning

It's never over

In later years in life, way after I had become an adult and tried on the garments of motherhood, I became engrossed in a television drama that aired on ABC called, *Grey's Anatomy*. Meredith Grey, the protagonist of the show, at many times seemed to be caught up in situations bigger than self. They spiraled out of control before she had time to blink. She wanted to give up on more occasions than just a few. A lot of times, it seemed to be the most logical thing to do because she couldn't foresee there being any other way out. I'm quite sure there were times she thought that having hard times would be all she would fish out of life's river and that would be so regardless of what bait she used.

But in the midst of all she had to endure, from her estranged father who abandoned her, to a mother who never really seemed to accept her, to even drowning when attempting to save someone else, and then losing her mother when it seems at last their relationship might stand a chance to be salvaged, she held it together. Just when it appeared as if one issue was resolved, another one was born. It's never over as far as Meredith's cares were concerned. Yet, the carousel never stopped turning. Time didn't stand still so that she might have the chance to play catch up.

I don't remember the name of the episode, or the season in which it aired, but in this particular episode, Meredith spoke words I found to be very powerful. Those words were: *The key to surviving is denial. We deny that we're tired. We deny we are scared. We deny how badly we want to succeed. And most importantly, we deny that we are in denial. We only see what we want to see, and believe what we want to believe, and it works. We lie to ourselves so much that after a while, the lies start to seem like the truth. We deny so much that we can't recognize the truth right in front of our faces.*

After listening to those words, I felt convicted in my spirit. It seemed as if Meredith was close to me. She was able to see through the façade I'd painted with colors of deception. She spoke to the little girl buried under the mask of adulthood. She still struggled relentlessly to make a life for herself beyond the streets of depression. All of the buildings were run down. There were no street light of possibilities, but many alleys infested with people who'd succumbed to the fate of morbidity.

It was a truth I couldn't make light of. I had denied a lot in my life. I thought that by denying the truth, it would be enough to make what I didn't want known to vanish from my life so I wouldn't have to deal with it anymore. But according to Meredith, denying the truth wasn't where things ended. She continued by saying: *Sooner or later, we have to put aside our denial and face the world, guns blazing. Denial: it's not just a river in Egypt. It's a freaking ocean. So, how do you keep from drowning in it?*

The question I wanted an answer to was, how had I survived so long without drowning when, many times, I hadn't even worn my lifejacket while paddling along in the ocean? I found the waves within the ocean to be quite turbulent. They tossed me around like a doll which had been emptied of its stuffing.

"Life is a beach," I've heard many say, but what good is a beach if all you're capable of doing is burying your head in the sand? So many days, I went through the motions because I didn't put forth all the effort I needed in order to assure I wouldn't have to continuously repeat certain lessons in life. It was like going to the bank expecting to make a withdrawal when I hadn't put anything into the account. It would not happen. Sitting there in anticipation would not yield unto me a favorable outcome. I would merely be sitting there in vain, growing more and more wearied instead of realizing what it was I needed to do.

While I was still a patient at Meadhaven, against the advice I had been given, I continuously allowed myself to deal with the guy I'd met. His name was Michael. It would come to my knowledge that he wasn't at Meadhaven alone for depression the way I was. He was an alcoholic, had done everything under the sun you could possibly think of to get his hands on the alcohol he wanted, including lying and stealing. He'd mastered Trickery 101. He had many tricks up his sleeve I, at the time, didn't even realize were tricks. He used them all on me. It was an effortless attempt for him. He was at the finish line long before I even realized I needed to run for my life.

Another story I read as a kid was one of the Aesop Fables, *The Tortoise and the Hare*. In the story, it was said that slow and steady is what wins the race. That couldn't have been farther from the truth in this scenario I found myself tangled in. While I was being slow, my so-called friend had what little confidence I owned clutched tightly in his fists, and the fragments of self-esteem I worked so hard to gain also as an award. I'd be his weakest counterpart because my arms weren't long enough to box with him. Yet, I had no problem with getting in the ring. I was silly enough to fight a battle I wasn't even prepared for.

Since I was ill-prepared, I got knocked out in the first round of the match. I just didn't have what it took to be to a man what he needed. That wasn't a bad thing. At that time in my life, I was supposed to be gathering the necessary tools I needed to take care of myself. I was who was important. I couldn't fix my issues, if I allowed them to be blindsided by an even bigger issue. I couldn't pretend like I was running through daisies in someone else's life, when in my life, I could very well drown in my own tears. The truth was, I trembled so hard from the breeze of hard knocks that levitated over me. I had nothing to shield me from how treacherous that breeze could be. Even with that being the case, the carousel never stopped turning.

The day came when I was discharged from Meadhaven some three-and-a-half weeks later, after I first became a patient. On the outskirts of my body, it seemed as if I had blossomed into a flower that had beautiful petals because it had been watered with the right nutrients needed for it to grow. It hadn't been taken over by the weeds you always find growing amongst flowers. Honestly, I wasn't much better than when I first walked through those double doors, scared out of mind of how I would be classified to everybody else. I didn't get to the root of my own issues because I was too busy visiting someone else's house of issues, sanitizing the walls within their house when my own was filthy and needed up keeping.

I wondered why I would do such a thing. When I took the time to think about it, I came to the conclusion that it wasn't often anyone showed any type of interest in me. I seemed to be a late bloomer as far as developing relationships with others, specifically those of the opposite sex. As much as I tried to hide it, that fact really got to me. Even my own twin sister seemed to be more acquainted with the opposite sex. I couldn't understand why it would happen for her and not for me when we were twins and had derived from the same egg during conception.

Whatever the reason, I wanted a relationship for myself. I wanted someone to love me so hard that maybe it would make up for the fact I didn't know how to love myself. I couldn't help reflecting on how it seemed as if everyone who I previously dared to care about always walked away without any form of notice. It was a battle for me to get over what I thought we had, while it always appeared as if my absence from their life couldn't have come at a better time. They'd move on with their lives as if I had never existed. That alone, made it so much harder for me to get over them.

After being dumped by my first boyfriend in the ninth grade, I only had one other boyfriend throughout my years in high school. I thought for sure things would work out between us because he lavished me with flowers, balloons, and candy for Valentine's Day. Wasn't that what guys was supposed to do to prove they loved you? At least that was what I assumed, if going by what I witnessed from all of the girls at school who had boyfriends.

I can't count how many days I walked around with a heavy heart because all of the other girls at school were getting the big boxes of chocolates on Valentine's Day. I felt left out and ashamed, went as far as to buy my own self a box of chocolates, hoping someone said, "Wow, she must really have someone special who loves her to have that big box of chocolates." I smiled heartily at the lie I wanted everyone to believe. You see, I had learned long ago that perception was everything, even if what was perceived wasn't exactly the way it was. It was okay for me to know I never received anything for Valentine's Day. I didn't want anyone else to know it. I wouldn't be able to take it if anyone else thought I wasn't good enough. Yes, those were my thoughts nestled deeply in my mind. If anyone else felt that way, I wanted to at least pretend it wasn't so. It was the only way I thought I could deal with the reality.

A way of escape

Prior to my being released from Meadhaven, I was allowed to come home on a 24-hour pass. During this 24-hour period, I was supposed to get reacquainted with the outside world. I was supposed to apply the serenity prayer to my life, *Change the things that I could, accept the things that I could not change, and obtain the wisdom to know the difference between the two.* I wasn't supposed to expect the world to revolve around me or to think that just because I was sensitive, everyone would treat me with the fragility I felt I deserved. Even if I did deserve it, everyone else wouldn't feel the same way. Therefore, I had to develop a layer of thick skin to protect myself, not to make me cold and unfeeling in the areas I was supposed to be warm, but there needed to be a balance. I couldn't wither like a rose planted in a garden of snow every time something didn't go my way or someone said or did something I thought to be cruel. I had to, "Suck it up!" as I heard the elders in the neighborhood say.

"Live and let live, that's how you survive," they assured me so many times, even before I could fully understand the meaning of their words. It was a breath of fresh air the day I walked into the house after being away for what seemed like forever. I stood in the living room, looking around at everything. Nothing was out of the ordinary. The same pictures hung on the wall. I looked at the big smile adorning my face on the family picture Tamara and I had taken with mom. My skin glistened with the glow of being carefree. My biggest issue, at the time, was convincing mom to let me wear the dress I wanted to wear to church.

My eyes continued to roam the home I'd lived in for most of my life. I heard the laughter shared throughout the years as I looked past the paneled walls and stared at the porcelain kitten sitting on the coffee table. Mom had it long before she allowed Tamara and me to come into her home. It was glued together where it had been previously broken. All of the pieces were in place. Unless you looked at it really hard, no one could tell that it was flawed. That's how I wanted things to be with me. Sometimes, I felt like I had been broken beyond repair. I was holding onto faith that my wounds could be healed. Though I had countless scars/flaws, no one would be able to tell because of how well I was put together. All of the pieces were visible. Unlimited prayers were the glue that connected all of my broken pieces.

I walked around in the living room, admiring my diploma and various other certificates mom had displayed. I had to admit that the familiarity of everything was giving me life. How could I feel anyway other than cozy as the warmness of being in my home reached down and hugged my soul? "Everything is going to be all right," I said, smiling bigger than I had ever remembered. I walked over to mom. She was sitting in her favorite chair. I stood before her and fell into her arms. The love emitted between us was like electrical currents. Yet, we remained fused together. I was so thankful I had her to come home to. I met a few people who were alright while a patient at Meadhaven, but there was no one who was comparable to mom, no place like home. There was nothing like walking into the house that morning and feasting on fish and grits. There was no greater feeling than having my pastor to meet me there to further counsel me, except the Bible was the textbook he used. He prayed for me, decreeing that God still was in control of my life. I had to allow Him to be who He was designed to be in my life. Also, I had to be willing to continue to live life to the fullest because the carousel never stopped turning. Even if I got a nauseating feeling from the continuous turning of the carousel, I had to deal with the sick feeling and keep it moving. Giving up wasn't an option.

A few rays of sunshine doesn't cast away the rain

Just as I heard the roosters crowing across the street, I lay in my bed trying my best to wake up. For whatever reason, I couldn't quite get to that point. Tamara hovered over me. I felt her hand on my face.

"Tamyra, Tamyra…Ta-my-raaaaa, you've got to wake up. Why are you acting like this? Please, wake up!"

But there was something on me. It was strong and heavy. I could hear everything going on around me, could distinguish between the different voices I heard in the room. For the life of me, I could not move a muscle in my body. I tried to scream out, noticing after much effort that I couldn't do that either. I had to lay there, until whatever it was that was on me decided at last to release me from its fury. The next moment, I arose from the bed, reaching for mom to hug me. I softly panted, scared to say the least. I tried to believe everything was going to be the way it needed to be so I could go on with my life.

As I lay my head against mom's chest, I thought back to my second week at Meadhaven. Mom had come to visit me. She brought with her an important letter I had received in the mail. When I saw University of South Alabama printed on the front of the envelope, I quickly tore it open, immediately learning that it was an acceptance letter for the fall of 1998. I had been accepted. I couldn't believe it. I screamed joyously, couldn't help feeling a little cocky as I waved the letter in the air. I was sure to show that letter to all of the staff at Meadhaven and the patients that I talked to as well. I even showed it to Dr. Holloway, when he came to see me.

"I'm so proud of you, Miss Walker," he said, holding the acceptance letter in his own hands and showing off a handsome smile as he admired the words it contained. "I knew there was more to you than sickness," he added. "You are a very smart young lady, and I know you will do well."

While reliving that moment, I once again felt the wonderful feeling of being proud. I was going to be somebody, if it was the last thing I did. I realize now, years later, after failing in so many areas I thought for sure I would be successful that going to college was a good thing, but it didn't make me the person who I was. College didn't have the capacity to make me somebody because I was already somebody the day I was born. What made me equate having a college education to being deemed worthy to being considered somebody was listening to the conversations I'd heard from the older generations. They were embedded with a lot of wisdom from their years of living. Although they meant well, everything they said wasn't exactly the gospel. There were days when I was lying on the floor watching television, pretending not to be eavesdropping on the conversations they shared with others.

"Child," they said, "did you hear about so and so daughter? She done got her college degree. Yeah, child, I knew she was going to make something out of herself."

As I listened intently to their words, I was left thinking, *if I want to be considered as somebody, I better go to college. People will love me then.* It never dawned on me how, if someone truly loved me, they would love me regardless of whether I had a college degree or not. I wouldn't have to do anything special to gain that love. Just waking up in the morning would be all I needed to do. What's even better, I wouldn't have to wonder if they loved me. It would be obvious by the way they treated me. It would show in the way they looked at me, and how they spoke of me to others.

I have to say, the sun had been shining pretty brightly in my life. I was coming along just fine. There were only a few things that got to me, specifically the waking up, feeling as if there was something on me holding me down. As hard as I always tried, I never got away from it. I would have been okay if it had only happened one time… maybe if it had only been two times. At that point, it had happened a few times. It didn't get better or easier with each time. I felt worst, began to wonder if I would ever be normal again. Those beautiful rays of sunshine that shone on my soul didn't have the strength to keep the rain away.

My thinking I was a mental nutcase caused depression to visit me once more. It didn't even knock on my door. It came right in and ransacked everything I had finally started to get in order. I knew the dangers of ignoring things, had seen on so many occasions what it had the strength to do. I found myself once more turning on that boulevard. I didn't want to deal with anything. I just wanted to live a normal life. I attempted to do this when I spent a night with my sister Sharmeen, along with Tamara. I always felt like I was doing something right when I babysat my niece. I had a nephew on the way, too. I was certain having the chance to babysit would make me feel even better. Maybe doing so when I was feeling low would be the spark I so desperately needed. I lay on the living room floor with my niece

Breonna, who had just turned four-years-old. The blinds were partially open. I saw the streetlights shining upon us through the window. Everything seemed to be calm and still. We were engaged in the biggest pillow fight inside on the living room floor. No one was exempt from getting popped upside the head or wherever the pillow landed. My plan of taking my mind off of the seriousness of life worked better than I thought it would. Once more, I had a smile on my face.

As the clock over the kitchen door alerted me that it was after midnight, I decided it was time for me to go to sleep for the night. I stuck the pillow I had just been having a pillow fight with under my head and pulled the covers up to my chin. It wasn't long before I was fast asleep. I'd actually prayed that I would get a good night's rest. However, I awaken only a few hours later with my sisters standing over me. The unthinkable had happened again. I lay on the floor grunting, trying hard to pull myself from the grip of whatever it was holding on to me. I'm certain I had awakened Tamara. She, in return, summoned our sister Sharmeen. The two of them stood together, yelling my name in unison.

Thankfully, the ruckus didn't stir my niece or any of the other kids from their sleep. When I was finally able to open my eyes, after Sharmeen smacked me in the face a few times, I glanced over at them. Their light breathing was proof of how they were resting well. Against my better judgment, I felt envious of the little ones. All I wanted was to rest well, to be able to wake up without it always being a chore. I was too ashamed to look up at the expression on either of my sisters faces. So I looked down on the floor and mumbled softly, "You can go back to bed now. I'm okay."

"Are you sure?" Sharmeen quizzed. "Were you having a bad..." "No, I wasn't having a bad dream," I interrupted, knowing already before she finished her sentence what she was going to say. "And, yes, I am sure I am okay," I said with my eyes still looking downward. I heard her take a deep breath. I glanced up briefly to find her rubbing her hand across her pregnant stomach. There were no words exchanged. I knew what that deep breath meant. It meant what she was witnessing from me, her baby sister, was more than she could handle. No, she would never tell me because above all else, she wanted to protect my feelings. She didn't want me to think she didn't love me. I understood perfectly well, refusing to hold how I knew she felt against her, although I was glad she decided not to be vocal about it. Hearing her say what I already knew was the truth would have hurt my feelings and brought the tears back on the scene. I didn't want to cry. I just wanted to go back to sleep.

"Go on back to bed," I said to my sisters, in my most convincing voice. "I promise you, I am okay." With that, I feigned a yawn, laid back down and pretended to be sleepy. It was my way of avoiding further conversation. Sharmeen took one more deep breath before she threw her hands up and went back to her room. When I heard the door close, I felt a wave of relief wash over me. Tamara sat back down on the floor. I could feel her eyes burning a hole in my back as I had it turned to her. *Please, don't let her ask me anything else*, I somberly thought. I got my wish when a couple of minutes later, I felt her getting under the covers next to me.

As I lay there on the carpeted floor, I felt the tears. They had decided to show up anyway. I let them fall down my face. Shortly thereafter, I glanced again at the clock on the wall. It was now four-thirty in the morning. Nearly an hour had passed. Everyone else was once again sleeping. There I was with my mind wandering aimlessly, not able to get any sleep. I went from lying on the pallet, to sitting on the end of the couch, to lying back on the pallet, to standing with the refrigerator door open, looking for a late night snack. I returned to my pallet and again looked at the clock on the wall. It was now just a few minutes passed five in the morning. I took a deep breath, wanting to kick insomnia's butt. As I kicked back the covers, my eyes fell upon my overnight bag. It was open. I saw a bottle of pills in clear view. I sat there through a haze of tears, staring at the bottle. I didn't pay any attention to any of the folded clothes I had in the bag or the toiletries.

The only thing I found interesting was the bottle of pills. It seemed to illuminate in my bag, so I wouldn't have any other choice but to notice it. Slowly, I began to scoot across the floor until I was close enough to grab it. I held it in my hand, looking at the label on the front. I found myself shaking my head in an attempt to ward off the unhealthy thoughts dancing in my head. A new set of tears fell down my face as I screwed the top off the bottle. I looked around the room a few times to make sure no one was watching and threw the bottle under one of the throw pillows on the couch when I thought I heard footsteps approaching. As soon as I knew the coast was clear, I poured as many of the pills in my hand as I could. With sweaty and shaky palms, I picked up the lukewarm Coke I had been drinking earlier in the night. There was a voice in my head telling me that I shouldn't do this. Another voice was telling me that I should do this. I decided to listen to the latter voice, and I shoved all of the pills into my mouth. Tears accompanied them. Along with the coke, they aided in helping the pills to go down more easily. I leaned over to retrieve a Kleenex off of the coffee table and wiped the snot that was dripping from my nose. That was when I caught a glimpse of my reflection in the glass top. Immediately, I turned my back so I wouldn't have to look at the girl looking back at me. More tears fell from my face as I allowed the bottle to fall on the floor next to my feet. A wave of shame swept over me, but I shrugged it off, pretending to be unbothered. I raised my knees into my chest and rested my head there… sobbing still, silently thinking, *it will be over soon.*

I don't know when I drifted back off to sleep. But I was awakened at around 7:30 in the morning with Tamara once more hovering over me. She had the empty pill bottle in her hand, demanding me to tell her what I had done. I sat there dumbfounded, staring at her. As if she had gotten the answer she was looking for from my eyes, she began to scream, "No, Tamyra! Please, tell me you didn't! Please, oh my, God!" She ran to Sharmeen's room and summoned her. Before the sun had time to rise, the house again was in an uproar. I didn't have a chance to object before I was being led out of the house to the emergency room. I didn't even get a chance to put my shoes on or to change out of my pajamas, for that matter.

I entered the hospital with my sisters still holding onto me. A nurse came from the back. She grabbed me by the hand, all but dragging me to trauma one, which was right in front of the nurse's station. Once the curtains were drawn, she helped me onto the gurney.

"We're going to pump your stomach, young lady," I heard a gruff male's voice talking to me. "You want to tell me why you took those pills?" he asked.

All I could think to say was, "I am sorry. I just wanted the sad feelings to go away." I looked around the room and saw a big tube with some form of lubricant on it.

"What's that?" I asked.

"It's called an endotracheal tube. It's what we're going to use to do your gastric lavage." "Gastric lavage," I repeated, confused.

"Pump your stomach, young lady. We're going to pump your stomach. This here is the tube that we are going to use." I could tell that the doctor was annoyed. His annoyance with me made me want to crawl inside of a crack in the wall. I actually saw myself staying there until I literally rotted away.

My nerves became unsettled as I looked at the thickness of the tube. I asked the doctor, “How will you do that?”

“We’re going to stick it down your throat,” the doctor responded, once more seeming to enjoy every second of what was going to be torture for me. He made sure to look me directly in my face so he could see the worried expression I wore.

“I’m sorry, sir,” I fumbled on. “Is that the only way you can pump my stomach?”

“Of course, we could give you something to make you throw up,” the doctor confirmed. “But I think this way will be more effective. And let me tell you now, young lady,” he said, coming closer to my face, “When we tell you to swallow, you need to swallow. If you pull the tube out, we will be forced to tie you down and stick the tube up your nose. I know you don’t want that to happen, right?”

I didn't say a word. I only shook my head, agreeing with the doctor that I didn't want him to stick the tube up my nose. "Is it going to hurt?" I yelled, becoming more fearful as the time went by.

"It's not going to be comfortable, I can tell you that," the doctor responded one last time before walking out of the room.

I couldn't help gagging as I felt the tube down my throat. I made sure to swallow when I was prompted to do so. Though it was very uncomfortable, I didn't get the urge to snatch the tube out of my throat. Just as I began to think to myself, *How long is this going to last?* I felt a nurse hand on my shoulder. "We are not punishing you, honey," she gently said. "We are treating you. I want you to be aware of that."

I nodded nervously, with tears burning my eyes, and I gagged uncontrollably. When it was all over, I panted anxiously, my eyes augmented with terror. I looked around for something I could hold on to for comfort, anything that would take my mind off of what I had just gone through. The nurse reached out her hand to me. "It's ok, honey," she softly whispered in my ear while using her other hand to wipe the perspiration off of my temple. "I promise you are going to be ok."

When I was taken to my room, I saw mom standing in the doorway, looking down at me. I could have sworn that her facial expression said that she had had enough of me and my antics. At least that was how I perceived things to be. With anxiety ripping me apart, I played with the loose ravels on the bland colored hospital blanket wrapped around my legs. I couldn't have been happier when the elevator finally dinged and opened up its doors. The nurse rolled me inside. The doors closed. That was the end of the stare down from mom.

Several hours later, I woke up gagging once more in the medical intensive care unit. The gentleman that had been sitting in the chair next to my bed grabbed the emesis basin off the bedside table. He stuck it under my chin. But nothing came up. One of the leads from the heart monitor came off of my chest. The alarm began to blare loudly as I grabbed a Kleenex. I wiped my forehead, allowing my eyes to make contact with the guy standing over me with the emesis basin still in his hand. I realized it was the psychiatrist who wore the thin-framed glasses at Meadhaven.

I immediately lowered my eyes to the floor. The jab of embarrassment was more than I could bear.

"You were doing so well, Miss Walker," he said. "What happened?"

"I don't know," I replied. My voice cracked with tears.

He put his finger up to his lip, ordering me to be quiet. "Don't worry. Just get some rest," he softly mumbled. He sat back down next to me and held my hand until the tears stopped.

I only stayed in the hospital for a few days. I had a lot of time to think about what I had done, and I was very sorry. If I had taken my life, there would be no do over. It would have been a permanent situation for an issue that was only temporary. Life was hard. There was no denying that. Things didn't always go according to plan. There was no denying that either. In other words, the carousel never stopped turning. I needed to play catch up and fast. If the truth was to be told, life for me had just begun. Now that I was approaching adulthood, things were even faster paced. I couldn't go off on the deep end wanting to hurt myself every time the events didn't flow the way I wanted or needed them to.

Roadblock

As the days and weeks passed following my attempt to take my own life, I will be the first to admit a change had to come in my life. I knew the road I was traveling would lead me into the neighborhood of destruction. God created me because He had a purpose for my life. He wanted me to fulfill that purpose and had set aside the tools I needed to be able to do just that. The scripture Jeremiah 29:11 comes to mind. *For I know the plans I have for you, declares the Lord, plans to prosper you and not to harm you, plans to give you hope and a future (New International Version).*

Long before I got the idea to try and self-inflict harm on myself, I'd heard about other people doing it. I felt bad for what they were going through and tried to imagine what could possibly be so bad to make them want to hurt themselves. I never fully understood the demons they fought because I wasn't going through it. Once it hit home for me, I was more than sympathetic. I was empathetic as well. I cried whenever I heard of someone committing suicide... sorry they didn't get the help they needed in time to keep them from doing such a heinous thing.

It wasn't long before it was time for me and Tamara to have another quarterly meeting with our social worker and a few other staff members at The Lowndes County Department of Human Resources. To be honest, I wasn't looking forward to it. I shook my head as I remembered how things had turned out during the last so-called quarterly meeting. I had gotten so upset that I got up and walked out of the meeting.

"Miss Walker," I heard my social worker calling after me. "You come right back here this minute and sit down." But I never looked back. I walked out of the conference room and out of the building. I found me a nice place on the side of the building and I allowed myself to slide down the side of the building. I placed my hands up to my head, thinking to myself, *Lord, these folks sure do know how to work my nerves. I don't know how much more of this I can take.*

"You were out of line to walk out of the meeting like that," mom told me later on when we were at home.

I sighed heavily and replied, "They weren't listening to anything I had to say. They only said what they wanted to say. When I tried to voice my opinion, they wanted to move on to the next topic."

"I don't care how you think they were wrong, Tamyra, you were out of line," mom continued.

"But that's not fair," I interrupted. I folded my arms across my chest with very much attitude.

I sighed again as I pondered how things would turn out in this new meeting. *As long as they don't disrespect me, I won't disrespect them*, I thought as I walked into the room where we usually had the meetings. I sat down to the first available table, silently praying things would not get heated. I didn't like being disrespectful. Even when I felt at the time I was justified in doing so, I always felt bad later and wished I had handled the situation differently.

It wasn't long before my social worker entered the room. Mom was already sitting across from me. I read the expression on her face. She also wanted things to transition smoothly. The last thing she wanted was for there to be more drama. I watched my social worker as she took a seat in her usual place. The supervisor, Mr. Davis, entered the room. The meeting began.

"Let's get straight to business," the supervisor murmured. He shuffled through papers. I rolled my eyes up in my head thinking, *if he had properly prepared himself, there would be no need for him to be shuffling papers.* He pushed his glasses up on his face and began to speak. "Miss Walker," he said, looking at me. I didn't respond, but I did look in his direction. He cleared his throat and continued. "It seems as if your Asthma Specialist, thinks you have some mental issues that need to be addressed.

Well of course he would think that...duh, even you ought to know that man has a few loose screws himself, I thought. Mr. Davis continued. "He has suggested you be admitted to Surcey in Mobile, Alabama..."

"What the hell is Surcey?" I interrupted. I had never heard of such a place. But going by the way he was speaking, I put two and two together. If I were right with my findings, Surcey had to be a mental hospital.

"I don't think you should go to Surcey," he went on, failing to answer my question. "Surcey is too harsh of a place for a young lady like you. I suggest Brice. It is located in Tuscaloosa..."

"What the hell is Brice?" I interrupted again. I had already risen from my seat.

"It is a hospital," the supervisor finally answered.

"What kind of hospital?" I wanted to know.

"It is a hospital for the mentally unstable."

"What makes you think I am mentally unstable?" I spat. Now I was completely irate. There was nothing anyone could say to calm me down.

"Calm down," Miss Walker, he had the nerve to say. "We, as an agency, only want the best for you."

"The best for me," I repeated, boisterously laughing. The thing is I didn't think anything was funny. Laughing was the only way I could keep myself from completely losing control. "The best for me," I said again, walking over to stand right in front of where he was sitting."

"Lord, Jesus" I heard mom say. She shook her head like she regretted what was about to take place. But I didn't pay her any mind.

"Tell me something," I said with my hand on my hip. "Why is it that you all are so ready to lock me up and throw away the key because this one doctor said you should do so? Whatever happened to a second opinion? Wasn't this the same doctor that told y'all I needed to go to National Jewish to get my asthma under control? You made sure you asked for a second opinion then. Even when you got the second opinion, I had to almost die before you decided to send me."

No one said anything. That was my cue to continue speaking my mind. "It seems to me ya'll only want a second opinion when it is convenient for you."

Still, no one replied. They all sat in their respective seats looking at me as I spoke. A couple of them looked nervous. One was even scratching his head. I continued talking. "What's going to happen, if I go to this place you are talking about?"

"Well, we would have to relieve custody of you, just until you were discharged," the social worker finally spoke up.

Again, I burst into laughter. "Oh, I get it," I said in between bouts of laughter. "You would be willing to send me to a place I don't really need to go just so you all can wash your hands of me? Then my voice shifted to the anger that I was really feeling. "It's obvious you don't care what happens to me. You only want to get rid of me. What kind of monsters are you people?"

By that time mom had taking all she could take. "I agree that Tamyra needs counseling," she spoke on my behalf. "She is angry, and she is hurting. But I think if anyone in this room had gone through half of what she has been forced to go through, you would be hurting as well. This child has a bright future ahead of her. A mental institution is not what she needs."

"I'm not going to no mental institution or any other kind of institution," I snapped. "If you don't want me, you can relieve custody of me. But you don't have to put me in a mental hospital just to justify getting rid of me."

"Oh, we can get a court order to make you go. You don't have a say in anything. If your doctor thinks this is what's best for you, then we have to agree with him." It seemed the supervisor had finally gotten fed up with my mouth. He flared his nostrils. I saw his breathing pattern had changed.

"Let's just all calm down," my designated lawyer (guidem ad litem) stood up.

"Don't fucking tell me to calm down!" I had completely lost my cool. Tears ran down my cheek as I sat back down with my chest heaving. I was so angry and hurt. The fact they saw me sitting there crying intensified my anger. I didn't want them to know they had the power to hurt me to the point that I cried. I couldn't help thinking, *DHR doesn't even want me. Nobody fucking wants me.* The tears quickly turned into sobs. At that moment I just wanted to be left alone.

"I'm sure there is another way we can handle this situation," the lawyer spoke again, holding up his hand. I knew that was his way of telling me that he would take care of things for me. I looked at him through the tears. He was a blur to my vision but I respected him for advocating for me. I really didn't mean to talk to him the way I had. I assumed he was the supervisor running his mouth once more.

I continued glancing at the lawyer apologetically while he spoke up for me. "Have you once thought about counseling," he asked, with a streak of aggravation coloring his face. "Don't you think it's jumping the gun a little to put this child in a mental hospital when maybe she can be treated as an outpatient?"

It was because of my mother and my lawyer advocating on my behalf that I wasn't forced to go to Surcey or Brice. DHR had indeed gone before the judge, trying to get me committed. Things didn't quite go the way they probably wanted them to go. The judge agreed that I should be counseled on a biweekly basis as an alternative. I sometimes wonder what would have become of me if no one had been willing to stand up for me. I knew my life would have never been the same. I probably would have been doped up on so much medication until I wouldn't have even remembered my own name. I thank God every day for the guardian angels he put in place to watch out for me.

Part 2: The Avenue of bad decisions

And Then I Was an Adult

"When I was a child, I spoke as a child, I understood as a child, I thought as a child: but when I became a man, I put away childish things." 1 Corinthians 13:11

College Days

The day I went to college started off on a beautiful note, marking its place in my life's calendar on a Sunday afternoon. I arose from bed early, just in time to see the sun peeping through my windowpane. As I sat gazing out of the window, breakfast waited for me on the wooden kitchen table that was dressed up in a red and white checkered tablecloth. I would have been content with a big bowl of Frosted Flakes cereal and a glass of apple juice. But once more, mom had outdone herself in the kitchen. It would have been hell on earth, if I thought for one second, I was going to eat cereal when she had slaved over the stove, getting popped in the process by the piping hot grits.

I yawned noisily as I pushed the covers back with my feet. Although I didn't vocalize it, I was happy God had allowed me to see another day. This was the day he had made. What better way to show my appreciation for another day of life than to join Him in His house for Sunday morning worship. Certainly, mom wouldn't have had it any other way. Despite the fact I felt like I was grown, I was still living under her roof. Her motto had always been, "In this house, we serve the Lord."

"God has been good to you. He wakes you up every morning. He promised me that He was going to save my household, and I'm not going to settle for anything less." Those words mom often said to me. So I didn't waste time debating the subject. Honestly, I looked forward to going to church this particular morning. I wanted to hear the praise team sing, *The Lord reigneth.*

I vividly remembered the term reign being one of the vocabulary words on my SAT test I'd taken for the second time in the preceding year. I knew it meant to be in control or to rule. It felt good to know God was in control of my life. It was confirmation He could handle the troubles in my world and, He didn't need my help to do so. He was capable of balancing the weight of my issues as well as everyone else who called on His name in their times of trouble.

"I want you to look at your neighbor and take the time to encourage him/her," my pastor said as he gave the benediction at the ending of service. I thought it was a good thing to fellowship with members in the congregation. They all smiled as they leaned in to give me a hug.

"All right, sister," one of the mothers of the church whispered in my ear. "There is nothing too hard for God. Keep your hand in His hand, and you will excel in life." I nodded at her advice as we embraced. I smiled myself as she loosened her grip. Those words alone had seemed to put pep in my step.

At last, I returned home to a hot dinner. In the South when something tasted good, we said, "Girl, you put your foot in this." Mom had definitely put her foot in the big pot of collard greens sitting atop the stove. She didn't half step with the cornbread either. The baked chicken was seasoned to perfection. It was so tender it was practically falling off the bones. The Lipton's iced tea washed everything down.

I felt like I couldn't have asked for more as I wobbled to my bedroom, cradling my full stomach as if I was pregnant with child, on the brink of going into labor. I lay peacefully across my bed, gazed out the window at the cedar trees mom had planted in what seemed to be many moons ago. As they grew, I noticed their branches eventually had to be cut. Otherwise, they would be unkempt and very unattractive. The same thing applied to me. I wasn't a tree, but at times, I had to cut some things out of my life so I could grow and prosper into the person I needed to be. I would then have the mindset needed to better myself. I wouldn't have time to sit pondering on things that would give life to more depression. I would be too busy walking into the light of my future. It was so bright. I needed a pair of shades.

I felt content as I continued to lie across the bed. I likened the feeling to the tranquility I most likely would have felt if I had been sitting on a porch swing with my hair blowing in the wind. I breathed in deeply, exhaling slowly, finally after finding myself about to dose off after a half hour or so. Realizing that I was forgetting to do something important, I suddenly sat up. "Oh, my God!" I yelled and hopped off the bed. This was the day I was supposed to move on campus. How could I have allowed it to slip my mind? I had a long list of things to do. Here I was lazing around the house as if I didn't have anything better to do.

My body became drenched with a surge of adrenaline as I began stuffing clothes of all sorts in as many duffle bags as I could get my hands on. I knew this day was coming. Yet, I couldn't pull myself out of my usual funk of procrastination. Now that it was time for me to be loading my belongings in the trunk of the car, I was just now packing. Surely when you found yourself rushing, you would forget something in the process. I had to make a mental note to pack my nebulizer and my breathing medicine. The last thing I needed was to get to wheezing on campus one night and not have my arsenal of weapons to put Cassie (my asthma) back in her place. Even though I was pressed for time, everything turned out the way it should have. I truly understood, at that moment, what mom had always told me about being an adult. It had nothing to do with age but everything to do with maturity. I had to be mature enough to handle my affairs in a timely manner without someone having to coach me along the way. Only then, could I officially debut as an adult.

Dorm life

It was about five-thirty in the evening when my uncles, Ronnie and Bobby, drove up on the campus of Alabama State University. I smiled brightly from the back seat of my Uncle Ronnie's car as I looked out of the mirror at the vast number of buildings surrounding the campus. They appeared to be arranged in a big circle.

Regardless of what I had gone through, it was a new year, a new chance to embark upon things having the ability to make a big difference in my life. Over the course of my years, I'd learned that until the day we breathe our last breath, we're always a work in progress. There will never be a time when we are perfect or free from mistakes. No matter how good we wanted to be, making mistakes were an epidemic widespread among all. It was sure to rock our world's a time or two. Even so, that didn't give us the right to be any less than our very best. I was happy to say I'd made some strides that had the potential to yield prosperity. But I hadn't been my best by a long shot. Thinking about it made me grimace at the fact my life had been filled with different levels of discord and feelings of uncertainty.

I wanted things to be different. I admit, I had overcome a lot to see this day unfold in the recesses of my life. I'd battled it out with the disturbing thoughts which had taken residence in my mind. They spoke untrue words to me, telling me, "Child, you are entering an era so out of your league. What makes you think you are college material? Girl, you better go on somewhere and flip some burgers or something. You might be a lot of things, but you ain't stuck up. So stop thinking you're supposed to have a college degree."

Naturally, I wanted to respond with the words, "You know what, you are right! What was I thinking?" For once, I took the road least traveled. Though I wasn't familiar with its curves, it was a great feeling to finally believe in myself, to finally make an effort despite the fear rising in my soul like acid up the esophagus of one suffering with reflux.

This day was one I dreamed about and reconstructed in my head so many times, playing the details over and over like a renowned saxophonist at a late night rehearsal. Now that it was upon me, I wondered if things would flow the way I hoped they would. Would I be able to function in a world new to me the way being outside of the womb was new for a newborn baby? Would I clap my hands to the beat of independence, allowing it to make its way down in my spirit, or would I crumble at the first sight of things being hard and extend my hand unto self-pity? Only time would tell as the words were written in this chapter of my life.

I stepped out of the bronze-colored station wagon into the sunlight and stretched my limbs. The feeling of excitement lingered while I stood before Bessie Wilson Benson Dormitory nodding my approval of what would be my life for the next four to five years. I was careful to take in the scenery, adoring the shrubbery and flower bed that led up to the front entrance. There were even sororities and fraternities who had designated areas under various trees to decorate with the colors that represented them.

While I admired their work, the sound of anxious students filled the air like the birds flying along here and there. They were everywhere, materializing from every corner of the university. Their voices held the tune of anticipation as they entered and exited the many dorms on campus. I continued standing there, making sure to watch everyone who walked up and down the sidewalk carrying their belongings to what would be their home away from home.

My uncles didn't waste any time grabbing my bags out of the trunk. After gawking at everyone else, I turned, at last, to help them. All of the bags sat neatly on the concrete. I reached down to pick up the bag in which I kept my toiletries, but then, my eyes locked with the girl who had gotten up off the steps leading up to the three-story building before me. She walked towards me in slow motion. I had all kinds of thoughts running through my head. If my eyes had been fire, they would have burned a hole in her flesh as I continued to watch until she was standing right in front of me.

"Hi, my name is Angela, but I prefer to be called Dee-Dee." Her voice was surprisingly cheerful.

"Hi," I responded, flashing a smile. I don't know why. But I felt like we were going to be the best of friends.

"My name is Tamyra, but you can call me Tee." I matched her level of cheerfulness.

"What room are you in?" she then asked.

I peered down at the blue slip clutched in my hand. Just when I wanted to feel embarrassed because it seemed as if I couldn't find the number fast enough, Dee-Dee gently took the blue slip out of my hand and looked it over. I felt like the helpless ninth grader again who was in his/her first year of high school, and needed help even with the simplest things. I quivered uncomfortably, wondering what she was thinking of me. *This girl is a lost cause. She doesn't need to be in college. She will certainly fold under the pressure*.

All of those things I assumed Dee-Dee was thinking of me when I didn't even know her. I just knew she had to be thinking the worst. Why would she even want to be friends with me when there were so many other popular girls that would have been more than happy to be her friend? They had far more to offer than I did. I was just an ordinary girl who wore her hair pulled back in a ponytail and jeans I made sure didn't accentuate my curves, for it was true that someone would notice. How dare I draw attention to myself by trying to look cute? Besides, I didn't know the first thing about being cool. I assumed that Dee-Dee, and the cool girls, would grace the clubs with their presence at night. They would probably dress in attire that hugged their frames like a long lost lover. All I ever did was read books. Occasionally I wrote in my journals. Sometimes, I watched reruns of my favorite movies. I had about as many VHS tapes as the cells in my body. I assumed what I did to past time couldn't have been the life Dee-Dee wanted. It would be what she got if she hung out with me.

"You're on the second floor with me," she finally said, after a few more moments of silence. "Come on. I'll show you what room you're in." With that, she grabbed one of my remaining bags off the ground. We walked into the building, giggling amongst ourselves.

"Girl, you're not going to believe this," she said while we walked side by side. "Can you believe the elevator is broke down already? So we've got to take the stairs. Good thing we're on the second floor."

I couldn't believe how confident she was. I had never witnessed anything like it in my almost nineteen-years of life. The way she conversed with me, it was as if we had known each other for years. There was no pretense present or no need to be someone she was not. I sensed that she was genuine, deciding myself to follow her lead. Above all else, I liked her style. She was 100 percent comfortable in her skin.

While unpacking my clothes, I listened to Brandy's, "Angel in Disguise." I felt grown up as I decorated my side of the room with my stuffed animals, porcelain angels, and water globes I had been collecting for a couple of years. I was eager to put my comforter set on my twin bed so I could place my throw pillows on top of it. I was indeed an adult at last. I planned to take full advantage of that fact.

Secretly, I wished, as I snapped my padlock on my closet door, that Dee-Dee was my roommate. I had only known of her for a couple of hours. I could already tell she was a cool person. I wanted her confidence to rub off on me because she was overflowing with it. I noticed it more so than her nice shape or pretty hairstyle she rocked with class. Nobody intimidated her. No one made her feel out of place. When she stepped out, everyone knew it. Most people watched with envious eyes, including me. She didn't set out to make anyone feel this way, but she wasn't with downplaying her happiness to pacify someone who couldn't stand to see it because they themselves weren't happy.

Unfortunately, Dee-Dee already had a roommate. They got along well. I felt slightly disappointed. I had already imagined us hanging together off campus. I wanted to see the days when we chatted with each other late at night and maybe even a time or two walked to class together. As I buried those thoughts in the grave marked with the head stone of not meant to be, the anticipation of finding out who would be my roommate was getting to be quite unbearable. I only hoped we would at least be cordial to each other, if not friends. I didn't want to feel uncomfortable in the one place I had to spend most of my time outside of class, the place where I got dressed in the mornings and laid down at night to sleep.

I liked my roommate, Romelle, alright. She walked in the room with a smile on her face about two hours later. I laid across the bed as she entered, dropping bags everywhere, and checking her cellular phone every few minutes. I noted that she was a cute girl. She was light skinned, medium built, and wore cornrows braided straight to the back of her head with the big beads at the end. We held a few friendly conversations throughout the few months that we were roommates. But then she became pregnant and decided to move off campus. Secretly, I was kind of glad. She had become to be kind of moody. I had enough issues myself. I couldn't stomach much more of her nice-nasty attitude. And I had tried. She just didn't know that my tongue could be as lethal as a razor. There were several days I literally had to grab my lips and hold them together to keep them from beating her little self-centered behind into submission. I had already made up in my mind that I wasn't going to be in control for too much longer. Pregnant or not, pretty soon I was going to say something to her that we both may have regretted.

My first semester on the campus of Alabama State University was a success. Because of my frequent hospitalizations, my doctor decided it would be best if I started school closer to home. Yes, I was disappointed. I had looked forward to going to Mobile, Alabama. But I was having so much fun at Alabama State that I didn't think about it for long. I was excited to be among such a large group of people. They were from all over the United States. Some of them were from as far as California and New York. Some were as close as Montgomery, where the school was actually located. Most of them, I didn't know. To me, that was a good thing. They wouldn't be able to hold me to anything having occurred in my past. I wouldn't have to secretly wonder if they knew anything about me, didn't have to worry about dodging the cold glares, or hearing the indignant whispers of those who constantly stuck their noses in other people's business. It was like being born again with no identity to be chained to like victims chained to each other during the Atlantic Slave Trade. But you could create one right then and there, one filled with the ingredient of promise. It could be as beautiful as you wanted it to be because you were the composer. Nothing was off limits.

The days when naivety clung to me like a needy toddler had been more than a few. They hadn't been long vacated the premises of my mind. I seriously thought if I was nice to everyone, I would get that treatment reciprocated when it came to me. As far as my eyes could see, being nice should have been a two-way street, instead of the one-way it often turned out to be in reality. Lord knows, I was in for a rude awakening. This was an all-new-ball-game I was about to play. The ball wouldn't always be in my court. Still I had to wear my catcher's mitt. Every ball I caught wouldn't be a good one. It was how I decided to handle the obstacles that oftentimes were fed to me in small doses that would determine if I would be successful or not. The decision was mine to make. No one could make it for me. I would have to be the one to live with the consequences of whatever decision I made. So if I made my bed hard, guess what? I was going to be the one to lay in it.

Distractions

I sat calmly on the steps of McGhee Hall, holding my journal and black ballpoint ink pen on my lap when he first stepped into my sight. I was feeling pretty down because of how things were turning out between me and Michael, who I'd met when I was a patient at Meadhaven. The only consolation I had, at a time when I thought I would be so happy, was knowing when I came to college, mom wouldn't be able to watch me 24/7. I knew there were a lot of things I could get away with. In other words, I could pull the wool over her eyes, and she would be completely clueless about it. While she was lying in bed at night tucked under her thermal blanket, I could be prowling the streets, if I desired to do so. I took those facts into deep consideration whenever I had dealings with Michael… my Meadhaven crush.

It was a good thing I lived on campus, so I could see him whenever I wanted to. I saw him at all cost, sacrificing my studies and much needed sleep to do so. There were a few nights I crept back into the dormitory very late, feeling like I had to sneak because even though mom wasn't there, I had the feeling she was lurking somewhere in the dark, ready to discipline me with the cowhide I considered to be a treasured memento she would never rid herself of. That Scripture, *Train up a child in the way he should go and when he is old, he will not depart from it,* weighed heavily on my conscience. Just as quickly as those thoughts ransacked the remnants of my mind, I shook them off, mumbling to myself at last, "Girl, will you relax. You are in a place where you can do whatever you want to do. Who's going to stop you?"

I wish now someone had stopped me. I gave everything imaginable to Michael: my time, my affection, my sympathy, and my virginity. I didn't think I was doing anything wrong by investing so much into this guy who I really didn't know. Furthermore, why continue to be a virgin? This was the perfect time, I assumed, to let it be a thing of the past. I had met the right person for me, and he was going to be all I could have ever imagined him to be.

Yes, I knew premarital sex (fornication) was wrong. I had attended singles ministry at my church for years. I almost heard Pastor Edwards reciting the Scripture found in 1st Corinthians about my body being a holy temple. And I heard many tales from the older generation about premarital sex as well. They made it seem like the worst thing in the world to have sex before marriage. If you did it, and they found out about it, you were all but shunned.

In the end, I did what felt good to my flesh. It didn't matter to me whether it was right or wrong. It was definitely acceptable by society's standards. As far as the older generation, my thoughts were, *Hell, some of them did it long before me. Not only did they have sex, but they had babies out of wedlock, too. That was all of the ones who didn't abort their babies to make sure their sexual indiscretions remained a secret. So who are they to point the finger at me? What was good for them is damn sure good for me, too. Some of them probably wish they could still get some and are just mad because they can't. It's not my fault their ovaries are old as hell.*

It was practically unheard of to be in a relationship where there was no sex involved. Besides, Michael was going to make me forget about the other guys who had made me cry in yesteryears, either because they were mean to me or treated me as if I wasn't pretty enough to suit their liking. I looked forward to it. There couldn't have been a better feeling than being in love. I wanted to be in love. I would make people see that if someone was in love with me, truly I was worthy of that love. Yes, I was still concerned about the thoughts of others. Despite any progress I'd made in any area of my life, I was still locked away in the cell of people pleasing, often I looked out of my cell with eyes smoldered with strife. It was a serious need of mine to be approved of. I was addicted to the thought of everyone loving me, had no idea what would be my sobriety, if there was even such a thing as sobriety in my case.

When things didn't turn out the way I wanted them to between myself and Michael, I felt bummed, pretty much like a child who wakes up on Christmas day only to find there are no toys under the Christmas tree for him. Though I cried, there was no amount of tears seeming to keep the blues from continuously serenading me with its songs of sadness. I thought about all the late nights and taxi drivers I paid just to be in his company, how at times I dealt with them flirting with me and wanting to put their greasy hands on me, all for the sake of making it safely to Perry Hill Road, so I could be with him. I couldn't believe such efforts were wasted. I pondered heavily on what it was I had done wrong. Why would he leave me when I had given him exactly what he wanted? He didn't have to fight for it.

I made it easy for him so he would know that I wanted him. In fact, it was so much deeper than simply wanting him. I thought I needed him. I'd unconsciously made a God out of him. But unlike the savior God, he wasn't taking care of me or protecting me from hurt, harm, and danger.

I longed to see the day where Michael and I actually went somewhere other than on the couch in the living room where he lived, to the bedroom he shared with a few other guys who were also recovering alcoholics. I never said anything about us not going to a movie or maybe out to eat because I always assumed that day would come when he, "Got himself together," as he would always say beforehand to discourage me from asking him for anything. I considered myself lucky if he actually brought me back to the dorm instead of having to catch a taxicab all of the time, spending unnecessary money I knew I needed to hold onto in case an urgent situation came up where I needed to have cash on hand.

Even though I didn't want to admit it, I knew things were doomed long before they completely fell apart. Even knowing this, I stuck my hand in the lion's mouth. I wanted to hang on to what my heart wanted to be real. I was hardheaded and tried to take on the role of God. I assumed I could make a nothing situation be more than just that. All it took was time. After a certain period of time, my warranty had worn off, and my sex appeal like dirty bath water was gone down the drain. I wasn't the shiny new toy in the box anymore. I had been taken out of the box and played with. Now I wasn't interesting, just lackluster, if anything at all.

In Michael's mind, it was time for him to move on to bigger and better things. Perhaps a fish that wasn't so easy to catch would hold his interest a little bit longer. Or maybe he would patch things up with his ex-wife. In recent weeks, he had talked about her a lot. She was no longer the "Selfish and inconsiderate bitch" he called her at

Meadhaven when we were alone in the day room talking and watching *Comic View*. Even though I didn't want to see it, I saw the love in his eyes when he talked of her. That was a look he had never given me, even when he considered me to be a hot commodity. I was now water under the bridge. He crossed the bridge without looking back once. It was never his intention to come back across this bridge either.

"Look, Tee," he said, one evening when I came over. "You might as well stop calling me, and there is no need for you to come over anymore."

"What do you mean?" I questioned. Really I don't know how I was able to say the words because my mouth had suddenly gone dry. My heart pounded with disbelief. I stood in the doorway of the house where I'd had several encounters with him, blocking the entrance. I hoped he would at least allow me to come in so we could talk about it.

"This is not going anywhere," he said nonchalantly, not budging from in front of the door. I felt disrespected, like I wasn't even as good as the dirt on the ground. "Why won't you let me in, Michael?" I asked hysterically. "You can't just tell me this all of a sudden and think I am supposed to be able to handle it."

As if my words were a weapon, he got irritated, like I didn't have a right to feel the way I was feeling, as if I was keeping him from doing something far more important than spending time with me.

"I don't want you, little girl," he spat. His eyes were pure venom as he gazed at me like I was a common whore on the street begging him for change. "Now I advise you to turn your little ass around and go on and get back in that cab and go back to campus. I don't have time to be explaining things over and over to you again. I swear all of you so-called women are damned crazy."

"But you said," I interrupted with long tears flowing down my face. I decided to ignore the horrendous words he'd just said to me. It hurt me to my heart. But I felt all of that would be forgiven if he stayed with me. I was willing to beg him if I had too. I felt it was necessary that I do whatever I had to do to keep him. But, before I finished my thought, he had slammed the door in my face. I stood there trembling, with the sun settling behind the clouds, knocking on the closed door for about five minutes before I got the strength to turn away. My dignity had long left my side. By then, the cab driver had left as well. I walked up the street, sobbing bitterly before I found a payphone to call him back. I knew Michael was looking out the window because I saw the curtains pulled back. The last thing I needed was for him to be laughing among his roommates about how torn apart I was. "That silly girl," I imagined him saying. "She actually thought I wanted her. Poor little thing, she has a lot to learn about life."

So, at a time when I was feeling like the world was about to close in on me, I was glad to have someone who turned out to be a great friend leaning over to talk to me. As he sat down on the steps next to me, I stuck my pen inside of my journal and closed it. My heart was heavy. It felt like it was going to protrude through my chest. Regardless of how bad I felt, from somewhere I mustered up the strength to say, "Hi." "Hi," the guy said. "Is it really that bad?"

"What," I asked, trying hard not to allow annoyance to besiege me. His chipper persona I found to be quite nauseating. "Well, I don't mean any harm, but you look like you are down and out," he responded, pointing at the expression on my face. "I just want to know, if it's really that bad?" I couldn't hold it in any longer. Tears begin to spill down my face right in front of this guy who I knew nothing about. It was very much embarrassing.

Though the release was what I know I needed. I didn't bother to wipe the tears away. I stood up instead, rushing away from him as fast as my feet would carry me. I went straight to my dorm room and fell across the bed without even removing my shoes. I cried until my head hurt and my pillow case was wet with my tears of sorrow. There in the privacy of my room, I soaked myself in the bosom of self-pity for about an hour before dragging myself out of bed to go to the dining room. I had seen the guy, who sat next to me on the steps of McGhee hall, parading around the campus several times. He had very distinctive features that made him hard to forget. He'd even waved at me a time or two as he shuffled through the early morning crowd of students, walking the paths leading to his various classes. Usually, he went to the large dining room for his meals. I didn't want to bump into him again, so I decided to go to the smaller dining room. To my surprise, he came to the table I sat at, placing his tray next to mine. "I take it this seat is not taken?" he asked with a half-smile on his face. I didn't respond, just continued chomping down on my hoagie sandwich, thinking to myself, *please, go away!*

"I didn't mean to upset you earlier," he mumbled, a few minutes later. Finally, I looked up at him and responded. "To be honest, I was already upset." He handed me my journal and said, "You left this when you stormed off." I motioned for him to put it down on the table. And I went back to eating. But the whole time, I wondered what he thought of me when I ran off like a baby in tears.

"My name is Tony," he finally said. The silence between us was very loud. I guess he wanted to make it be quiet. "You seem like a cool person. Whoever the dude is that's got you so upset, he is not even worth your time."

I never told him what I was upset about. So I don't know how he knew. I simply nodded my head in response to what he had just said. Then with a few furrows in my head I turned and asked, "Did you read my journal?"

"Me," he said, pointing to himself. He had the nerve to look shocked that I asked him such a question. However,

I wasn't falling for the okey doke. He could play dumb all he wanted. "There's no one else here but you and I," I stated, beyond aggravated.

Surprisingly, he burst into laughter. "I would never be caught reading anyone's journal. I mean I'd plead temporary insanity if I was ever caught with my eyes in one of those little books. I leave all of that sentimental stuff to you girls, you know what I'm saying?"

"Well, how did you know I was upset about a guy," I continued, not ready to let him off the hook. He laughed again and said, "Duh, it's quite obvious. I mean look at yourself, why else would you be so torn apart. I'm sorry for laughing because it's really not funny."

I didn't know what else to say. It was obvious I had sunk my claws into this guy for no reason at all. Knowing that I had made a fool of myself, I stood up, even though I wasn't finished eating, and I went and dumped my tray. I walked out of the dining room without looking back, but I felt Tony eyes on me or maybe it was all in my head. The only thing I knew was I had to get away from him. Once more, I had tears in my eyes. It wasn't a good feeling to be called out, although, I knew he meant no harm. Maybe it was his way of helping me to see my worth, a worth I thought was washed away from the shore of my existence like a message in a bottle lost in the sea

The friendship of a lifetime

True friendship is a gift often hard to come by. This was a lesson I had to learn the hard, painful way, after dealing with several people who I thought were my friends. They looked like my friends, even for a while acted like they were my friends. As fate would have it, they turned out to be nothing more than snakes, slithering into my life when I wasn't paying attention, or when I was feeling so desperate for someone to call my friend that I took the first thing that came along. They didn't stick around when things got rough.

They weren't even around long enough for things to get rough. Just as soon as they slipped through the doorway of my heart, they slipped back through the same hole once they no longer had any use for me. They didn't bring anything to the table with them. But willing they were to take everything I already had established on my own. It's funny how when they were done draining me, I didn't have enough for myself. I felt used, as if I didn't have the needed strength to go on from day to day.

My insatiable desire to feel like I belonged to someone got me caught up in a lot of situations not so easy for me to get out of, at least, not without it having an adverse effect on my well-being. After a dozen or so upsets, I realized a true friendship was not something that happened overnight. It was not quick and easy like a microwave dinner that you just popped into the oven for a minute or so, and it would be ready for you to indulge. The right ingredients had to be mixed together. It had to take time baking the way you would bake a cake. The batter alone wouldn't make the cake be the way it needed to be, just the same as the ingredients needed to form a friendship alone without being used in the right way wouldn't be enough.

Once the friendship was formed, you would have to constantly do updates to it because just like a house will eventually fall apart if you don't do what is necessary to upkeep it, the same theory applies when it comes to a friendship. You cannot expect it to stand alone on its own. It has to be fertilized constantly with love, patience, honesty, and understanding. In addition, you have to pressure wash drama off of the walls of friendship, for surely it would have it grimy and in such bad shape, you wouldn't want to be around it.

A friendship could very well be compared to a rose. Though a few petals on the rose may have withered over time, if you deadhead those petals, still the rose will continue to bloom.

Like a kid who always wanted the trendy things he saw his friends with, I wanted a few friendships of my own, felt I would be the perfect candidate for several friendships since I was nice and gave my very last to whoever wanted it. Anyone who graced me with their friendship should have, as far as I could see, been happy about doing so. If I couldn't do anything else, I could definitely be the perfect friend.

When it seemed as if it wasn't going to happen, I adjusted what I wanted, rationalized that maybe I was being greedy by thinking I should have more than one friend. One good friendship was perhaps all I needed. So I played the waiting game once more, hoping since I had adjusted my needs, I would soon get what I wanted. However, it seemed as if that one friendship was far beyond my reach. I watched so many peers of mine as they engaged in different friendships. I noticed how it appeared as if they always got along, and they were constantly together: laughing, reminiscing, enjoying each other's company, and being there for one another the way you would expect two or more people in a friendship to be. Sometimes, I saw one of the parties in the friendship not actually being a good friend. He/she was rude, obnoxious, selfish, or maybe even all of the above. At times, the issues they had could be worked out while other times, the friendship fell through the cracks of time. But it wouldn't be long before the individuals from the broken friendship had a new person whom they called friend. I watched all of this with care, wondered why it happened for them and not for me. After many years of feeling rejected, I considered God to have opened up the windows of heaven and poured me out a blessing when He allowed me to cross paths with Tony.

Tony and I were different in so many ways. He woke up in the morning thinking about baseball and laid down at night to sleep thinking about baseball. Many evenings, we met up at the batting cage on campus. Even though I had no interest whatsoever in baseball, it meant the world to him for me to come and watch him practice in the batting cage. It would be an added bonus if I would listen to him rant on and on nonstop about his love for the game and how he was certain one day he would be a pro. I heard the excitement in his voice when he spoke, which is why I was all smiles when I listened to him talk. This wasn't a one-sided thing. He treated me with the same courtesy when I talked to him about my passion for writing. Regardless of how he may have truly felt about it, he allowed me to read to him poems I often wrote late at night while I lay in bed at the dormitory.

As we continuously hung around each other, I noticed Tony could be kind of obnoxious. He was a little too cocky sometimes. Really, it got on my nerves. I whined about it, throwing a hissy fit every now and then, which in return, got on his nerves, instead of handling the situation like an adult. I was an adult at last, so I had claimed. If that was the case, it wasn't something I could be straddled the fence about, grown today, a child tomorrow, and somewhere in between the day after. Consistency was the best way to handle my new status. After all, I was the one who was so ready to wear the garments of adulthood as if having a chance to be an adult was a coupon that was only good for a limited time. Despite the few misunderstandings that surfaced, for the most part, Tony and I got along well. A genuine friendship must have been what the doctor ordered for me to move on with my life.

It wasn't long before Michael was only but a dull memory in my mind. I had the friendship of a lifetime. I didn't think there was nothing more I could ask for to make me feel more fulfilled at that given time in my life. Yes, I was putting all of my eggs in the same basket. There was nothing Tony would do to make me not want to be friends with him anymore. He never raked me over the coals, leaving me to burn into the ashes of bitterness like so many other people had done. My past was a different story. It had a dark side it wanted to reveal in my new life. It wanted to upset the joy that had me smiling from ear to ear. It didn't want me to be happy because it was so used to seeing me down. If it got in the way, maybe Tony would feel as if he would've been better off had he not met me.

Past interferences

When it comes to the game of football, there is a term called, pass interference. According to google, it is a foul, occurring when a player interferes with an eligible receiver's ability to make a fair attempt to catch a forward pass. When this happens the referee throws a flag, resulting in certain penalties administered as punishment to alert the guilty player that he had done something he should not have done. But what happens when a person's past interferes with his/her future? Is there a referee available to throw a flag? What would be the penalty?

Throwing flags only existed in sports. If I wanted my life to be free from past interferences, I had to be the one to bid farewell to it once and for all. Without reservations, I would have to bury it in its final resting place, wipe the tears from my eyes, turn on my heels, and walk away from the graveyard of the past and into my future.

After several months of being friends with Tony, I finally got the chance to meet the coach. The coach was a serious person, fierce, and not really down for childishness of any sort. I'd heard many stories about the coach. I knew right off that I never wanted to rub her the wrong way. Yes, the coach was a she. It was Tony's pet name for his mom. *What if she doesn't think I'm good enough to be her son's friend?* As usual I allowed my mind to throw its darts of destruction. I'm certain Tony had mentioned me to his mom on an occasion or two. She had to know of me. Yet, I was so insecure that I quivered when I extended to her my hand.

Her eyes were fastened on my eyes. She did not smile, or give any kind of indication that would prove whether she liked me or not. That only intensified my level of insecurity. "Pleased to meet you," she said as she shook my hand and released it from her grip.

I'm happy to meet you, too," I shyly responded, dropping my eyes to the ground. I was glad when it was all over but felt bad later in the evening as I walked into my dorm room. "Why wouldn't she like you?" I asked myself aloud. "Even more, why do you care? Why do you always have to center your life around whether someone else likes you or not? I think the question at hand should be, do you even like yourself? Of course you're not concerned about that because you think if someone else likes you, it will lessen the blow of the fact you don't like yourself."

To further understand why I felt the way I felt I'm going to go back into my past a little bit. I don't want any of you to be confused, as at this point in life, I am close to

Yesterday's Woes

Kids will be kids

When I was in my impressionable stage in life, I learned a nursery rhyme I found to be very funny. It told the difference between boys and girls, relaying that boys were made of snips and snails and puppy dog tails, while on the other hand, girls were made of sugar and spice and everything nice. I believed those words to be true until I became acquainted with my teenage years and put away childish things. That included childish thoughts. I knew then that children's behavior was defined by how their parents raised them. Where rules and boundaries were set, you most likely had a well-balanced, obedient child. If there were no rules to follow, you could not blame the child when he/she lacked basic manners and proceeded to embarrass you in public and then, looked at you as if you were crazy when you tried to correct them.

I am not Sigmund Freud, but I know from experience that it is not wise to confuse a child by assuming he/she should know how to act when out in public, especially when allowed to do whatever he/she pleased while at home. It would be best to instill the desired traits you want your child to have within at all times, for whatever seeds planted will sprout. Its' fruit will not be denied. You can't expect to go outside and pick oranges off an apple tree.

Regardless of what you teach your children or how you stay on their case about doing the right thing, saying the right thing, and thinking the right thing, at times, they will be rebellious. They will test the waters. Even when they know they should not do so and are certain there will be consequences to follow. They will find themselves caught in situations that you as parents, never thought would be possible because you had discussed with them why they should not be involved many years before it presented itself before them. They will work your nerves, get smart at the mouth, and have you wondering, *Lord, where did I go wrong*? *What could I have done differently*? Sometimes, you may even cry late at night and want to throw your hands up declaring there is nothing more you can do. You may be beating yourself up trying to figure out a solution. It is not always something you did wrong. Even when you do everything right, the outcome will not always be the way you hoped it would be. It is no more than kids being kids. I think it is in their genetic make-up to, at times, act out. Besides, how normal would they be, if they did not occasionally get their hands wet with mischief? How much better would you feel, if they just sat around like cute little decorative pieces on a mantle, collecting dust?

Things were slightly different from the above theory when it came to me. I had so many want to be psychiatrists and psychologists analyzing me. Not even a fraction of them had gone to school to have the right to solicit their unwanted analysis and diagnosis when it came to my life and why I behaved the way I behaved. They were no more than outsiders looking in. Sometimes their children went astray. It was all because they were too busy trying to figure me out. Instead, they should have been investing time and energy into being concerned about what their children were doing right under their noses or how they were burning the midnight oil at night cursing and stressing because they couldn't get their children to obey even the simplest of rules.

I could not understand (I really tried) how they came up with their analysis. If I happened to stray away from rules and regulations the way it was normal for kids to sometimes do, I found a mass amount of people saying,

"Oh, she did that because she is a foster child." Really? Whatever happened to, "Oh, she did that because she is hardheaded, or she did that because she is a kid, and kids will be kids?" Yes, I grew up as a foster child, but long before I was a foster child, I was simply a child. That was a fact that cannot be changed, regardless of what else came along to join it.

The stipulations were different when it came to me, although, I noted how some of the kids who came from the homes where everyone expected them to be successful were way more unruly than I had ever dreamed of being. They were smoking, and I am not talking about cigarettes. They were sneaking out at night, drinking excessively, and the list goes on. Fortunately, for them, their behaviors were swept under the rug so that they remained in the good graces of those who would have surely gossiped about their, "Not being perfect after all," if it were made public.

Since a large number of people assumed I did certain things based on the fact I was a foster child and did not know any better, I found they treated me differently. I was the odd ball to them, kind of like the child in the classroom who no one wanted to play with because it was something noticeably different about him everyone else felt was not acceptable. They did not put as much effort in to going to bat for me or encouraging me because they did not expect me to flourish. They expected me to be less than second best simply because I grew up as a ward of the state. There is no way I can recollect how many times I heard the words, "You'll never amount to anything," rolling off the lips of those who I never thought for once would say those words to me.

It is very true. I did not come from a home where both parents were present and asked their children as they came home from school, "Son, daughter, how was your day?" It was not customary to be tucked into bed at night or have mom sing lullabies while I fell asleep in her arms. The pages in my beginning were dark, and oftentimes, dreary, for I came from a situation where the Department of Human Resources had to get involved. They had to disrupt what I thought was a home. They had to put me in a situation where I was really in a good home that would be conducive to what I needed as a child. It is the hardcore ugly truth that my biological mother did not want to be tied down with children. Therefore, DHR had to find someone who would be willing to take on her responsibility.

My foster mom did her best to rear me according to the Christian standards she herself had been raised to have. The seeds she planted were not in vain. Still, I had underlying issues. I was scarred from my past. Even so, I was not the menace to society many people wanted to believe I was. I never got in any serious trouble at school. I wasn't beefing with any of my classmates. I honestly wanted all of them to be my friends. Nevertheless, whenever there was a problem, you can bet your bottom dollar if I were present at the time it took place, the blame was put on my shoulders. This happened even without the accuser knowing what had truly transpired. “That gal ain’t nothing but a trouble maker. That’s all she will ever be,” they had the tendency to say while dismissing me, embracing the child they assumed was worthy of love, the child who had started the drama.

The seed took root

I wanted people to see me for who I was. The shell I was encased was marred to the point no one wanted to look any further. I sat on the shelf alone, constantly picked over while everyone reached for the merchandise they considered to be beautiful on the outside. *Oh, you are the Pastor’s daughter or the District Attorney’s son. So I know you will go far in life*, I assumed they said to themselves with huge doting smiles glued on their faces. The same face on more than one occasion, fell to that of sheer disappointment when they looked at me. I felt like Cinderella, dressed in the raggedy clothes, forced to slave for her stepmother and stepsisters, who were considered to be superior.

It wasn't just thoughts. Sometimes, I heard them discussing me. "Oh, yeah, she'll be in and out of jail just like her ole good for nothing mother. She's going to find herself in an early grave. Mark my words."

To the contrary, I was hell bent on getting those closeminded individuals, who only wanted to think the worst of me, to see it was what was on the inside that counted. After all, I never saw anyone throw away a Bentley just because it had a few scratches and dings here and there. The paint may have chipped from the storms it weathered. But what about the good engine on the inside that hummed silently as it took you wherever you had to go? What about the second looks it received from others, who could look beyond a few small scratches on its exterior and still note that it was a fine car.

I wanted to be accepted as an equal. As much effort as I put into trying to make that happen, I secretly thought I was undeserving. Over the course of listening to the disdain others appeared to have for me, I started to not like myself. I allowed their seeds of criticism to take root in my soil. Its vines, as they sprung up, were filled with everything designed to ultimately destroy me. That was why, as the years came and went, I constantly sought validation from everyone. I was always extra nice but always assumed the worst. *He/she do not like me.*

What I realize now that I did not realize back then, is how I could not expect anyone else to like me when I was having a hard time liking myself? My own negative vibes may have told them to stay far away from me. Maybe they knew they could not fix the issues I had, and in the process, knew I would bring them down.

The higher up the ladder of success the one I conversed with seemed to be, the more intimidated I became. I wanted to be near them. I wanted what they had to manifest in my life so I could levitate out of the slums of unworthiness to a place I felt I could be proud of. I even constructed a plan to start a conversation with some of them. But when it was time to release the pearl out of the shell, I "chickened out" as I heard a lot of people say in regards to reneging on a situation.

More than just a handful

I know as we've traveled along life's tempestuous journey, there have been times when we have heard someone close to us say, "Oh, so you think you're mad. Well, I'm going to give you a reason to be mad for real." I will not say it was the right attitude to possess. It was the one I picked to wear out of the closet. I put it on and decided I liked the way it fit. So then, I made a vow to myself that I would not take it off for anyone. If they did not like it, they didn't have to deal with me. I was not going to spend any more time trying to convince anyone how good of a person I was. They wanted and expected Tamyra to be a bad girl. They finally were going to get their wish. They would now have a reason to point their holier than thou fingers' and whisper under their condescending breaths. I was going to be more than a handful.

Now truthfully speaking, it was not all about going astray because everyone expected me to. I willfully took a walk down this path because I did not see the point in trying so hard to be good. I had accepted in my mind that I, more than likely, was going to be a failure. So now, it was time to see it through. Even when I decided I was going to do that, I was angry because I truly wanted more for myself. I thought about the conversations I'd had with teachers who actually cared about me and other authoritarian figures who asked me, with a big smile on their faces, what I wanted to be when I grew up. At that time, I thought I wanted to be a teacher. Then, I thought I wanted to be a social worker. I felt as if I was good enough to make it happen. I wanted to grow up to be a well-respected woman. I wanted the right man to find me and make me his wife. I wanted to have children of my own, who I wanted to raise to be better than I was.

Now that I was older, and it was time for me to be about my business, doubt was hanging around like a third wheel. It all seemed to be an unattainable dream. Out of my mind, I had to be if I thought I was going to have any of that. I felt like a kid who gazed longingly at the doll sitting on the top shelf in the toy department. She wanted it so badly, had already imagined how she would play with it for hours at a time. Her mom told her she couldn't have it. She felt it was unfair and threw a temper tantrum. I did not throw a temper tantrum. I did take my anger out on innocent bystanders, becoming rebellious and hurting people in the process.

The day came, sooner than later, where mom could not tell me anything. I stood toe-to-toe with her plenty days, thinking I was just as grown as she was. My mouth was "flip" as I'd heard the old people say. It was going to be my way or no way. Mom was not the only one I got diarrhea at the mouth with. I got smart with any adult who I felt had stepped out of line. My specialty was being sarcastic. I was known to try to play it off as if I did not know I was being a smart aleck.

I never raised my hand to hit mom. I knew if I had done such a thing, I would not be alive now to be writing this book. I did not curse her out either, for I was well aware that the dentist would not have been able to fit me for a nice pair of dentures to replace the teeth mom knocked out of my mouth. I was not into sneaking out of the house. When I was younger, I heard about how mom had waited for one of her biological daughters when she sneaked out. When she went to get back in the same window she had sneaked out of, mom grabbed her by the hair and pulled her in. I did not want that to happen to me. I did, however, do everything else you could think of.

I had a change of heart one evening when mom sent me in her room to get something for her off her nightstand. As I was turning the lamp off to walk out of the room, my eyes fell upon a book she was reading. I picked the book up and read the title. It hurt me to my heart that mom had to read a book like this. It was called, “How to Talk So That Kids Will Listen, and Listen So That Kids Will Talk.” Up under that book was another one titled, “If the Devil Made You Do It, You Blew It.”

“What have I done?” I asked myself on the brink of tears. Had I really been that bad? Mom had been good to me. She had taken me in when no one else would. And she kept me, even when everyone advised her to send me back to where I had come from. She had gone far and beyond the call of duty, doing things for me she didn't even do for her own biological children.

"I'm going to change," I said aloud. I actually did do better, for a while. Even when I felt myself getting annoyed, and I wanted to spew my sarcastic words, I thought long and hard about the Scripture found in Exodus 20:12. It said to, *Honor thy Father and thy Mother that thy days may be long upon the land which the Lord thy God giveth thee*. It played like a musical in my head. Ephesians 6:2 came to mind as well. It said, *Honor your father and mother (this is the first commandment with a promise).*

Even with me knowing the word of God, it wasn't too long before I slipped back into my old ways. I always had to be told more than once to do something. I had the audacity to mumble under my breath when I finally did decide to do what was asked of me. If that wasn't enough, I even had the nerve to tell mom when she mentioned how she had taken us in, "Well, nobody told you to get us. You did that because you wanted to." I had my hands on my hip as if I was grown, looking at her as if she was my equal.

Those choice words were followed with a hard slap to my face. Mom walked up to me, so close, in fact, that I fell backwards into the chair behind me. "Don't you ever in life talk to me like that, you little ungrateful heifer," she said with trembling lips and tears flowing down her face. "I'm the one who does everything for you, not DHR. It is me who miss out on sleep when I have to carry you up the road late at night to the hospital. And you think you shouldn't listen to me? Huh? I tell you what then, go and pack your stuff. I'll take you back to DHR tomorrow!"

There were no words left to say after that. Mom went to her room. I sat back down in the chair I'd just found the strength to get out of when mom hovered over me with her fingers only inches away from my face. I spent the rest of the evening wondering where would DHR put me once mom took me back. I felt all kinds of remorse as the words,

"I'll take you back to DHR tomorrow," continuously taunted me. I couldn't believe how I had acted. I couldn't believe how I had talked to the one person who would have never done me wrong.

"I want to at least apologize," I said to myself later in the evening. We'd sat at the dinner table in total silence. Mom wouldn't even look at me as we ate. She was deeply hurt by my level of disrespect. I had been very disrespectful. There was no need for me to deny it or justify it in any kind of way. *I don't want to leave with mom thinking I don't appreciate her*, I solemnly thought. I realized how I would miss everyone I had gotten the chance to know throughout the years. I allowed my mind to take me back to the summer of 1990. The house was in total chaos as we were getting ready for our annual Peterson/McGill family reunion. I was excited as ever. Family reunion meant I would get to see family from all over. This particular year, I met more family than I had ever met before. Some of them were not really my biological family, but you couldn't tell by the way they treated me. "Come on over here and give me a hug, cuz," some of them said with outstretched arms.

I raced outside with a big smile, my heart fluttering with joy as the out of town guests began to pour into mom's driveway. When the three 5.0 mustangs screeched to a halt, I came face-to-face with a tall, bald guy as he stepped out of one of the cars. I scratched my head. *I've never seen him before*, I thought. He looked at me, smiled, then said, "Give me five," while sticking out his hand for me to hit. I soon found out his name was Mitchell Daniel. I called him Cousin Mitchell instead. Mom had told me you were never supposed to call an adult by his first name.

Cousin Mitchell and I became close very fast. I was so sad when the family reunion was over and he and his wife and children made the trip back to Detroit, Michigan. Throughout the course of our relationship, it got to the point where Cousin Mitchell never showed up without bringing a gift for me and Tamara. The most exquisite had been a gold herringbone for me and a pearl bracelet for Tamara. He even paid for our hair to be braided for back to school one year. He planned to allow us to come to Detroit to visit him the following summer. It was a total blow to my heart when he suddenly died from a heart attack. I heard about the news one evening when I was in the drugstore picking up a new bronchodilator pill for my asthma, called Volmax. I fell to the floor when mom came busting through the drugstore doors with tears flowing down her face. "Cousin Mitchell is gone," she said, hardly able to contain herself. I wanted to die right along with him. I knew family reunion would never be the same without him. And it wasn't. Even with him resting in his grave, the thought of how disappointed he would be in me, if he knew how I had acted, made me cringe. I was now totally embarrassed by my actions.

While in bed that night, my mind continuously showed me previews of what I was going to be missing out on now since mom was washing her hands of me. I could hear her soothing voice, comforting Tamara and I throughout the years. She'd gotten us through some tough times… times I literally thought my heart would split in half because it was harboring so much pain. Our pain didn't drain her of any of her strength. Instead, it filled her up with a feeling of satisfaction, knowing she was helping us in our time of need.

I silently wept, thinking of the time mom allowed us to bake cookies and a cake in an attempt to cheer us up. We didn't have a date to the school dance that was going on at that very moment and was feeling the blues as a result. "How about you two have a date with me," she said. "We can bake some sweets and watch movies all night long." Soon enough, we'd forgotten about how sad we were feeling and waited anxiously for the cake we'd baked to cool off so we could put icing on it. The laughter and memories from that night, back in the day, still had an effect on me. I heard it all as if it was happening right then. Mom sat in a chair in the kitchen giving orders. We smiled heartily, not minding at all. I was careful not to bump into anything as mom had said, it could cause the cake to not rise.

Then there was the time mom attempted to teach us how to drive while we were in our early teens. We were fourteen-years-old to be exact. At the time she had a navy blue LTD. One Sunday when we got out of church I noticed that she drove out through the field behind the house that she grew up in when she was a little girl. Her father, granddad Joe, lived there up until his death. And now that he was gone, my Uncles Ronnie and Bobby still lived there. I really wasn't alarmed because we had a lot of family land. Oftentimes mom would drive through to make sure nothing was going on that shouldn't have been going on. She pulled up in the middle of the field and stopped the car.

Okay, I silently thought, looking at her as if she had lost her mind. She smiled and said, “So, who is going to drive first?” I stretched my eyes in amazement. “Are you serious?” I asked. She repeated her first question. “So who is going to drive first?”

I didn’t waste any time getting out of the car. I twisted my little nickel worth of hips around to the driver’s side and waited for mom to get out. I snapped my fingers and did a little silly dance while she scuffled to get out. She walked around to the other side of the car and sat down in the passenger seat. I was sitting there grinning like a Cheshire cat after I had adjusted the seat to suit my height, or lack thereof. Before I took off mom said, “Oh Lord, Titty, you are under the wheel of the car. Let me put on my seatbelt.” I usually would’ve been pissed about her calling me Titty. I had dealt with Nana calling me that God awful name for many years, and there was nothing I could do about it. I could hardly put up with anyone else calling me that. But of course I wasn't going to gripe about it today. Not when mom had graciously allowed me to get under the wheel of her car.

I put the car in drive. "Ease your foot off the brake," she said, bracing herself. Of course I didn't pay any attention. I took off driving like I was in a high speed chase. When I hit the first bale of hay I looked at mom and said, "Oops." Then I hit the second bale of hay. Again, I looked at mom and said, "Oops." By the time I decided to look back in front of me, I had hit the third bale of hay. Of course I looked at mom again. And yes I said, "Oops," with a silly smirk on my face. Mom was laughing so hard. She could hardly breathe. By the time I stopped the car she'd almost peed on herself. I smiled a little myself as I thought about that memory. She clutched her heart like she was about to have a heart attack. But I was thinking, *Aye, you ain't got to tell me I did good. I know it for myself. Yeah, I see this driving thing is going to be a breeze.*

Teaching me how to drive was something mom didn't have to do. Still, she did it just the same as she had done so many other things for me.

Eventually, I fell asleep amongst my thoughts and tears. The next morning, I dreaded getting out of bed. My pillow was soaked with tears as I'd cried every time I woke up during the night. I'd packed a lot of my things the evening before but couldn't pull myself to finish the task as it pained me to know I would no longer be able to call my bedroom mine. I probably would be sleeping on a hard twin-size bed in a room with lots of other girls. These girls probably would be far more messed up than I was. I would probably wake up to find one of them standing over me with a knife. I wouldn't be able to make pallets on the floor the way I'd done so many times in my room, or fall asleep watching movies. My new residence would be a facility, I was sure, where you had to use a community bathroom. Lights out probably would be not long after the stroke of dusk. It was good for me, though. That's what I got for having the nerve to be disrespectful.

I got dressed and made my way to the kitchen. I peeked around the corner at mom. She was sitting in a chair, facing the window, having a cup of coffee. I wanted a bowl of cereal. Although I felt like I didn't deserve to have anything mom had bought because of how I'd treated her. I desperately wanted to ask her to forgive me. The thought of her rejecting me made me nauseous to my stomach.

"Don't just stand there," mom finally said. I wondered how she knew I was there when she never once looked up from the mug she nursed as if it was ointment to heal the hole in her heart. "Come on in here and get yourself some cereal," she went on. Relief fell over my face as I dared to enter the same space as mom. I was more relieved when I realized she wasn't going to take me back to DHR after all. She sought help for me instead. So, in the year of 1997, I became not just a foster child, but a therapeutic foster child. I didn't know what it meant to be a therapeutic foster child. I decided to do an Internet search to find out. I was surprised to find out that according to Google, therapeutic foster care was a clinical intervention, which included placement in specifically trained foster parent homes for youth with severe mental, emotional, or behavioral health needs."

Therapeutic Programs, Inc. (TPI)

I heard a knock on my hospital room door in the early part of the afternoon. I sat in the middle of the bed with one foot dangling over the rail. *Days of Our Lives* played on the television attached to the wall. The weather outside was hot as I had spent a significant part of the morning sitting in the windowsill looking out at the shining sun and everyone who came in and out of the hospital. Mom was there visiting me. She sat in the chair next to the bed, glancing at the soap opera from time to time. We both looked at the door as the loud staccato knock rang in our ears.

"Come in," we said in unison. A tall, dark-skinned gentleman emerged. Immediately, his eyes fell upon me. I pulled the ugly gray blanket on the bed further around the thin hospital gown I had on as attire. I had no idea who this guy was looking at me as if he had a problem. It was obvious that mom knew who he was. She didn't have the same, "Hey, who are you?" expression outlining her face as I did.

The gentleman walked over to me and extended his massive hand. He introduced himself, his voice a combination of tenor and baritone. He informed me he was from TPI which was an acronym for Therapeutic Programs, Inc. I immediately rolled my eyes up in my head, thinking, *Great, he's here to so-called psychoanalyze me*. My body language didn't disguise how I was feeling, and I didn't care one bit. "Be nice," mom mouthed to me when I looked over at her with the, "You couldn't tell him to wait until I was out of the hospital," expression on my face. I looked back at him and clearly saw he had noticed my bad attitude. Yet, he didn't seem to be moved by it. He maintained the same calm expression. His tone of voice did not change.

"I'm sorry you're in the hospital," he bellowed.

I didn't respond. I glared at him like, "Yeah, so am I, but I probably would get better faster, if you weren't here trying to act like you are my savior." I took in a deep breath, exhaling it slowly. I thought about how I promised mom I would give the new caseworker a shot. I promised not to be rude or possess assumptive behavior. Now that it was time for me to keep my word, there was nothing more I wanted than to let this guy have it. The longer he stood there with that goofy smile on his face, the fouler my mood became. I just wanted him to scram so I could continue watching my soap operas. It was about all I could do laying in the hospital. *He can think I'm mental all he wants, but I'm not fixing to tell him anything*, I silently thought.

"I just dropped in to see you," the social worker went on, communicating with me, regardless of how difficult I tried to make it. "I know it has to be tough lying here in the hospital. I know I wouldn't like that. But I hope you get to feeling better real soon, and I look forward to seeing you in the office next week."

"In the office…" I finally spoke up for the first time. "What office are you talking about?"

"Our office located on McGhee Road," he responded. "You'll have the chance to be in group sessions with other therapeutic foster children and meet other therapeutic foster parents as well. You'll also get the chance to see the nice lady who will be making home visits to your home on a weekly basis."

I don't know who they think they are. DHR doesn't even make home visits on a weekly basis. I got better things to do than to be staring in their ugly faces all the damn time, I thought as he continued to talk. I'm sure he was aware of how I was ignoring him by now. He finished what he had to say, extended his hand to me once again, and then, left the room after I reluctantly shook his hand.

"Well, this is just great," I said with disgust, covering my head with the same gray blanket I considered to be beyond putrid and pouting like a baby.

TPI wasn't as bad as I assumed it would be. The social worker who came to see me in the hospital name was Joe. He often led the group sessions that Tamara and I attended on a weekly basis. The social worker who came to visit us weekly was also nice. She always allowed us to express how we felt, never once showing that she was aggravated in the least.

I thought the CEO, who was also the founder, and owner of the TPI in Montgomery, Alabama, and about thirteen other TPI's throughout the state of Alabama would be over the top stuck up. But I was so wrong. Dr. Mitchell, was probably one of the most down to earth people I had ever met in my life. He had a genuine love for foster children and truly wanted to see them overcome their issues. I came on board just in time to join the other teens on the trip to Six Flags over Georgia that Dr. Mitchell paid for. As if that wasn't enough, he threw a Christmas party for us as well. When I was twenty-four-years-old he allowed me to be a secretary in the same office I had been affiliated with when I was a teen. I also met another friend whose name was Romeo. Ever since the day we first met we have been great friends. Had it not been for TPI, our paths would've never crossed.

The Garments of Maturity

Emancipation

Finally, came the day, after much preparation and anticipation, when I turned twenty-one-years old at last. I do not know why it was so important for me to turn twenty-one. I did not feel any differently from how I felt when I turned twenty-years-old. In fact, I didn't feel any differently from how I had felt when I turned nineteen-years-old. I didn't do the things most needed to be legal in order to do without getting into trouble.

I was not a drinker, not even socially. Ever since the day I choked on the smoke from one of my uncle's cigarettes, after I snatched it out of his mouth, and decided to take a pull, I knew I would never be a smoker. Coughing nonstop that day taught me a valuable lesson I never saw myself forgetting, even when the peer pressure to do so was at its peak.

Furthermore, I did not grace the clubs with my presence, therefore, needing my ID to verify I was of age to be in the place. Quite a few of my peers lived for the weekend, so they could be in the clubs all night long. I didn't see what the big fuss was all about. I was what many considered to be a party pooper. I was too afraid of a stray bullet intended for someone else hitting me instead. Whether it was an accident or not, I was going to be just as dead, if it hit me in the right place. If that wasn't enough, I didn't want any guys so-called grinding on me or asking me to dance, for that matter. I knew I wouldn't have ever been confident enough to dance with them, if they asked. Therefore, I didn't put myself in the hot seat where I would wind up feeling embarrassed and out of place. There was really no need for me to be excited about turning twenty-one except for the simple fact, I knew I was legal.

With adulthood, came more responsibilities. I didn't realize it then, when I was so excited to be on my own, but there were many days I wished to be a kid again. Adulthood didn't come with instructions on how to do it the right way. It was a learn-as-you-go process. I made many costly mistakes. Some of them were hard to recover from. On those days when everything seemed to be so hard, I longed for the days where I didn't have to wonder where my next meal came from or where I was going to lay my head. I wouldn't have to be responsible for providing for kids or making wise decisions. All I had to do was get up every day and follow the instructions already set for me.

Now that I was grown, it was time to see if the independent living conferences I attended as a teen would make the difference in my life they were designed to make.

I remembered the retreats we had during the summer where Tamara and I got the chance to meet up with lots of other foster children from all over the state of Alabama. The first Independent Living Conference we got a chance to attend birthed a level of excitement in my world I'd never before experienced. I hardly slept the night before we were to leave for Eufaula, Alabama. I'd sadly watched a few years before as my brother packed his bags to go to the conference. At the time I was too young. It didn't seem fair to me at all, although waiting to have the opportunity to go myself gave me something to look forward to. Once we arrived at the conference, Tamara and I participated in many activities and were given an abundance of information on how we could be successful once we moved out on our own or in my case, when I was emancipated out of the custody of the State. There were quite a few people I met at the conference I wanted to remain in contact with. I couldn't help feeling flattered as I noticed how there was this one particular dark-skinned guy who glared at me every chance he got.

I didn't know what his name was, didn't even bother to ask him. I simply allowed my mind to take me on one of those, "What if," excursions. Maybe we could have been great together. I realized I would never know as I watched him and the other teens from his county load up in their vehicle to head back home at the ending of the conference. It was like hope evaporating into nothing right before my eyes. I thought about him for a while after the conference, smiled brightly while I visualized his gleaming white teeth. He'd flashed me several smiles throughout the conference. What was even better was the carefree demeanor he had. He flaunted it like it was muscles he'd obtained from bench-pressing weights.

Fate allowed us to see each other again twenty years later. I didn't remember him as we approached each other near an elevator. But he definitely remembered me.

"I know you from somewhere," he said as he pressed the button to go to the third floor. I didn't know how he could know me. But I chose not to debate the matter. Instead, I said, "Well, my name is Tamyra. I went to Central High School. Maybe that's where…"

"No," he interrupted. "It is not school where I know you from. But I swear when I figure it out I'm going to let you know." I nodded my head and walked off. A couple of weeks later he came to the table I was sitting at for lunch and sat down in front me.

"I finally figured it out," he said with a smile. A look of excitement came over my face and I responded, "Well, what are you waiting for? Tell me, please."

"Do you remember going to ILP conferences as a teen," he asked with his eyes still fastened on mine.

"Oh, my, God," I mumbled in response.

"That's where I know you from," he said. So that I wouldn't think he was trying to run game on me, he told me that I had a twin sister and he specifically mentioned that we'd attended an ILP conference together when we were both teens. I learned that his name was Marcus and he was from Greenville, Alabama. It was a good thing our paths crossed again. There had never been anyone else who I'd felt such a connection with. We had so much in common, much more than I ever imagined possible.

Truth of the matter was, I considered those ILP conferences to be great. During those times, I was surrounded by people who knew what it was like to be a foster child, not because they had read about it in a textbook, but because they, themselves had lived the life.

The day I turned twenty-one, I was still a student living on the campus at Alabama State University. Recently, I had been promoted to the editorial staff of the Hornet Tribune. Now, not only could I write articles, since I was an editor, I got the chance to write a commentary every week. It did my soul good to see my words published in the Hornet's

Living Section of the paper. The things I decided to write about, I considered relevant among the college population. Surely, if I felt a certain way about things, I couldn't have been the only one who felt that way. There were others who weren't always brave enough to speak out. I wanted to reach them, wanted them to know someone cared about what they were going through.

As fulfilling as writing on the newspaper had been for me, there were other great things I had done as well. Just a few weeks prior to my twenty-first birthday, I had spoken at a legislative luncheon, telling the legislators and other dignitaries sitting in their three-piece suits and wiping lunch off their mouths with their satin handkerchiefs, about my experiences in foster care. I was appalled to see how my words moved some of them to the point of tears. I thought as I looked around the room, *these macho men are actually crying about something I said.* To sweeten the deal, I saw myself on the six o' clock news that afternoon. I didn't realize as I was speaking that there were any news anchors present.

This was not where the greatness sprouting in my life ended. There were other ways in which I defied the odds. Several times I appeared on the panel at GPS (Group Preparation and Selection) trainings, where I shared with prospective foster parents, my experiences as a child growing up in the system. They appreciated my testimony, giving me their undivided attention as I spoke. It was all worth it knowing that maybe they would take into consideration some of the things I said when they became foster parents.

I was even a mentor at Bellingrath Junior High School, had won first place in one writing contest, and second place in another one. I'd successfully gotten over my fear of my friend Tony's mother not liking me. I had even made another friend who was just as special to me as Tony. His name was Cecil. He was from Mobile, Alabama. He went to special lengths to make sure I didn't do without any of the necessary things I would need to survive on campus. That meant wherever I had to go, he was willing to take me. He never once complained about lugging me around as if he was my personal chauffeur. He was about as humble as anyone could be. So, yes, I considered my life to be pretty good at that point. I still fell in my funks from time to time. Although, it wasn't as bad as it had been in the past. I found I was able to bounce back quicker than I had before when I held on to pain as if it was my lifeline.

Out of all the things I considered to be going well, nothing compared to the day I was emancipated out of foster care. Tamara had been released from custody a couple of years before me. Because of my, what they called extenuating circumstances, due to my severe asthma, I was allowed to stay in custody until I was twenty-one. I did not consider that to be a particularly good thing. I longed to see the day when I could put the social workers I'd dealt with and group sessions I'd attended, out of my life. I felt it was time for that chapter in the book of my existence to come to an abrupt end. It was time for me to move on to the point of where I would wear the fine garments of maturity.

It was a cold day in the month of February, the day I was emancipated. I ended my classes early as the Department of Human Resources (DHR) had decided to host a celebration in my honor. They'd made me so mad at times that I had changed DHR from meaning Department of Human Resources to, "Do Harm Regularly." But I have to say they went all out of the way for little ole me, which I truly considered to be shocking. I was certain on many days, there was nothing they wanted more than to sever all ties with me, to finally be rid of the headache that had been difficult and given them a hard time. Seemed as if I could see them praising the Lord in their minds as the day my departure came nigh. It reminded me of a movie I'd enjoyed as a kid called, *Problem Child.* When the little boy finally got a family who were willing to adopt him, the nuns at the orphanage he'd lived at threw a party because they considered it to be a time to celebrate.

But the party being thrown on that day in 2001, as I entered the same room we'd had several conferences, was all for me. I saw a beautiful cake made for me sitting on one of the tables. All of the tables were tastefully decorated. There was even a program with my name on the front of it. "A new beginning for Tamyra," it said in big purple letters. I smiled as I looked up to the front of the room and saw there were an abundance of gifts. They were all for me. Every last one of the case/social workers at Lowndes County DHR, even the ones who didn't specifically work with me, were in attendance. My social worker, who'd toiled with me for many years, sat amongst a panel of other prominent individuals. I'm sure I'd caused her to have many nightmares. She nodded her head as our eyes met. A few more people drifted into the room and the program promptly began.

After it was all over, I felt lightheaded from the thought of the responsibilities I now had to tackle. DHR was not going to be my crutch anymore. It was time to apply what I learned throughout the years. It was time for me to be grown and wear the garments of maturity I'd been trying on for so long.

The bitter taste of responsibility

When I was a kid and found myself sick with the common cold, sinus issues, and pretty much any other ailment, mom lined up me and my siblings in a single file line, and spoon fed us castor oil. It had the most God awful taste. Not only that, it was thick and not very easy to swallow without the urge to puke. I tried to play mom a few times when it came to chugalugging the castor oil. But after I got a glimpse of her switch she always kept at her side, I knew I had better take heed and swallow. My lips trembled as the medicine dripped down the sides of my mouth. Tears followed suit while I made one final attempt to get out of taking the medicine. "Please, mom. Don't make me swallow this," I pleaded, gurgling the medicine in my mouth.

"Girl, do you think I am playing with you?" mom asked me. "Swallow that medicine now, and that includes what you allowed to drip down the side of your mouth." I panted like my life was about to end. Finally, I was able to completely swallow it. Talking about mad, I was mad as hell as I plopped down on the couch afterwards with my arms folded, giving mom the coldest stare ever behind her back. It was only a matter of time before it sent me to the toilet, where I spent a couple hours or so as it cleaned out my system.

I didn't like the taste of the castor oil one bit. When it was all said and done, it got rid of the impurities in my body that made me sick. It did for me what I needed it to do so I could be the healthy young lady I was supposed to be. When it came to me being responsible in life, it would not always be an easy task. At times, it would leave a bitter taste in my mouth. Even so, I would have to do what I needed to do. To not do so would stagnate my growth. It would create more issues in my life.

Up until the point where I turned twenty-one-years old, I had never had a job. I always wanted one. I felt having one would make me feel more complete. So I was beyond elated when I walked into Winn-Dixie grocery store one afternoon to put in an application, and the store manager was available for me to talk to right then. I had my hopes up for a position as a cashier. Quickly I had to readjust my expectations when I learned there was no such position available. The manager informed me they only had openings available on the stock crew. He wanted to know how I felt about working overnight. I had no idea what I was getting myself into. The fact I was going to be given a chance without having to put forth much effort was more than enough to make me squeal with delight. I spent the rest of the day and the days following, thinking about how my first day in the work force would be.

A week or so later, I walked into Winn-Dixie at a quarter to eleven p.m., ready to work my first shift as a part of the stock crew. I felt as if I was really accomplishing something great. I don't know if excitement or nervousness was more prevalent as the stock crew manager walked me to the backroom of the grocery store to show me how to clock in and out on the timeclock. He introduced me to all of the guys who were already standing there, gaping at me as if I was a piece of meat about to be filleted. I sheepishly glanced at them, feeling out of place, and at last, raised my hand to wave at them when they asked me how I was doing. My voice came out as a shrill, as I mumbled, "I'm good," and I inadvertently lowered my eyes to the floor. I heard one of them whistle as I turned around and headed back out of the backroom with the stock crew manager by my side. Most girls I knew would have been flattered. It would have done numbers for their self-esteem. I, on the other hand, was reeling with embarrassment, couldn't wait to be out of sight of the guys I considered to be hounds.

I handled my first few weeks as a new employee about as well as could be expected, especially being the new kid on the block. It wasn't always easy to stay on task. I lacked discipline, wasn't use to being told what to do. I found myself complaining about how cold it was. But I perked up when I heard, Destiny's Child, "I'm a Survivor," blaring through the speakers in the store.

After dropping a few jars of pickles and mayonnaise when I tripped and fell off the step ladder I had been using to help me reach the top shelf, I felt really discouraged, wanted to give up. Besides, it was still hard for me to keep my eyes open. I did okay until around two-thirty in the morning. After that, I was beyond miserable. After my first night working, I went back to the dorm, stripped down to my undergarments, hopped in the bed, pulled the covers over my head, and slept the entire day away. I didn't even bother to show my face at any of my classes the morning after my first night of work, refused to even get out of the bed until way after five-thirty in the evening.

Now, after a month had passed, I still struggled to keep my eyes open. Some mornings, after work, I literally had to drag myself to class. Other mornings, I skipped class, deciding with little to no coercion how my bed needed me more. Possessing a job was definitely an honorable thing to have. I will, however, admit it wasn't a necessity. I lived on campus. I didn't have to pay any out of pocket bills. I didn't have any other urgent expenses either. I simply wanted to keep up with all of the other girls on campus, who always seemed to have the latest styles. They seemed to have everyone's respect. I wanted that same respect, even when I knew without a moment's hesitation that everyone who hung around them weren't really their friends. Some of them wanted to boost their level of confidence by hanging with the most popular, while others suffered with low self-esteem the way I did, and wanted any kind of attention they could get from the ones who seemed to have it all. When would it dawn on me that the ones who were so popular at school, probably were lacking attention at home? So they equated their popularity status as meaning they were loved. I was not built to fit in with the crowd. Sooner or later, I would have to accept that fact.

Game Time (Misconceptions)

Eventually, I lost my job at Winn-Dixie. I couldn't fault anyone for this mishap but myself. Over the course of the couple of months I had been employed, I had been given several opportunities to get my act together. I chose to behave immaturely as if I hadn't been raised to have respect for authority. When I was terminated, I felt as if my world would fall apart. It wasn't a good feeling to have something taken away from me, even though I had proved a countless number of times that I didn't appreciate having a job. So why should I have expected to hold onto it is beneath my comprehension. That was another one of those painful lessons beneficial for me to take notes and learn from. However, my fate was not the end of the world. In spite of all of the mistakes I had made, I could grow up to be a very prosperous young woman.

None of this came to the light until after I had involved myself with another guy. When I became smitten by what I thought to be love, it had been a couple of years since I had dealt with Michael. But now, I was twenty-one-years-old, and I could handle my own, or so I thought. I wasn't the same weak little nineteen-year-old I was when I let Michael control me as if I was his personal puppet.

Willie, my new boo, worked on the stock crew at Winn-Dixie. He was three years older than me but seemed to be wise beyond his years. Quite a few times, I found myself awestruck by the conversations we shared with each other. He had my full attention, so to the point you could barely get me to blink while we were talking. It was not until later on, after things went south with us, that I made the painful realization how some of the things he told me were for the purpose of wooing me. He had taken time before we began talking to each other on that level, getting to know me. He knew what irked me. He knew what made me smile. He knew what excited me. He knew me enough to have his way with me.

His approach was different from how Michael's had been. His game plan was to constantly make me feel as if I was doing something wrong to him. I allowed him to make me feel as if it was my job to be there for him in every way possible, when he didn't do the same for me. What was sad was, he never showed interest in me until he learned I had a brand new, 2001 Mitsubishi Galant. Deep down within, I think I knew he wanted to use me, but the thought of being in love and having him, at least pretend to be in love with me, kept me from taking the necessary steps I needed to protect myself. I should have told him to get the hell on and drive the same beat up Ford, Taurus, he wouldn't even give me a ride back to the dorm in one morning when I didn't have a way. Instead, I reached out for him. I was eager for him to hook me and reel me in.

It wasn't long before my car was being used as if it was a taxi cab, except I wasn't getting paid. My so-called boyfriend had gotten himself a DUI. His license was suspended. He approached me to ask me to be his personal chauffeur. We were sitting over to one of our co-workers house. I noticed his spirit seemed to be down as he wasn't talking much. He had his hand up to his head as if he was completely stressed out. He even got up and stormed out of the room, telling me he needed a little time to himself. When he came back in, I gently asked him if everything was okay. This was when the game began.

"Look, Tee," he said as calmly as he could. "I don't want to be a burden to you. The situation I am in has nothing to do with you. So, if you can't help me, I will understand." He paused his conversation to see if I would respond. As he expected, I took the bait he fed me. It made me feel good to think he was concerned about me. Such realization only made me want to do even more what he really wanted me to do. That was what he was counting on anyway. I didn't know. But he knew I would offer to do whatever it was he wanted me to do.

"Well," I said, a little too excitedly. "I will help you with whatever you need, baby. Just tell me what it is," I purred in his ear while massaging his leg. He inched a little closer to me, looking me directly in the eye. He sighed heavily, lowered his eyes to the floor, and acted as if he wasn't going to speak after all.

"Please, tell me," I begged. "I'm willing to help you. I want to be the person you can depend on."

After a few uncomfortable moments, he looked back at me and began to pour out his heart. "If I get caught driving by the police, I will be in serious trouble. It would help me out if you could take me a few places sometimes. I know you have classes and all, but I promise it would only be a few hours and not every day."

"That's it," I asked, surprised. The way he had been looking, I almost thought he wanted to ask me for a kidney or at least a hefty amount of cash. Sadly, if that had been the case, I would have stressed myself out trying to do what he wanted me to do. If I couldn't, it would've depressed me so much. I wouldn't have been able to focus on anything I needed to do for myself. It didn't dawn on me how sometimes, you had to say no to a person. It didn't mean you didn't care or that you were being mean. It meant you couldn't do it. I have learned since then, that people will sometimes get angry when you can't do what they want you to do. Even when they do get angry, it won't kill them. They will find someone else to do it or ultimately figure out how to do it on their own. Sometimes, they even appreciated you for having a backbone, not allowing them to walk all over you. It seemed as if no one truly wanted a person who constantly played the mousy victim role.

As much as I wanted to be there for my new man, I eventually became wearied. Every single day the good Lord sent, he wanted me to take him somewhere. It was way off from how he assured me it would be. I even missed classes several times because what he wanted didn't permit me to get back on time. If I hinted around that I needed to go to class, he pretended like he thought I was trying to leave him hanging. He knew I wouldn't be able to handle him thinking that way of me. He knew above all, I wouldn't want him to be mad at me.

Over the course of what I really assumed to be a relationship, nothing made me feel worse than the time I came to Winn-Dixie on his lunchbreak. There he was, as I approached the building, sitting in front of the store on his cellular phone. When he saw me, he got up from where he was sitting and went around to the side of the building to finish his conversation. It was pretty obvious to me it was another female that he was talking to. When he finally decided to get in the car, he asked me, "Why are you looking so pitiful?" I shrugged my shoulder in response. I didn't want to start an argument. I knew if I tried to defend myself, he would be on my case. "It's your job to take care of me," he then yelled. "I don't know why you are acting like such a broad."

"Why the hell are you calling me a broad?" I asked, matching his tone. "You got some fucking nerves."

He threw his hands up and responded, "I think you need to lower your voice when you are talking to me." As if he was my dad, I did exactly what he asked me to do. "At least I didn't call you a bitch," he then snapped.

"I'm just saying," I mumbled, my voice a lot lower. "There is no reason for you to call me out of my name. I never call you out of yours."

"That's because I never give you a reason to. You know what, I am out of here. Your ass just wants to argue." With that, he hopped back out of the car, slammed the door, and walked away from me without looking back.

I left his job that day in tears. But it was obvious I hadn't had enough of his cruel treatment. He wasn't going to treat me better, if I didn't demand it. Nothing changed on my part. So, nothing changed on his part. He continued to play Russian Roulette with my heart for as long as I allowed him to. This was all fun and games for him. His heart had safely made it to shore while my heart felt like it was about to drown in pain.

The next day, I parked in the same spot I had the day before, ready to take him to lunch. That day, he decided to stand me up. I angrily wiped the tears flowing down my face away as I sped off, after he refused to get in the car. It wasn't two minutes later before I heard my phone chiming as he was calling me. "Your attitude is really bad," he yelled into my ear when I answered the phone. "You promised me you would be there for me, but if you want to renege now, you can."

"I'm not reneging," I cried into the receiver. Before I could say anything else, he hung the phone up in my face.

"Dammit," I screamed as I threw my phone on the floor. We didn't talk after that for a couple of days. Every time I tried to call him, he wouldn't answer the phone. When I finally got the strength to stop calling him, he called me.

“Are you done tripping?” he asked me when I answered the phone. I didn’t say anything, so he continued talking. “Come pick me up. I want to take you out to dinner.” He had never before offered to take me anywhere, so the thought of us going out together caused me to perk up a little. Only when I got to his house, the plan changed completely. “What’s up?” he asked me as he sat in the passenger seat. He strapped on his seat belt, then turned to me, waiting on a response to his question.

I smiled. “Nothing is up,” I said as I drove off down the street.

“Look here, Tee,” he said. Take this right on Patton Street. I need to go to the nearest ABC Store.” My heart sank a little. I tried to remain optimistic, thinking after we left the ABC Store our next stop would be at Applebee’s. Applebee’s was the restaurant we agreed to go to.

I went back to the dorm that evening once more in tears. After taking him to several places all over Montgomery, he acted as if he was tired. "He stretched and yawned noisily. "Ugh, Tee, I'm going to have to take a raincheck, boo! I'm tired and just want to go back home. Let's do this another time, ok." I was so hurt. I felt like my body would explode with pain as I lay in bed that night. I cried so many tears until my head began throbbing like I had an aneurysm about to rupture. My spirit was broken, I thought beyond repair. I felt hopeless as a penny with a hole in it. He knew exactly what to say to make me feel that way. For the first time in years, I entertained the idea of wanting to take my life. I didn't think I could feel any lower than I did at that moment, even if I had wanted to. I couldn't understand why he would treat me so badly when I was doing everything he wanted me to do.

The truth finally comes out…

One television show I always counted on Nana allowing me to watch when I was a kid was, *The Cosby*

Show. She absolutely loved Bill and his wit. I didn't say so out loud but I loved the show as well. There was this one particular episode when the main characters played this game called Charades. They had to act and everybody else had to guess what they were doing. Whoever got the answer right obtained a point.

I wondered why the game was called Charades. So I took it upon myself to look it up. According to the Webster's dictionary, it relayed that in addition to the word charade being a game in pantomime, it also meant to be transparent or to pretend. Willie had been doing a lot of pretending, pretending to care about me. I also had been doing a lot of pretending. I had long figured out he wasn't really into me. I knew he was only using me for his personal gain. Because I didn't want to see it that way, I didn't do anything about it. I only allowed myself to become more deeply involved. But in every situation, there comes a point in time when the truth can no longer be denied or ignored. You have to deal with it head on. You have to know that it is the truth. That truth cannot be altered to suit anyone.

The painful truth came to my realization one afternoon. I'd had an argument with Willie, as usual. In ending the conversation, he relayed to me that I wasn't his girl. Silence fell over the phone line when he said those words to me. I literally did not know what to say. I could feel my eyes watering with tears.

"Look, Tee," he said after a few more moments of silence. "You are not my girl. We are working towards a relationship."

By then, I was all but sobbing as I turned onto Norman Bridge Road. "If I am not your girlfriend, why do you expect me to do so much for you?" I angrily asked. I didn't even attempt to hide the fact that I was crying.

He knew I was crying. Still, he laughed at me. "You said you would be there for me. If you want to be my girl, I got to see what you are made of. I don't need anybody who can't do simple little things for me."

"What about me?" I snapped. "What are you doing for me?"

"I deal with you and your extra-sensitive ass," he coldly stated. He then hung up the phone in my face.

By the time I got to the traffic light where I would turn onto the Boulevard, my vision was blurred with the tears that were still rolling down my cheeks. I didn't pay attention to the fact the traffic light was red. So I didn't stop. I ran the light. Consequently, I was side swiped by a lady who drove a Mercury Grand Marquis. My head hit the steering wheel as the airbag on the passenger side deployed. I could feel my nose throbbing when I lifted my head off the steering wheel. I sat there mute, scared out of mind to even move a muscle, not knowing if my body was even intact.

I heard the sirens of the police and paramedics approaching the scene. *Why is this happening*? I thought as I laid my head back down on the steering wheel. The owner of the Grand Marquis had already gotten out of her car. I saw her when she shot me a cold glare. Usually, I would have been upset about someone looking at me like that. That wasn't the case on this day. Her cold glare couldn't make me any worse than I already felt. A couple of minutes later, I heard tapping on my window. I looked to the side of me and saw an officer standing there, motioning for me to let the window down.

"Are you okay, ma'am?" he asked me. I didn't respond. I just stared at him. "Is this your driver's license on the rearview mirror, ma'am?" he then asked. I nodded, but still refused to talk. He reached over me and popped the hood to the car. "I'm going to disconnect your battery ma'am," he said in a take charge manner and disappeared seemingly into thin air.

An hour or so later, I watched with sadness as my car was towed away. Another officer had cleared all of the debris out of the road from where I'd had the wreck. I had a ticket in my hand for running the light. I was at fault for the accident. A claim would be made with my insurance company to fix the lady I'd collided with car. My tears had dried up. I was all cried out. I knew it wasn't the right move to call my so-called boyfriend. But I wanted so badly to take my mind off the accident I'd just had.

"I had an accident," I somberly spoke into the receiver when his voice came alive over the phone. There was silence, so I continued to talk. "Did you hear me?" I asked. "I wrecked my car."

"Yeah, I heard you," he muttered. "I'm trying to figure out what that has to do with me. I'm at work. I'll call you later."

Once more, there was silence. I had no idea what to say after that. He didn't leave me much time to think about it before hanging the phone up again in my face. Our conversations became even more limited after that day. The majority of the time, he rejected my phone calls when I tried to call him. When he did answer, he was very short with me. I knew I should have stopped calling. But I refused to acknowledge what I needed to do for myself. It was easy for anyone to see that I would've rather been in pain than to leave alone someone who wasn't treating me right.

About two weeks later, I wound up in the hospital. Stressing over a situation I couldn't change had caused me to have another asthma attack. I thought for sure, after everything I had done for him, he would come to visit me. I was wrong. He didn't care the least how sick I was. One of his co-workers, who had become friends with me as well, decided to defend my honor. He spoke to him about how cruel he was to me. The entire time he talked on the phone to him I knew it was the worst mistake ever. I knew it was only a matter of time before he called me and let me have it.

When he called, his words were, “I didn’t make you sick! I didn’t have to come see you.” I couldn’t have been more heartbroken. I didn’t want to talk to anybody about the pain I felt. I assumed they wouldn’t understand or would scold me for being so dumb. How could I look anyone in the face and relay to them how I had allowed myself to be someone’s personal fool? There was no way I could do it. So I did the only thing I knew to do. I didn’t have any notebook paper to write on. I grabbed a paper towel and began to pour out my heart in written words. It was the only thing that kept me sane when I felt so unworthy.

Dear heart of mine. You certainly are a trooper. You’re stronger than I gave you credit for. I don’t understand how you still work when you’ve been stomped so many times… how you continue ticking when your rhythm should be no more. It seems as if I should have a transplant. I just want somebody to open up my chest and take this pain filled heart away from me... the pain runs deeper than the Nile...it's width is as far as the East is from the West. Where is the healing? I need it to reach out its hand to me. People see me smiling. But Lord knows I'm dying inside. Dear heart of mine. Your steady pace lets me know I'm still alive. I don't understand because I feel so empty. I feel barren in the epitome of my soul, like a womb that can't produce a child.

When I looked up from writing my poem of sadness I looked at the television screen. The same breaking news was on every channel. The headline read, "America under attack." My voice caught in my throat and my eyes quickly filled with tears as I witnessed the twin towers in New York falling down to the ground. People were screaming and running for their lives. And I couldn't help saying as I witnessed it all unfolding right before my terror filled eyes,

"Oh, no! Jesus no! Oh, my God! Why is this happening?" I never knew that the time when I was feeling so heartbroken would be the day of 9/11. It wasn't a coincidence to me that the month and the date of the incident was 911. I knew that my pain was nothing compared to what the world was going through at that moment. So, I pushed my pain aside and allowed myself to think about all of the innocent lives that had been lost because of terrorists.

Life is What You Make of it

Wasted years

I left Alabama State University after the spring semester of 2001. I knew I wanted my degree, however, I wasn't focused on my studies the way I should have been. I allowed myself to fall into another rut of depression. It was true, I had been at this point so many times in my life. I knew what I needed to do. Nobody had to preach to me because whatever they had to say, I already knew. The problem was I lacked willpower. Instead of really putting in the work to get myself together, I took the easy way out. I quit.

As time went on, I began to learn of how some of the students I'd gone to college with were about to graduate. It pierced my heart in the worst way possible. I knew that could have been me. It should have been me about to receive something that was never out of my reach in the first place. It wasn't long before I was inflicted with enviousness. I didn't want to be around anyone who finished school because I thought they would look at me the same way I looked at myself… as a failure. I had the same opportunities as the next person, and therefore, knew I couldn't fault anyone for the bad decisions I made other than myself.

After engaging in a pity party for some time, I made a vow to myself that I was going to go back and finish what I started. One year turned into two years. Two years turned into three. Before I took the time to realize it, the year had gone from 2001 to 2005. I was no longer the young woman who no longer had any responsibilities other than going to school. I had gone out into the world and created more bills for myself by getting an apartment. It felt good to be out on my own. I soon realized, after all the bills started to pour in, that I would be in a better position if only I had finished my college education. Since I had left school, I really hadn't done too much. The only thing I had to account for in the past years was getting my heart broken again from another guy I should have never involved myself with. If it was one thing I was good at, it was definitely with picking the wrong guy.

A quick fix

In the year 2002, I met a guy who I quickly fell hard for. Our relationship didn't last long because he got into trouble and found himself in jail. I wrote letters to him while he was incarcerated. When he got out, he called to let me know he was okay. I was under the impression that we were going to be together. I waited by the phone for his call to let me know we were going to be a couple. We had talked about it before he got locked up. But that day never came.

Just when I started to feel bad about the situation, I got the sad news that he'd been killed in a motorcycle accident. That was news I didn't find out until one week after his funeral. By that time, I'd gotten another job. As I stood at work, thinking of him, with tears of sadness streaming down my face, I was once again feeling like my world was going to end.

There was no closure to our relationship. It seemed to be too much to handle. I even had dreams about him where I was calling out for him. He could hear me calling him because he answered me. His voice was distant, but he answered. Right when I was about to reach out to touch him, he suddenly disappeared. I screamed for him louder. I even became frantic. No answer I received. I woke up sadder than I was before I went to sleep. With my face wet with tears, I leaned over and retrieved his obituary from under my pillow. I pictured the sadness emulated in his mother's eyes when I dropped by her house after finding out about his death. She burst into tears when she saw me. Once she was able to calm down, she handed me a copy of the obituary. I glared at the picture on the front, thinking how unfair it was that he was gone. "I didn't get to say goodbye," I said before bursting into a gut wrenching sob. His mother comforted me as well as she could, considering that her heart too was broken.

I finally got the nerve, after sitting with his mother for a couple of hours, to ask her what had happened. "He hit a water hydrant… knocked it out of the ground," she sadly recollected. "Had it not been for just a small piece of skin holding his head in place, he would've been completely decapitated." I sat there with a fresh set of tears streaming down my face. I wasn't expecting her to tell me that. It was definitely too much for me.

Nearly two months passed. I was still feeling the blues. Reminiscing on our last conversation had initially numbed the pain. I even smiled. Now it wasn't working so much. I needed something to take away the pain I felt. It was getting the best of me. I was hardly functioning the way I should have been. As much as I didn't want it to be the truth, my friend was gone. He wasn't coming back.

I decided to get a second job at the Waffle House in an effort to take my mind off of how badly I was hurting. That was one of the worst decision I ever made. I'd never been in a work environment where the servers could get into it with other servers while guests were in the store. When they weren't arguing with each other, sometimes they got into it with customers. Yes, you read that right. Yet, they didn't get fired. Their job was secure as if they hadn't done anything wrong at all.

It took me a minute to get used to calling the orders. The cook had no problem with embarrassing me, if I didn't say it right. He made me repeat it over and over again until I got it right. Even if I called the order right and I wasn't standing on my mark, he wouldn't prepare the food. There was one particular cook who all together refused to cook any of my orders. He was upset with me because, in his attempt to make passes at me, I wouldn't give in to what he wanted. That was to have sex with him in the back room. I can't say how many tips he caused me to miss out on because of his desire to be petty. I approached him nicely and told him I had an order. At first he didn't respond. He eventually said, "Well, I'm sorry but I'm doing my prep work!"

It didn't take me long to realize that this job wasn't going to cut it for me. But I tried to hold on. I had a few regular customers who kept me on my toes with laughter. And they left good tips. I guess that could be accounted to the fact that I worked at the store in Hope Hull, Alabama. My location was only a few minutes away from the

Hyundai Plant. Many of the workers decided to come to the Waffle House on their lunch break. They had big appetites and were willing to leave big tips if you got their orders right.

There was one guy who came in and sat in my section. I had gotten pretty good at calling the orders. I asked him if he wanted anything on his hash browns. He looked at me and smiled, “Why yes, I do, you pretty little thang, you.” I was expecting him to say, smothered, covered, and chunked. Instead he told me, “I want my hash browns tied, slapped, and talked to dirty. You think you can fix em up like that for me?” I couldn’t help laughing. He just didn’t know, his wit helped me to deal with the job as long as I had. That was until one night the worst thing that could have ever transpired happened. Business was slow. I’d done all of my side work. A couple of guys came in that I’d gotten used to associating with. They sat in my section. I knew what they wanted.

(We didn't have to summon the cook to make waffles for us. We had the right to get some batter and put it in the waffle iron ourselves).

I gave them their waffles, deciding to sit down at the table with them. I had a big cup of hot chocolate that was too hot for me to even attempt to drink at that moment. I found myself dosing off several minutes later. I thought I was dreaming when a guy came into the store with a twelve gauge shotgun. He had a shirt tied around his face. He stood before the cook, with the gun drawn, ordering him to give him the money out of the register. I wasn't sure, but this seemed a little too surreal to be a dream. Ever so gently, I tapped the guy next to me on the shoulder. I leaned over and whispered in a panicked tone, "Are we being robbed?" He nodded, yes, in response. But he never uttered a word.

Oh, my God, I frantically thought as I cowered down in the booth. I hid my face as best as I could in my apron.

Luckily, the robber only wanted the money out of the register. He didn't come for any of the servers. Still, I was shaken up to the point where I poured the whole cup of hot chocolate in my lap and didn't even feel it. If I wasn't sure before, I knew then that was my last night at the Waffle House.

I watched as the detectives swarmed the tiny little diner. They ransacked the place and asked for the surveillance tape. Only a few minutes later, the store manager walked in with her eyes bugged. It didn't take long to realize she didn't care one iota about us. Even when I told her I was too shaken up to stay, she insisted that I did. At the end of my shift, I walked out of the Waffle House. I got in my car, drove off, and never looked back.

As far as thinking about my friend, I was doing a lot better. The right medicine truly came along, I thought, when I met this guy I was working with at my primary job. It was my only job now, since I'd quit the Waffle House.

He turned out to be my emotional Tylenol, extra strength, I might add.

Truthfully speaking, it wasn't my intention for anything to get started between us. Just having someone to talk to on lunchbreak seemed to be enough to keep my mind from aimlessly wandering to the death of my friend. After a few friendly conversations, I started to feel some type of way about him. Whatever it was, I soon realized that whenever he came around, I felt butterflies in my stomach. My mind was telling me to take my time. My heart said otherwise. "Girl, make him yours before someone else scoops him up," it warned me.

Unfortunately, for me, I followed my heart. I already knew the heart wouldn't always tell you the right things to do. But I felt like this light-skinned guy was perfect for me. Even though he was eleven years older, he was pretty easygoing. Our conversations never seemed to be out of sync. He was quick to let me know that, though he was older, he'd never met a woman like me. The fact I could write appeared to turn him on even more. Sometimes, he sat and watched me write in my journals. He even got the nerve to ask me, "What you be writing about in them journals of yours?"

I smiled, and replied, "Whatever comes to mind."

"Well, I would like for you to read them to me some time," he said, pushing the issue. Turned out, he was hoping I would've put something in one of the journals to incriminate myself, something that would show him how I wasn't all I was cracked up to be.

The same brick wall (Two years later…)

The year was now 2005. I was still tangled up with this guy. Initially, in 2003, we talked for about five months. He eventually broke it off because come to find out, he had another woman who he had a child with.

I was upset when I found out he had another woman. The word was, they had been talking about getting married. I was too ashamed to talk to mom about my latest situation or anyone, for that matter. I'm sure they would have wondered why I didn't see the warning signs. I pined over him for a while. Then, I turned my attention to my Aunt Mary (Nana).

The year was now 2004. Slowly, her health began to decline right after we celebrated her 93rd birthday. Only recently, she'd been diagnosed with cancer. I was so overcome with grief knowing this but did my best to not show how I felt. Every day I made sure to go to her house so that I could help mom with her. It did my soul good to sit next to her bed for hours, reminiscing on past years, and savoring the final moments of her life with her. Even when it got to the point where the cancer had metastasized to her brain, and she talked out of her head, she made sure to tell me and Tamara, “God is going to bless ya’ll for taking care of me.”

Sadly, my Nana died on November 13, 2004. I knew the moment she slipped into eternal rest because, even though I wasn’t at the hospital when it happened, I felt the emptiness in my heart. Her death took its toll on me. I was sure to write a tribute to her in her obituary.

As I sat with my family at her home going service, I thought on all the times I thought she was being mean to me when I was a child. I chuckled at some of the memories as my cousin, Crystal, stood up to the front of the church singing, “I’m Going Up a Yonder.” We then marched out of the church behind the pallbearers and the flower bearers.

Things will never be the same, I solemnly thought.

I viewed her body for the last time at her grave. The funeral directors decided to open the casket one more time so that one of her granddaughters, who didn’t make it when the funeral first started, could see her.

"Who else wants to see her?" they asked before closing the lid for the final time.

"I do," I said, full of emotion as I stepped up to the casket. I reached down and touched her face. I stared at her hard. Moments later, I started to tremble and sob uncontrollably as one of the church members grabbed me and hugged me close.

It took a while. Slowly, I started to feel better about losing my Nana. I took consolation in the fact she was no longer in pain and was in a better place. I was even more elated when I learned the guy I had been involved with had parted ways with the woman he'd been involved with.

Deep down, I knew I shouldn't have gotten back involved with him. I'm sure you all know that I did it anyway. Beforehand, we used to simply meet up with each other. Now it was different. I had my own place. He often came over to spend the night. At first, everything seemed to be okay. He was very affectionate. He appeared to truly care about me. That was until I mentioned doing something for someone I considered to be a friend. It would have been okay, if the friend had been a female, like me. Since the friend was a man, and he wasn't gay, he wasn't having it.

"I don't want to hear shit about nobody who is just supposed to be a friend," He pretty much came unglued. His sudden change of behavior shocked me. I sat on the couch staring at him with my mouth wide open. The menacing look correlating from the cornea of his eyes and spreading abroad let me know I had better cut my talking out about doing something for any other guy besides him.

Accusations then showed up on the scene. He started accusing me of everyone he could think of. At one point, he even accused me of getting too cozy with his oldest son who was just a teenager. I don't know what kind of person he thought I was. I had never once given him a reason to think I was being unfaithful.

For starters, I didn't go anywhere. Neither did I really have any friends. That was just the way he wanted it to be. Yet, he still wanted to believe somehow, I was messing around with someone. My neighbors who lived down the hall from me and across the hall from me, became suspects. They were males, leaving my insecure boyfriend under the impression that every chance I got, I was over to either one of their houses getting it on. I did everything I could to convince him I wasn't doing anything. No matter what I said, it was never enough to ease the ramblings of his wayward mind.

One day when I came home from work, I noticed he had moved all of his belongings into my apartment. He called me that day at work. I made sure to answer right away so he wouldn't think anything.

"Hello," I answered in my most chipper voice.

"Hello," he responded. "I hope you are having a good day at work."

I didn't say anything and that was his cue to continue talking.

"Listen," he said. "I was just calling because I got a few boxes in your house. I didn't want you to come home and see them without me letting you know. It's just a few things though."

"Well, that's fine," I responded, hurrying up to end the call. The last thing I wanted was to get caught on the phone. I was definitely going to get written up, if that had been the case. When I got home, what turned out to be a few boxes was everything he owned. He'd even taken the liberty to hang all of his clothes up in my closet. I walked into the bedroom to find him sitting on the bed looking sad.

"Look, Tamyra," he said, reaching out for me to sit on his lap. "I just need to stay here with you for a couple of months so I can save up some money and then, I'm going to get my own place."

I was okay with that until one day, about three months later, I asked him if he had been looking for a place. I didn't mean any harm by asking him that. I was only trying to show that I was concerned about him.

"Why the hell you asking me that?" he snapped. "You must want me out of your house or something?" Once again, his behavior caught me by surprise. I wound up apologizing to him when I knew I hadn't done anything wrong. He didn't forgive me right away. He acted like he was angry with me for at least a couple of days. I knew then, not to ever ask him that again. I guess he would've just told me when he had found a place of his own.

That day never came. I soon realized, he never had any intention of moving out on his own. I felt violated. I clearly remembered telling him, in the beginning, that I didn't want to live together. He'd walked up to me only about a week later, after we started back talking, and asked me, "So are we going to live together?"

"No," I answered in a blunt tone.

"Okay," he said, backing away with his hands up in defense. I glared at him with my arms akimbo.

When I thought about how he lashed out at me the first time I asked him about getting his own apartment, I decided not to say anything about my discovery. I let it go just the same as I did so many other times when it came to us. The accusations continued. He wanted to know my every move, even if I went to lunch with any male co-workers at work. With the help of a friend, who was a little more knowledgeable than I was when it came to guys, it didn't take me long to realize all of the things he was accusing me of were things he probably was doing to me behind my back. I didn't say anything to him, even when I started to notice his phone would ring all times of the night.

I asked myself, *Why do I keep running into the same brick wall?*

All I wanted was for someone to truly care about me. *What is it about me that always send the wrong guy my way*? I silently thought. I couldn't pretend like I was really happy, although I knew I wouldn't be able to let him go. Long had he started to call me all kinds of foul names. "Bitch" seemed to be his favorite one of all.

The name calling turned into him hitting me. I could take it, I thought, until late one morning, I was doing some typing. He came into the living room and decided to watch a movie. He tried with all of his might to distract me from what I was doing. He always seemed intimidated when I was doing something that didn't involve him.

When he saw that trying to distract me wasn't going to work, he picked a fight. Pretty soon, I couldn't concentrate at all. I found myself arguing back and forth with him. He seemed to be a little more irate than normal. I decided it was in my best interest to try to get away from him.

Everywhere I went, he followed me until he had me cornered.

"Oh, my God, he's going to hit me," I mouthed to myself, completely terrified. As soon as I said those words, he threw me on the floor, got down on one knee, and started punching me. I balled myself into a fetal position to try to ward off some of the blows. Then he started kicking me, harder and harder as he thought about how angry he was.

"Please, stop!" I screamed. However, my screams fell on deaf ears. He continued to kick me until he was satisfied that I'd had enough. After it was all over, I lay on the floor still, crying my eyes out. It wasn't until the next day, I noticed I had a big black bruise on my back. I don't think I ever felt so low in my life before. No matter what I had been through, no one had ever put their hands on me. I kept thinking to myself, *He saw me lying on the floor. I was defenseless, and yet, he continued to kick me over and over again.*

What happened that day when all I wanted to do was get some writing done turned out to be a sad matinee I had to see in my mind so many times. I couldn't get it out of my head no matter how hard I tried. There was another time after that that he actually threw rocks at me. I thought, *I wouldn't even throw a rock at a dog. I can't believe he thinks less of me than he thinks of a dog.* Later on when I got the courage to ask him why he would throw rocks at me, he became very angry and told me. "Those weren't rocks. They were pebbles. Why you always got to try to make things seem worse than they really are?"

A life outside of my own

What I thought would finally be the relationship I longed for all of my life, turned out to be an on and off type situation. No matter how hard I tried for things to be right, peace didn't last very long when it came to me and Chris who I refused to kick to the curb. By now, I'd been called everything in the book. When he felt that wasn't enough to completely shatter my self-esteem, he looked for other ways to do it. Things I told him in confidence about my upbringing, he started to use against me.

"The only thing you will ever be good for is someone screwing," he said. "That's why your mom left you when you were a child because she already knew what a bitch you were going to be. You ain't nobody, bitch, and you never will be."

"You know what," I finally said with tears streaming down my face. "I am so sick and tired of you calling me out of my name. I'm tired of you accusing me of other people. I'm just tired of you. All I have ever done is be nice to you. I guess calling me out of my name wasn't good enough for you. No, you had to go and throw what I told you about my mom up in my face. I want you to get your stuff and get the fuck out of my apartment."

"Fuck you and your mammy," he then responded. "If I was her, I would've left you, too, and I ain't going anywhere. I'm sick and tired of your crazy ass thinking you're going to use this apartment against me whenever you get mad. You think you all high and mighty. I'm just trying to bring you back down so you'll understand me better. I tell you what, bitch, give me back my two hundred dollars I gave you for the power bill and then, I will leave."

"What do you mean?" I snapped. "That is the first time you have ever helped me with a bill since you have been here. The whole time you've been here, I have paid all the bills. And then, on top of that, you expect me to give you money, too."

For a minute, he just stared at me. I think he really believed I had lost my ever loving mind. I had never heard such nonsense as a woman having to take care of a man, when all he had to offer to her was his penis. He was getting all he wanted from me as far as sex was concerned, so I didn't understand why he thought he had to get more from me just because we were sleeping together. He wanted me to be his mother, lover, chauffeur, and everything else in between.

Finally, he said, "I swear you ain't shit. I don't know what I was thinking about getting involved with you. Every other woman I have ever had has taken good care of me, cooked for me, and gave me money…"

"Why should I give you money?" I interrupted. "You see I have this apartment that you don't help me with…" I allowed my voice to trail off. The only thing I was getting was a headache from arguing with him. Even if he understood what I was saying, he was going to pretend like he didn't. I went in the room to lay down while he continued to mumble under his breath, talking about me as if I was the scum of the earth.

"You one crazy ass, stupid ass, retarded ass, nothing ass, stanking bitch!" These were the words I heard echoing through the living room wall as I tried my best to drown out how badly the words hurt.

A few months later, I discovered that I was pregnant. I was now working the nightshift. I noticed I was extremely fatigued before the shift really got started. In fact, I could barely walk up and down the halls. I had never felt this way before. So I knew something had to be wrong. The next day, I went to Wal-Mart and purchased a home pregnancy test. When no one was paying attention, I went into the bathroom at my sister's apartment, to take the test. Almost immediately, the two lines appeared, indicating that I was indeed pregnant. I couldn't believe what my eyes were seeing, so I bought two more tests, different brands from what I'd previously bought and took those as well. The same results showed on the little stick. I knew then, it had to be true.

"Oh, my God," I whispered with my hand over my mouth. "I'm going to be a mom!" I began to cradle my stomach to see if I would feel anything. I smiled to myself as I thought of if I would have a boy or girl. I'd always assumed I wanted a girl so I could dress her up in the little cute frilly outfits and style her hair in many ways. She would be so spoiled, would for sure have a floor sized dollhouse and kitchen set, two of the toys I'd always wanted as a child, but I never got.

The next week, I found out I was eight weeks and four days pregnant. As I looked at my baby on the computer screen at my first ultrasound he was no bigger than a peanut. When I heard the heartbeat, my smile was never ending. I had another ultrasound before I was sixteen weeks pregnant. I didn't think I would learn the sex of the baby. I was surprised when the ultrasound tech asked me, "Would you like to know the sex of this baby?"

"You mean you can tell me now?" I asked excitedly.

She simply smiled. With her mouse, she made a circle around his private area. "You see that?" she asked, pointing? "That's his penis. You're going to have a little boy."

"Oh, my God," I squealed, forgetting all about the fact I thought I had always wanted a girl. Since I now knew I would be having a boy, all I could think about was boy names, boy clothes, and boy toys. The first thing I bought for my baby boy was a rainforest bouncer. He would love it. I wanted the absolute best for him.

Throughout my pregnancy, I experienced a lot of highs and lows. I didn't have the crazy cravings I knew some pregnant women to have. Neither was I mean the way I knew some pregnant women to be. I had to be the friendliest pregnant person ever. I always had a smile on my face. That was until I got into it with Chris. I should've known better than to think just because I was carrying his child that would stop him from abusing me. He continued to call me out my name, even ripped my shirt off of me one day because he was angry I'd discovered how he was messing with another woman on his job. As he was preparing himself to drive off, I asked him, "How could you do this to me? You see that I am pregnant."

He looked at me, with his face twisted. "I don't give a damn. The motherfucker can die for all I care," he said. I stood there, watching him, with tear streaked eyes, of course, as he floored it, leaving out of the parking lot. I would've rather stood naked in the freezing cold, welcoming hypothermia with open arms, than to feel the chilliness from his heartless words. His words froze my heart with sadness. It was all too much.

Intuition can be a powerful thing and mine wasn't substandard by a long shot. I always knew something had to be going on between him and someone else. For one, all of the women on his job hated me with a passion. There was no basis to their anger. They didn't know anything about me. He had them fooled, convincing them that I was about as conniving as they came. I tried relentlessly to defend myself to them. I eventually became weary with doing that. I just argued with him back and forth, wanting to know why he was telling lies on me.

"It seems to me you want to portray yourself as a victim!" I screamed at him one day, after he told me what people at his job were saying about me. He only said those things to me when he wanted to further convince me that I wasn't being the woman to him that I should have been. Supposedly, others had noticed it as well.

"I am a victim," he had the audacity to say. "You know better than I do that you are crazy as hell. DHR didn't want to put you in the crazy house for no reason. There had to be a reason. But, naw bitch, you want everyone to think you are a fucking angel. Angel my ass, bitch."

A few months later, when I was almost seven months pregnant, I received a phone call from an unknown number. "Hello," I said, as I picked up the receiver.

"Hello," the voice on the other end came alive. "I'm just going to get to the point. I want to know what you and Chris had to talk about the other day." I felt my heart as it began to beat rapidly. I thought this part of my life was over when I no longer had to deal with the little young psychotic woman he had decided to mess around on me with. When he discovered she was at the job he worked at to perform community service, he should have known then not to mess with her. He was thinking with his head, just not the one with the brain.

Not again, I thought as I listened to this woman breathing in my ear. Words cannot describe how upset I was, but I decided I wasn't going to let her see me sweat.

“What does it have to do with you?” I asked. “Why do you want to know what we were talking about?”

“He’s my boyfriend. That’s what it has to do with me. In fact, I’m three months pregnant from him.”

I began to hyperventilate. There was nothing more I could say, nothing more I wanted to say. With shaking hands, I placed the receiver back in the cradle. I couldn’t stop the tears flowing at the speed of lightning.

This can’t be happening! No, she didn’t just say that to me! The caller ID said Janna Hinton. That’s the same girl whose number I saw programmed in his phone. She called him one day on his off day wanting him to come up to the job. He swore to me nothing was going on. Oh, my God, he lied to me... he fucking lied to me. My thoughts were on a rampage.

At first when I asked him about the girl, he denied it. Finally, he admitted to it, making sure to tell me if I had been taking care of him the way I was supposed to, he wouldn't have had to go and get another woman.

The next couple of months, I spent in a very depressed state of mind. I literally felt like I was nobody. I never thought I would be a woman who would get pregnant from a guy and he leave before the baby is born. This was the kind of mess I felt sorry for other women about. How in the world did I become that woman?

One thing I was certain about, I now knew that was the reason he'd accused me so many times. He knew what he was doing. He figured since he was getting away with it without raising any alarms with me, I had to be doing the same thing, too. The only thing that made me feel better was when I felt my baby kick. I put my hand on my stomach where I felt the kick and I talked to my baby. "I promise I am going to always love you," I said, wiping the tears from my eyes with my other hand. "And I know you will always love me, too."

As the end of my pregnancy approached, most of the time, I couldn't get in contact with his father. Every time I tried to call him, his phone went straight to voicemail. When I started to have contractions at exactly midnight on August 25, 2008, I had to wait until later in the day, when he was at work, before I was able to call him. Tamara and my cousin, Robert, loaded me up in the car. They rushed me up the dark road, from White Hall to Baptist South Hospital in Montgomery, Alabama.

By the time we got to the hospital, the contractions were already two minutes apart. When I got to labor and delivery, my nurse helped me into bed. She proceeded to check my cervix. I was two centimeters dilated and progressing pretty quickly. My water hadn't completely broken. But it was seeping.

"Can I please have the Epidural now?" I managed to ask in between the contractions. *I know he is with someone else, but I sure do wish he was here to hold my hand through this. Why do I have to feel like the other woman at a time when I really need him to be here for me*? I thought.

I dared not let the nurse know for a second that I was having these kinds of thoughts. I told her with a smile, "I can handle this on my own," when she'd asked me, "Are you going to have this baby alone?"

Christian started having dips in his heart. And he constantly kicked so hard that the belts came off of my stomach. Every hour or so the nurse came into LDR4 (labor delivery room 4) where I was and helped me to turn from my left side to my right side or from my right side to my left side.

"Your baby doesn't like how you are laying," she said to me with a smile. I smiled back and drifted back off to sleep. I was very depressed and wanted to sleep as much as possible. My nurse then gave me something through the IV to make me dilate faster.

"We just want you to have this sweet baby boy quicker," she said to me, making sure she didn't alarm me. By the time I was seven centimeters dilated, my doctor came and broke my water all the way. Within one hour I jumped from seven centimeters dilated to nine-and-a-half centimeters dilated.

At 1:15 in the afternoon, my son was born. He weighed exactly eight pounds and was twenty-one inches long. I smiled when I heard his first cry. It was the sweetest sound ever. No other sound has ever come close to how it made me feel.

After he was wiped off a little and suctioned, the nurse put him on my chest. "Give him a kiss, momma," she said with a big smile on her face. I reached down and touched the bundle wiggling on top of me. As I looked him in the face, I was sure to grab his little hand into mine. He looked at me and I leaned over, giving him a kiss on the forehead.

The nurse grabbed him, swaddled him in a blanket and took him to the nursery.

The doctor then delivered the placenta and sowed me up. Christian had torn me, as he was a big baby. His feet were so big that the newborn socks were too small.

My eyes lit up like a Christmas tree when the nurse brought him to me, after I was moved into a room on the second floor. I sat upright in the bed as she gently lifted him and handed him to me.

“Hi, there,” I said as I held him close to my heart. I was so engulfed in spending time with my newborn that I almost didn’t hear the knocking on the door. Whoever it was knocked again. He then, walked into the room. It was his father. To my surprise, he seemed excited about seeing the baby. He sat on the edge of the bed with me and moved the blanket wrapped around our son so he could get a closer look. “Do you want to hold him?” I asked.

"Yes, if it is okay with you," he answered, reaching for him.

Time for a change

It would have meant the world to me if things could have remained the way they were when my son's father saw him for the first time. I sat on the bed watching him hold the baby. He was so gentle, far from the monster he had been to me before and during my pregnancy. As he sat there, gently rocking him, he said, "Christian, I think you should name him Christian."

Christian was a beautiful name to me. I named my baby, Christian Deshawn Walker. Deshawn was his father's middle name.

He eventually came off of his high of having a newborn baby. The next day, he was yelling at me. He stormed out of the hospital room without as much as a goodbye. He'd gone to the doctor's office with the other girl he'd gotten pregnant while she had her ultrasound. I didn't want to be bitter, but it pissed me off. I couldn't help thinking how I almost had to have a C-section, had to push for a whole hour before I dilated the last half-centimeter before it was time for the doctor to come and deliver my baby. I went through that alone. He wasn't there for me but willing he was to go to an ultrasound with the woman he'd cheated on me with. Naturally, he thought I shouldn't have had any feelings about it. "I'm here now, dammit, he said. "Why you got to be so fucking ungrateful?"

After he left, he didn't call to see if we had a way home from the hospital. It was the worst feeling ever to have to call mom to pick me up from the hospital. I tried hard not to worry about it as I dressed Christian in one of his brand new outfits. I sat with a heavy heart, holding him in my arms, waiting for the photographer to come and take his newborn pictures. I then strapped him in his carrier. We were on our way home. We didn't see his father again until Christian was three-weeks-old.

Once again, he played the role of the loving father until he was out of sight. The disappearing acts became more frequent. Soon afterwards, he started to deny my son by telling everyone he could get to listen, that I was trying to pin another man's child on him. But he was willing to accept the child he'd cheated on me and gotten.

My heart was broken. I was depressed, tired, stressed, and overwhelmed all at the same time. I didn't know the first thing about taking care of a newborn baby. I did my very best. As my baby lay next to me at night, I cried. I thought about all of the lonely days I spent without my biological mother and father in my life. I didn't want this to be my son's fate. What was even worse, was that I had hand-picked the same guy to father my child as my father had been to me… a deadbeat.

My whole life, up until the point I became a mother, I had dealt with depression and low self-esteem. It seemed to be a part of me, just as big of a part of me as the veins and vessels in my body. I tried to escape its strong grip. I wanted to be free. I wanted true happiness, not just drippings of what I once thought was happiness. You see, the crust of my heart was so deeply wounded that the drippings of happiness didn't have the capacity to irrigate it with what it needed. It was hard, just the same as the crust of the earth would be if it went for an extended amount of time without water.

I realized it was time for a change. I not only had myself to think about now. I had a baby who couldn't take care of himself. It was time for me to put aside everything that had ruffled me the wrong way. It was time for me to fall down on my knees and pray. It was time for me to ask God for the guidance necessary to be the type of mother my son needed. The type of mother he himself demanded me to be.

That precious little boy He loaned to me to bring up under His word, to nurture, nourish, and protect, needed me. If I gave him back to God, I didn't have to worry about my issues taking over his life. The moment I gave birth, it didn't matter what I had gone through in life or how it hurt me. I was now secondary. My child had to come first. In order for him to thrive, I had to turn off the blues. I couldn't let the depression sing to me any longer. I had to create my own melody. The melody that said I was fearfully and wonderfully made. That melody would saturate my soul. It brought about healing at last. It was not beneath me to have a healthy self-esteem. If only I trusted in God. He had the ability to raise me up.

The LORD is close to the brokenhearted; he rescues those whose spirits are crushed,

Psalms 34:18 (New Living Translation)

Reincarnated

Together, hand in hand, Christian and I walked through the grassy area of Vaughn Road Park. He was now four-years-old. With strides of excitement, we made our way to the playground to engage in an afternoon of high octane fun. He'd just asked me right when I pulled into the first available parking spot and killed the engine, "Mommy, will you push me on the swing, please?" I peered at him sitting in the back, still fastened in his seatbelt. A smile found its way across my lips. Sometimes, it was hard for me to accept that I was a mother, and I had taken part in making such a handsome little boy. Having a child of my own was an awesome responsibility, one that I actually enjoyed and wanted to get better at with time.

"Yes, I will push you, baby," I answered as he looked at me with curious eyes. He offered me his own little crooked smile, thanking me for being what he called a, "fun mommy." He unfastened the seatbelt and immediately opened the back door. Before I had time to put one foot out of the car, he'd already hopped out and took off running up one of the paths leading to the playground.

"Wait for me, boy!" I yelled. *Anxious little rascal*, I thought as I rushed to catch up with him. But as soon as Christian spotted a game of football being played, the whole idea of pushing him on the swing was rendered null and void. He stopped in his tracks, watching with anxious eyes until he couldn't take it anymore. He looked at me pleadingly. Those brown eyes with the curly long eyelashes were asking me if he could join the boys he saw playing his favorite sport. Once my eyes relayed to him that it was okay, he ran as fast as his legs would take him over to play. I sat down in the grass to watch, not wanting to let my precious baby out of my sight. His laughs were beyond infectious. They echoed throughout the park as he threw the ball with a bunch of kids who were total strangers.

Later, he opted to be the running back, successfully making his way through the scramble several times. Soon enough, I was laughing too at how adorable he looked with the football clutched tightly in his arms. He held onto it for dear life, running the last yards before reaching the designated end zone and yelling to the top of his lungs, "Touchdown!"

I noted, while sitting there as if I had the best seats in a football stadium, that he had a lot of heart playing the game. I admired his short frame gracefully zipping back and forth. I couldn't help wondering, *How does he know so much about football?* Above all, he was happy to have someone to play with. I was just happy to see him smiling.

Slowly, the sun began to meander its way behind the clouds. The sky acquiesced to turn an orange-red color. Night was in full effect as it prepared to release its stars abroad. Lightning bugs did their thing. The mosquitoes were vicious. I stood up and brushed the grass off of my jeans. Then, I saw the sadness disseminating throughout the irises of Christian's eyes. Night coming on to the scene was the cue for the other boy's father's to whisk them away to their perspective vehicles and head home for the evening. Having to say goodbye to his newfound friends, caused Christian's demeanor to shift from that of cheerful to melancholy.

"It's time for us to go, too," I said. I watched him watching the boys until they were out of sight. He walked over to me, head hung low. He lightly tapped me on the shoulder and calmly asked, "Mom, where is my dad?"

Totally caught off guard, that question appeared to be a thrusting punch to my ribs. I found myself doubled over in pain, not knowing what to say. I was almost too ashamed to look my child in the eyes. All kinds of thoughts ran a marathon through my head as I considered the best way to answer my son.

Do I poison the well, I silently wondered? My eyes ran over with hate. For a second, I felt like my son deserved to know what a deadbeat his father was. He deserved to know that he wasn't making any kind of efforts whatsoever to be in his life. It wasn't that he couldn't have been in his life. He chose not to be. Like any mother would, I only wanted the best for my offspring. When a mother witnesses her child hurting, it hurts her as well. My heart ached profusely for my sweet baby who still stood, waiting for an answer to the simple question he'd asked me.

I chose not to scar my son any further than he already was. Trust me I wasn't doing his father any favors by sparing him. But it was obvious that Christian was aware that a vital part of his life was missing. I didn't want to make the pain fester by saying things I shouldn't say, even if what I was saying was the true. "Would your motives be pure," I asked myself as I dismissed the thought of saying anything negative about my son's father.

"Christian, mommy is sorry, baby, but I don't know where your dad is," I softly responded, at last. I looked up briefly to notice his eyes were fastened deeply into my eyes. I would have preferred to bare the pain there was to gain from a third-degree burn than to have my child looking at me in the manner in which he looked at me. It pierced my heart even more having to tell him that I didn't know where his father was. No words he said. He simply fell into my arms. I rubbed the small of his back as he whimpered. It took every bit of self-control I had not to break down and cry too, or call that bastard of a father of his up and curse him out. He thought he was hurting me by not having anything to do with Christian. His desire to see me in pain was much stronger than his desire to be a father to his child. I thought it was sad how he didn't realize that it was his son, his own flesh and blood who was taking the loss.

Christian didn't dwell on it for too long. I couldn't have been happier. As a peace offering, I bought him an ice cream cone from Brewster's. A smile was born across his lips as he greedily licked the birthday cake flavored ice cream, allowing it to get all over his face in the process. His eyes glistened with delight, obviously thankful I'd bought him a treat.

"Whew, I said to myself, thinking I was off the hook. That was until several months later, Christian asked me again, "Mom, where is my dad?" There was no way I could ever prepare myself for that question. It didn't matter how many times he asked me. Each time made me feel as if my breath was cut off by a blood clot nesting in my lungs. I was fed up with having to feed him the same tired lines I'd told him before. It always seemed to make anger erupt out of me like lava out of a volcano. Eventually, those words were going to lose their strength. I would have to dig deeper into my soul to pacify Christian's growing desire to have his father in his life. No matter what I did, I couldn't be a father to him. He longed to have someone who he could tackle and build things with. I was a nurturer. I didn't have that tough nature he had growing inside of him. I couldn't teach Christian how to be a man. I was his mother, not his father.

"My dad doesn't love me, does he," Christian finally asked, after I'd repeatedly run the same line on him. Though small in stature, he'd put two and two together. He was wise enough to know there was something I wasn't telling him.

"Awwww, don't say that baby," I cried. My voice completely broke as tears ran down my face. "I'm sure he loves you. He just.... well... he.... the thing is baby." I rambled on nonstop for the right words to say. Once again,

Christian was in my arms. I felt his little heart pulsating with sadness as he hugged me tightly.

"I'm not going to be depressed. I refuse to be depressed. I rebuke depression." I said these words over and over again to myself in the following weeks to come. I felt my spirit descending like Jack and Jill down the hill. I'd done all I knew to distract Christian from asking me about his father, not because I didn't think he had a right to know. I couldn't stand to see the sadness in his eyes. I realized I had a hand in hurting my own child because I'd chosen the wrong person to have a child with. The train table I bought with his name monogrammed on the front to soothe my conscience, only worked for a short period of time. He'd always eventually ask me again those hard questions I didn't know how to answer.

In the few years he had been alive, Christian didn't have anybody but me, my twin sister, and my other sisters and brother. He didn't know any of his family on his father's side. This was déjà vu in my eyes. I hadn't known any of my family on my father's side either. We'd traded places. My son was me, reincarnated. The child I once was had transformed, wounds and all, into an adult. But behind the shell, I still quivered from the cool breeze of disappointment. It was a hard pill to swallow, realizing that the answers Christian wanted now I'd never gotten as a child.

The questions Christian asked me about his father made me secretly wonder what was going on with Carolyn. The last time I'd seen Carolyn was the year 2010 when she suddenly appeared in Montgomery, Alabama. I didn't say much to her when she walked into my house. But I didn't be mean to her either. I even allowed her to sleep in bed with me at night as I didn't have another bedroom set in my guest room she could sleep on.

"This is a nice place you have here," she reluctantly mumbled as her eyes roamed around the room.

"Thank you," I said, turning to face her. We shared a glance for a few seconds, turned our backs to each other once more, and fell asleep amidst hard feelings and unresolved pain. That time, Carolyn stuck around for a couple of weeks. Then, as the fairytale came to an end, it was back to the disappearing acts I'd grown so accustomed to over the years. Honestly speaking, it felt weird that she stuck around even for two weeks. It had never happened before. The thought of walking into my house one day and seeing her finally gone without as much as a goodbye, caused me to feel unsettled. I would rather have her leave early on than to get used to her being around, and then, she decided to leave. When she did leave, she didn't leave a phone number for anyone to contact her. So I was doomed. I was crushed. I was lost. Before I knew it, four years had passed.

It was now 2014. I couldn't shake the gut wrenching feeling that maybe Carolyn had died and the city buried her because they didn't know who to contact about her death. She suffered with congestive heart failure, along with high blood pressure, and COPD. The COPD resulted from many years of her being a heavy smoker. She was taking several pills a day. I could see the great deal of swelling she had in her feet as she propped them up on my ottoman during those two weeks she stuck around back in 2010. Her breath was often short, too, as having congestive heart failure often caused her to have a build-up of fluid around her heart.

When the feelings of uncertainty had reached their peak, I tried calling all of the hospitals in Birmingham, Alabama, to see if she was a patient. Because of HIPAA Privacy Rules, they couldn't give me any information. I even contacted the Birmingham Police Department. I gave them the last address I'd known her to have. They assured me they would send a unit out to check on her. But I never heard anything back from them. Their failure to help me wasn't how I decided to let the story end. I had to know the truth, a truth I was going to find one way or another. I would've never been able to rest not knowing if she was dead or alive.

Once I made up in my mind that I was going to find her, I began to ponder about what my next move should be. It was definitely an, "Aha" moment when I realized what I should do. I would go to the Social Security Office to see if they could tell me anything.

The following Monday morning, I walked into the Social Security office wearing the mascara of worry upon my face. I wasn't sure I would get the answers I needed/wanted. Such realization made me feel queasy as I walked over to where you check in, grabbed my number, and found a nearby seat. Less than an hour later I heard my number being called over the intercom.

"Please have your ticket and ID in hand when you approach the window," the voice said as I hurriedly gathered myself to talk to the customer service representative.

"I don't want you to break any rules," I stammered, when I was seated before her. "I just want to know if my mother is dead or alive. I know she get a SSI check monthly. Will you please tell me if she still get the check or not? If she doesn't get it, I'll know that she has died. Please, help me. I haven't been able to sleep and I…I…I, well, I just don't know what else to do."

The customer service representative looked at me long and hard. I felt like I'd bared my soul in those few moments I explained to her what was so embarrassing for anyone to know. She didn't judge me the way I assumed she would. I saw the smallest hint of compassion resting on her features as she listened to what I had to say. I silently prayed that this day, compassion worked in my favor.

"Excuse me for a moment," she said as she stood and went to talk with her supervisor. It seemed to take forever for her to come back. I quickly noted that only five minutes had passed when she sat back down before me.

"It's limited what I can tell you," she spoke again, after pecking away on her computer keyboard.

"I'll be thankful for whatever you tell me," I replied, my voice seasoned with that of gratitude. I tried to disguise the nervousness I felt. But obviously, my skin was very pale. I looked like I was about to faint as I waited to hear the words I'd longed to hear for so long.

"Are you alright," asked the customer service rep with an edge of concern in her voice. "Are you sure you can handle this?"

"Yes… yes... I… uh... I can handle it. I… I… I need to know. Pl… please, tell me!"

"Well, Ms. Walker, I can tell you that she is alive."

"She is? You mean, she's not dead?"

"No, sweetie, she is very much alive."

"Oh, thank you, Jesus," I said aloud, not at all ashamed of whom may have heard me praising his name. It took me several moments to collect myself. I'd gotten worked up, thinking the customer service representative was going to tell me that Carolyn had passed away. I didn't know how I would be able to deal with knowing that. Once that heartbreaking information was relayed to me, it would become my responsibility to relay the bad news to Tamara and my other siblings, therefore breaking their hearts as well. Thank God, He spared me of the pain and the burden of having to do such a thing.

The tears flowed long and hard as I sat there, soaking up the information I'd just heard. With my peripheral vision, I could see the customer service representative dabbing at her own eyes with a piece of tissue, although she did her best to remain poised.

"Would you like to write her a letter?" She finally spoke to me again, once she knew I was calm. She had a big smile on her face, indeed happy she'd been able to help me to discover the truth.

"I… I… I can do that," I stuttered.

"Sure, you can, honey. We cannot give you her address. But you are more than welcome to write her a letter. We can forward it to her with her next check. It'll be up to her whether she responds or not."

"Yes… Yes… I want to write her a letter. Oh, my God. I can't believe this is happening." I grew more excited.

Not only was Carolyn alive. I could write her a letter. This was far more than I ever bargained for, much more than I expected to receive. Unfortunately, I did not get a chance to write her the letter. As fate determined, she decided to contact me. On that day, I was sitting on the floor in my apartment with my son watching television. The phone rang. I noted it was mom as I hit the "Talk" button on my cellular device.

"Someone called me today," she said before I had a chance to say anything. "The caller ID said it was a Carolyn Walker."

I took in a deep breath when I heard those words. "For real," I squealed.

"Yes," mom continued. "When I answered the phone, she hung up. I tried calling back a couple of times, but she didn't answer the phone."

"Give me her number, mom. I will call her," I interrupted. This had to be too good to be the truth. But I would never know unless I called. I was going to risk being disappointed to see if by any chance it was the truth. No soon as I ended the call with mom, my fingers were dialing Carolyn's number. She didn't answer for me either. I hung up and called again. After the third time, I left her a message. "Please, Carolyn, call me. This is Tamyra. Mom said you called her phone. I just want to hear your voice. I won't ask you any questions about why we haven’t seen you. I promise. Call me, please!"

I was beyond happy when she finally decided to call back about an hour later. As soon as I saw the 205 area code flash across my screen, I answered. "Carolyn, is that you," I yelled into the phone.

“Yes, it’s me,” she replied, almost inaudibly.

“Oh, my God, this can’t be. I have missed you so much. Are you ok? Can I come to see you?” Please let me come to see you!”

“I guess that will be ok,” she remarked, accepting my invitation to come visit.

“Are you for real, Carolyn? You’re really going to let me come see you.”

“Yes, Tamyra, it is ok,” she reiterated.

After that call, I took a quick shower, dressed myself in some decent clothing, and decided to go to Birmingham to pay Carolyn a visit.

"After all these years, finally we can have somewhat of a relationship," I said to myself as Tamara sped up I-65 North. Our older sister, Sharmeen, decided to tag along as well. I couldn't wait to tell them that I had talked to Carolyn. "I'm going to see her," I said to Tamara.

"Well, I'm coming too," she matched my excitement.

It was my desire for things to be better. But as soon as Sharmeen saw Carolyn, she became very upset. "I don't understand how you could go four years without contacting anyone, Carolyn. Why would you do that? Didn't you know that we were worried about you?"

Not knowing what to say, Carolyn took a cigarette from her pack and lit it. "I was going to call," she said after taking several pulls, looking hurt like a child who'd just been reprimanded for being disobedient.

"You have seven grandchildren and a great grand on the way," Sharmeen continued. "Since you didn't have anything to do with us, you could at least try to get to know them. Don't you think they want to have a relationship with their grandmother? We didn't even know if you were dead or alive! How could you put us through that?"

It is unfortunate that things did not go the way I hoped they would. Carolyn, as always, slipped back into her old ways. We never talked on the phone after that day. We sent text messages to each other for a while. The text messages became limited before they altogether stopped. This latest account of events caused a rift to find its way to my heart.

Depression was more than willing to come and chill with me. But I wasn't having it. I made up in my mind I was not going to spend the rest of my life hoping for something I probably would never get. I was not going to be bitter and angry either. I was simply going to live. I was going to be there for my son, and by the grace of God, I was going to help him to be unscathed by the fact that his father was not in his life. We were going to laugh together until we became dizzy from doing so. We were going to comfort each other with the unwavering love we had in our hearts for each other. I was going to teach him all the things I knew and research things I didn’t know, so I could teach him that as well.

It was true that Christian loved me. God knows I loved him, too... beyond infinity. Everyday wasn't going to be a good day. One thing was for sure, there wasn’t anything in life that we couldn't conquer. God was our captain. He knew what was ahead of us. He could help us to get through each part with as less pain/turbulence as possible.

Depression had been on life support in my life for a few years at that point. I wasn't giving in to it the way I had done so many times in the past, but it was being ventilated and kept alive in my heart. After years of torment, I finally decided to pull the plug. Depression had to die once and for all because I had to live.

Once I pulled the plug, its heartbeat slowly trended down until it had flat lined. I didn't stand around weeping, the way one would over the loss of a loved one. What I was gaining as a result was so much better. I simply scraped my heart of the fragments depression had left there. I took a deep breath. I smiled. I laughed. I moved on.

The End!

Contact Tamyra
deshawnlashae@gmail.com

Other books by Tamyra

Seeds:
Poetic Words of Power
Amazon

Made in the USA
Columbia, SC
28 January 2022